RITUALS
OF RESPECT

Inge Bolin

RITUALS
OF RESPECT

The Secret

of Survival

in the

High

Peruvian

Andes

University
of Texas Press
Austin

Requests for permission to reproduce material from this work
should be sent to Permissions, University of Texas Press, Box
7819, Austin, TX 78713-7819.

∞ The paper used in this publication meets the minimum re-
quirements of American National Standard for Information
Sciences—Permanence of Paper for Printed Library Materials,
ANSI Z39.48-1984.

Library of Congress Cataloging-in-Publication Data
Bolin, Inge.
  Rituals of respect : the secret of survival in the high Peru-
vian Andes / Inge Bolin. — 1st ed.
    p. cm.
  Includes bibliographical references and index.
  ISBN 0-292-70866-1 (alk. paper)
  ISBN 0-292-70867-X (pbk. : alk. paper)
  1. Quechua Indians—Rites and ceremonies. 2. Quechua
philosophy. 3. Quechua Indians—Social life and customs.
4. Herders—Peru—Chillihuani. 5. Festivals—Peru—Chilli-
huani. 6. Chillihuani (Peru)—Social life and customs.
I. Title.
  F2230.2.K4 B65   1998
  813'.54—ddc21   98-8930

To my parents, to Ron, Greg,
and Andrea with love,
and to my friends and teachers,
the herders of Chillihuani,
who know so much and who
allow me to share the warmth
and wisdom of their lives.

Contents

Illustrations

Preface

It all began in February 1988, on a hot, sunny morning in the marketplace of Cusipata, a Peruvian village in the Vilcanota Valley of Peru between Cuzco and Sicuani. My *compadre* Antolín, with whom I had worked since 1984 on the organization of irrigation and other aspects of Andean life, introduced me to Juan Mamani, the *curandero* (healer) from the high-altitude herding community of Chillihuani. *"Imaynallan kashanki,"* Juan said, wishing me a good day with a loose embrace in Chillihuani fashion. We talked about the upcoming fiesta, an ancient celebration called Pukllay in Quechua and Carnavales in Spanish. Pukllay, which literally means "game" or "play," reaches far back to Inca and pre-Inca times. It celebrates fertility, procreation, and new life. On this occasion Pachamama, the great Earth Mother; the Apus, powerful mountain deities; Illapa, the god of thunder; and other spirits of nature receive offerings and are entreated in return to protect the herds and make them prosper and multiply. Love and solidarity between villagers are reconfirmed in many intriguing rituals which take place during the eight days of Pukllay festivities.

In previous years I had participated in the rites of Carnavales among sheep herders in the valley, where Christian elements mingle with ancient practices. In the remoteness of Chillihuani, I was told, Andean religion remains authentic, as do pre-Columbian dances and songs and pentatonic music played on ancient instruments. I was eager to participate in the fiestas of

Chillihuani, but did not dare to ask. I knew that many of the rituals are secret, practiced only within the intimacy of each family. The health of the animals and the economic well-being of the family depend on the precise execution of the rituals. An outsider could bring disaster for the entire year.

"It is time to return to Chillihuani; Carnavales begins tomorrow," Juan Mamani said in eager anticipation of this great event. There was a moment of silence, and then, hesitating somewhat, he added, "Señorita, please come to celebrate Pukllay with me and my family." I could hardly believe my ears. It was a dream come true.

In 1984, when I first met herders from Chillihuani who had descended to the valley, I was struck by their appearance and the elegance of their movements and gestures. Two well-known Peruvian anthropologists, Oscar Núñez del Prado and Jorge Flores Ochoa, have also noted a very special elegance of high-altitude herders. Soft-spoken yet self-confident, they exchanged their goods at the Sunday market. Then they retreated again behind the towering mountains in the distance.

Chillihuani can be reached only by a narrow path that winds alongside steep ravines and across mountain creeks up to the perpetual snows of the Andes. The higher ranges of the village are at a day's walking distance from Apu Ausangate, which at 6,384 meters is the highest and most sacred mountain of southern Peru. This is the realm of condors and pumas. Occasionally vicuñas can be seen in this, one of the most mountainous and rugged regions of the Peruvian Sierra. Due to its inaccessibility, ancient Andean ways of life have remained relatively undisturbed.

The ancient celebration of Pukllay to which I was invited was only the beginning of a love for the people, their culture, and their mountain wilderness that was to deepen with time, transcending the inconveniences which life at a high altitude can bring. There is neither electricity nor running water in this village, where high winds, lightning, and hail are frequent and the nights can be icy cold. A few weeks later I left Chillihuani during a thundering storm that washed away all paths and made the journey to the valley still more treacherous. Yet, I knew that I had to return to Chillihuani. I was ready to focus my studies on Andean culture on this village under the clouds. I had found a second home.

When I returned to Chillihuani for fieldwork in 1990, I was received with joy. "Things are very good," Juan Mamani assured me with a big smile. He took me to the corral and pointed to a white alpaca with light eyes which had been conceived during the fiesta of Pukllay in 1988. "Never before in my life has this happened," Juan confided with joy. I was relieved. My ritual performance had not been a disaster. The gods must have been pleased, and so were my hosts. Yet, I had much to learn and I made many mistakes over the years. People forgave me with patience and understanding.

With every year my insight into the way of life of these mountain pastoralists grew. I began to better discern the symbolic patterns that give structure to their lives and that are so thoroughly expressed in rituals. I began to see that the key value of this society, the focus of all rituals and celebrations and the basis of all social interaction, centers on respect.

Respect is the essence of life, and like the life force itself, it knows no boundaries. Respect is owed to other human beings, to animals, to the deities—to Pachamama, the Earth Mother; to the Apus, the mountain abode of ancestral protective spirits; to Illapa, the powerful god of thunder; and to all sacred places, including rocks, springs, lakes, and meadows. Respect is the moral code that permeates all thought and action. Regardless of the fiesta celebrated, rituals of respect are always central. They take place in tiny adobe houses, in the sacred corral or *muyukancha,* on the fields, and during daring horse races near the perpetual snow.

The respect for others that is so consistently reinforced in all rituals carries over into everyday life. The people of Chillihuani are aware of the tremendous importance of respect, without which they feel society cannot be sustained. Respect is at the very root of their social relations. Juan Mamani, the healer, and his wife Luisa receive patients by day and night. They offer medical help, comfort, and food from the little they own without charge. Respect is at the basis of Chillihuani's superb organizational strategies during fiestas, communal work parties, and other events. Out of respect for the people in attendance and the deities worshiped, ceremonies, meetings, and work parties begin on time and are executed with care and precision.

Animals are not considered inferior beings, but are also treated with kindness and respect. When a llama or an alpaca must be slaughtered, the owner holds its head in his or her lap, giving the animal *coca* leaves and comforting it while its soul soars to Apu Ausangate, the mountain god who is implored to return the animal's spirit in the form of a newborn.

The ancient customs and the ideology of the people of Chillihuani reflect on the way Inca and pre-Inca societies lived and thought. The very heights of the province of Quispicanchis, where Chillihuani is located, have been much less affected by the conquest and the shock waves that followed than lower regions. This is because of its remoteness, the low pressure at high altitude, the absence of roads, the severe weather conditions, and the lack of any modern facilities. Furthermore, Chillihuani has never been under the control of a *hacienda,* and intermarriage with people from lower lying villages has been minimal. An indomitable spirit resides in these people, who have strong ties to their ancestors. Energetic and dynamic, they know their worth. "We are Incas, true Incas," they exclaimed when asked about their heritage.

Chillihuani is not, however, a utopian society. Conflict does arise and hostilities sometimes penetrate the predominantly harmonious existence of these llama and alpaca herders. But the efforts that are made to avoid and to resolve conflicts are deep and far-reaching. Whether community members are dealing with interpersonal conflict or problems that arise between people and the natural or spiritual worlds, rituals are always at hand to maintain and restore harmony. Thus, for example, before each community meeting *coca k'intus* (offerings of three perfect *coca* leaves arranged in a bunch, green sides up) are blown to the deities, who are asked to watch over the ensuing conversations so that disrespectful speech will be avoided.

In some of the ancient rituals that took place during *tinkuys,* ritual encounters between people of the different *suyus* (sections) of the village, blood had to flow to assure fertility and to reaffirm *suyu* borders. Yet, even in seemingly ferocious ritual battles, the rules of the game have always been observed and respect between the adversaries has been maintained. Today these ritualized battles find symbolic expression in dances.

Whether we are dealing with *tinkuys* or with spectacular horse races, the competitive element is minimized. The concept of winners and losers does not fit into this highly egalitarian society. I remember the first time I attended the Fiesta de Santiago in 1990, when the four sectors of the village "competed" in most impressive horse races. The riders virtually flew through the air on their sturdy horses, their ponchos fluttering in the wind. Yet, the winner was not loudly or publicly declared. In a society where respect for others is a key value, no one wants to set himself above the others.

Unfortunately, this society, to which respect means so much, has for centuries been scorned by people from Peru's valleys and coasts for its "backward" lifestyle, "false" worldview, and "pagan" religion. The truth is that this stereotyping is based on total ignorance and gross distortion. This in itself is tragic. Honesty is much valued by the herders of Chillihuani. My friends and teachers, in telling me of their ancient customs, made sure that everything they said was correct. "We must tell about the good and bad things that happen here," Roberto, my centenarian teacher, often stated. The proud people of Chillihuani know the value of their system and they want to maintain it.

In the following chapters I hope to convey an understanding of these ancient rituals and the impact they have on a society so dynamic and energetic, so full of wisdom and insight, yet so vulnerable. The people of Chillihuani wage a daily struggle to eke out a living from a marginal environment. But the struggle to survive does not deter them from engaging in an equally exhausting struggle to maintain a decent society. The forces that disrupt harmony and peaceful coexistence are controlled through rituals during fiestas and in everyday life. The rituals of the llama and alpaca herders of Chillihuani assure that respect flows with the force of life throughout time and space, animating the eternal *pacha* (the universe of both space and time).

In the remoteness of their mountain retreat, the herders of Chillihuani recognize that respect for others is the central and most significant element of all thought and action. Without respect, no society, no civilization, can flourish for long. Without respect, humanity is doomed and so is the earth, sustainer of all life.

Acknowledgments

Writing this book has been a pleasure not only because it tied me so closely to the fascinating and inspiring world of Chillihuani, but also because it gave me the opportunity to exchange ideas with people from all realms of life in different parts of the world.

Many individuals and organizations have been instrumental in making the research that led to the writing of this book possible. My 1984–1985 doctoral study, on the organization of irrigation in the Vilcanota Valley of Peru, was funded by the Wenner-Gren Foundation for Anthropological Research, the German Agency for Technical Cooperation, and the Canadian Fund for the Support of International Development Activities at the University of Alberta. That study led to my work in Chillihuani three years later.

Malaspina University College reduced my teaching load by one course in the spring of 1996 to facilitate finishing this book. I value the support I received from Interlibrary Loan and Communications at Malaspina University College. The students I have taught over the years have stimulated my research with their enthusiasm and interest in Andean culture.

Following my first visit to Chillihuani, simultaneously with my anthropological research, I began to cooperate with the villagers on their grassroots projects. As we worked toward common goals, I became more closely acquainted with their organizational strategies. At the same time, this cooperation permitted some reciprocity in return for the herders' generosity, patience, and understanding throughout so many years. For much-appreciated funding of small grassroots projects and an occasional flight to Peru, I thank the German Red Cross, Landesverband Baden-Württemberg. In coordination with the Red Cross, the Landkreis of Böblingen in Germany and the NGO Change for Children in Edmonton, Canada, also helped to promote reciprocity by contributing to a small health clinic, several first-aid stations, a drinking water system, solar cooking and solar water heating projects, a project to bring back ancient Andean medicine, Mother's Club projects, and a small library in Chillihuani. Much appreciated are the funds from the Wirtschaftsministerium in Stuttgart for the NGO "Yachaq," where we deal with traditional Andean medicine, nutrition, and ecology. I would also like to thank friends and family in Germany, the United States, and Canada for their assistance, especially when emergencies arose in Chillihuani and other villages.

The support I received as research associate in 1992 and at other times from the Centro de Estudios Regionales Andinos Bartolomé de las Casas in Cuzco is much appreciated, as are the stimulating conversations with Henrique Urbano, Jesús Guillén, Juan Carlos Godenzzi, and other members of the staff.

I am also much indebted to the insightful writings of many authors who helped me to more fully understand Andean life in the past and present.

Theresa May, executive editor of the University of Texas Press, approached this project in a warm and efficient way. I would like to thank her and the readers for valuable comments and suggestions. It has been a pleasure to work with Carolyn Cates Wylie, Sue Carter, Margaret McDonald, Sharon Casteel, and other members of the University of Texas Press.

I am grateful to Rolf Olsson for converting my color prints and slides to black-and-white prints.

For good times, exciting discussions, and insightful comments, I owe many friends and colleagues, among them Reinhild Boehm, Nancy Gibson, Olive Dickason, Ronald Wright, Ross Crumrine, Margo Matwychuk, Tom Zuidema, William Mitchell, Patricia Lyon, Hank Lewis, David Johnson, Joseph Bastien, Melanie Wiber, Lucila Flores, Llanca Letelier, the Diez Canseco family, Anneke and Peter Van Kerkoerle, Kate Khan, Anneliese Cooley, and the students and faculty of the University of Alberta and Athabasca University. Scott Raymond gave me the first taste of Andean culture in an academic setting. My friends from Vancouver Island and Germany, too numerous to mention individually, assisted me in every way and never became tired of Andean topics.

Friendship, hospitality, and intellectual stimulation were always plentiful in Peru. Lucho Millones conveyed his much-valued approach to Andean culture and ethnohistory. Manuel Chávez Ballón shared his unique way of perceiving Andean archaeology and anthropology and his humanitarian work on finding ways to curb hunger in Peru. With the late Oscar Núñez del Prado we discussed the value of applied anthropology. Alfredo Tupayachi Herrera helped me identify Andean plants, Julinho Zapata shared exciting accounts on archaeology, and Antenor Vargas helped me with the new Quechua orthography in my translations from Quechua to Spanish.

Directly involved in my studies of Andean culture and in my practical work in support of traditional Andean medicine were many friends. Antolín Maza introduced me to the *curandero* Juan Mamani, who then invited me to his village under the clouds. Antolín, Ana Caviedes, Dina Pantigozo, Catalina Durán, and Juan Pablo Canchari are wonderful friends who helped me in every way, and together with all the other members of the Andean Medicine Group and their families, we forgot space and time while discussing the intriguing world of the Andes.

Solón Corazao, the late Manuel Orihuela and his wife Joséfina, José Cáceres and his wife Dori, Edmundo Pantigozo, Genara Lizarraga, Anton and Regia Ponce de León, Rosas Quispe, Zonia Rozas Huacho, César Palomino Diáz, José Altamirano and his wife Gloria, Isaias Cárdenas, the Durán-Cevallos families, and other friends and their families in Cuzco, Cusipata, and the Sacred Valley of the Incas helped me in many ways and opened their homes to me at all times to talk about culture, religion, and medical practices.

My appreciation for the herders of Chillihuani cannot be put into words. Throughout the years they received me with love, initiated me into their rituals of respect, and made me a member of their unique society. To my Chillihuani friends and mentors I owe the wonderful experience of living and studying in their high mountain village; they have enriched my life in every other way as well. The adobe house of the *curandero* Juan Mamani and his family has become my home away from home and my Chillihuani friends and *compadres,* too numerous to mention by name, have become an extended family.

Finally, I want to thank my family in Europe and North America, who shares my great love for the high Andes. My parents in Germany, together with my family in Canada—Ronald, Andrea, and Greg—have given me steady support in my Andean endeavors from the beginning and have tolerated my long absences from home. My husband Ron read this manuscript, gave constructive advice, drew the map, and helped with the computer. Without the understanding and the much-appreciated help of so many people, this book could not have been written.

RITUALS
OF RESPECT

Introduction

Doña Escobar, her daughter, and other neighbors shook their heads in disbelief as they heard of my plans to go to Chillihuani. Having lived all their lives in the Vilcanota Valley, they had never ventured to the *puna*, the high, windswept region above their village where only a few tubers can grow, and they know little about this society of herders. At times young men from the high mountains come to the valley to help during harvest time or to sell or barter their goods at the Sunday market, but they communicate little information about their society. Some people from Cusipata had heard anecdotes about the herding way of life, and they too advised me not to go. The mountains are precipitous, they said, the weather is unpredictable, and the society—well, no one really knows what goes on up there. One university-educated man from the valley told me about powerful shamans—too powerful for him to dare to venture to those heights.

The people in the villages and towns of the Andean valleys are not alone in their comparative ignorance about the ideology and life ways of the inhabitants of the high mountains. Until quite recently, the scientific world has also lacked systematic knowledge of high-altitude herding societies. In 1963 anthropologist Bernard Mishkin deplored the fact that the literature contained so little reliable data on the extent and nature of Quechua herding societies even though these same societies are the foremost custodians of ancient Andean customs and life ways which go back to their Inca and pre-Inca past. Sergio Quijada Jara (1957:29) agreed with Mishkin that the people living high in the Andes have conserved the purest traditions and are the guardians and faithful interpreters of thousands of years of Andean culture.

For centuries, perhaps millennia in pre-Columbian times, the seat of power and the highest demographic density in the Andes were found at altitudes above 3,400 meters (Murra 1985a:3). Settlements in the Andes are older, denser, and are found at higher elevations than those in the Himalayas. John Murra (1988:57) found that in Nepal, Sherpa settlements were very sparsely populated, while the *altiplano* of the Titicaca and the Charcas had high population densities; and Isaiah Bowman (1938) found the highest house in the world at 17,000 feet (5,182 meters) above sea level in the Andes. The well-known Peruvian researcher Carlos Monge (1953:5) wrote: "Andean people are born, live and reproduce at altitudes up to 17,000 feet above sea level."

The Vilcanota Valley (also referred to as Willkamayu Valley—*willka* means "sacred"; *mayu* means "river"), which lies far below Chillihuani at an altitude between 3,100 and 3,300 meters, was densely populated and of considerable importance already in pre-Inca times, as indicated by the ruins from the Wari civilization which are found there. "The Vilcanota Valley played an outstanding role in the development and elaboration of Inca civilization," wrote Daniel Gade (1975:18). Inca canals and astonishingly shaped and polished stones attest to the fact that the Incas lived and worked in and around Cusipata and up toward Chillihuani.

Cusipata, capital of the Cusipata district, which includes Chillihuani, is located in the province of Quispicanchis 80 kilometers south of Cuzco, between this former capital of the Inca Empire and the town of Sicuani (see map). (See Jacques Malengreau's 1972 study on Cusipata.) Extensive trade routes have long existed throughout this area as well as to the south to Lake Titicaca, which, at 3,800 meters above sea level, is the highest navigable lake in the world. This lake is strategically and economically important and is the hub of many ancient myths and legends. Legend tells that the first Incas originated in Lake Titicaca, traveled along subterranean channels, and emerged in a cave in Pacariqtambo. These children of the high lake founded an immense empire in Cuzco that eventually included what is now Peru, Bolivia, Ecuador, southern Colombia, northern Chile, and upland Argentina.

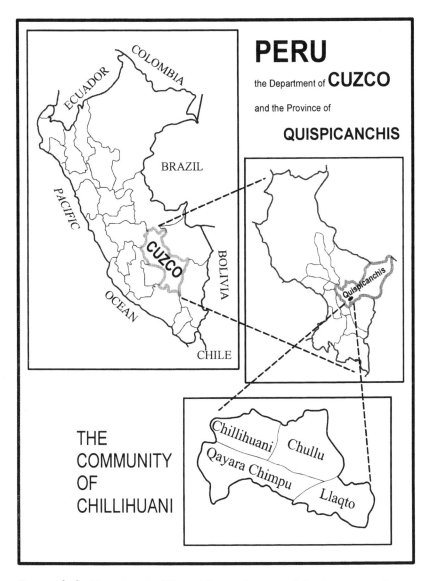

Peru with the Department of Cuzco, its provinces, and the four *suyus* of Chillihuani.

Archaeological remains reveal the impressive achievements of the ancient inhabitants of these regions of the Andes, and reports from early chroniclers as well as the oral histories of today's inhabitants verify the grandeur of these past times. We find enormous structures in stone and adobe, earthquake-resistant architecture, outstanding irrigation works, and superb agricultural terraces. The Incas knew about astronomy, practiced brain surgery, and organized their empire in ways unlike any other known society. Tawantinsuyu—the Inca Empire (literally, the United Four Quarters)—became the largest native empire that ever arose in the New World.

Apart from mythology and important archaeological evidence that reveal Inca and pre-Inca occupation of the Vilcanota Valley and the mountains above, significant events took place here in colonial times as well. The provinces of Quispicanchis and Canchis received major attention, for example, in the early 1780s when José Gabriel Condorcanqui, born in Tinta as a direct descendant of the Inca royal lineage, took the name Tupac Amaru II, and together with his wife Micaela Bastides, led an ill-fated revolution to prevent the outrageous exploitation of the native people by colonial authorities. Contrary to the plans and intentions of Tupac Amaru II, Micaela Bastides, and their followers, the uprising turned into the bloodiest rebellion of the colonial epoch (Sallnow 1991:285), in which both the native people and the Spanish suffered devastating losses. After a series of unfortunate circumstances, Tupac Amaru II and his followers were defeated and taken to Cuzco, where on May 18, 1781 he, his family, and other leaders were executed most cruelly in Hawkaypata, the large central plaza. Tupac Amaru had to witness the execution of his wife, his son, and other relatives. Then his limbs were tied to horses which were chased into the four directions of Tawantinsuyu. According to witnesses, his body never divided. Finally he was chopped into pieces (see Fisher 1966 and Walker 1991 for details). Although Tupac Amaru II and Micaela Bastides were defeated and killed, they live on in the memories of the people today as heroes.

These historic and prehistoric events occurred at the very margins of Chillihuani. Although a remote village today, it may have been within a far more frequently traveled region in pre-Columbian times. Its location in the high mountains and its proximity to the sacred Apu Ausangate must have conferred religious and economic significance to the region. Intriguing rock engravings, Inca canals, and remains of ancient inhabitants indicate that Inca ideology was at home in the stormy heights of Chillihuani.

Fieldwork

To undertake fieldwork in the former Inca Empire is an experience of a very special kind. Although one is reminded at all times of the Spanish conquest, which devastated Andean society with disease, forced labor, and gruesome efforts to extirpate ancient religion and life ways, the impressive remains of this once-magnificent culture still speak loudly of the strength, courage, and creativity of the people who built it. These characteristics have survived among the people of the high Andes and are most pronounced in the remote region where Chillihuani is located. Arguedas and Stephan (1957:179) wrote that the settlements of the high region of the Vilcanota were densely populated and "had not been reduced to a state of servitude like the majority of the populations in both the hot and temperate valleys of Cuzco, and like the Indians of the farming and cattle-grazing regions of the plateau."

Chillihuani is situated in precisely this rugged and inaccessible area, the inhabitants of which have preserved an indomitable spirit and pride in their culture. These characteristics of the Chillihuani herders actually facilitate fieldwork. Respectful and polite, yet with utter self-confidence, they tell about their lives and the lives of their ancestors. A sense of perfectionism and total honesty guide their conversations.

Yet, some aspects of their worldview are not easy to comprehend, particularly because people often speak in metaphors, using ancient myths and legends to describe actual phenomena. Therefore, it is important to analyze the mythological accounts of the indigenous people. In turn, what we know about the Inca and pre-Inca societies can clarify and explain the metaphors through which Andean people see the world.

To help minimize potential misunderstanding of what I saw and heard, Chillihuani residents participated in group discussions regarding certain metaphors and symbolic actions after I had observed a ritual or conducted an interview. On such occasions each person explained the issues from his or her own perspective. Flannery, Marcus, and Reynolds (1989:xii) realized in the course of their fieldwork among llama herders of Ayacucho that "it is one thing to collect a series of concepts in an American Indian language; it is quite another thing to have their underlying meaning revealed by someone who spent his entire youth thinking in that language." Similarly, the preeminent anthropologist Victor Turner (1969:11) suggested that in the study of ritual, one must try to discover how the indigenous people themselves feel and think about their own rituals.

In order to get a deeper grasp of Andean culture the way the Chillihuani herders see it, I made sure that people would on many occasions speak for themselves. Our discussion sessions were always held in the form of a dialogue. And, while I was interested in Andean phenomena, I was also open to the curious questions of the Chillihuani herders about people and places in other parts of the world. I found that even though most herders had little knowledge of geography and the people who populate the world, their questions were consistently formulated in such a way that they made sense. The facility with which the people of Chillihuani were able to perceive new phenomena and the speed at which they learned was astounding. I was often reminded of the school principal of Cusipata who had told me that the children of those Chillihuani herders who came to the valley to study were always at the top of the class.

The people of Chillihuani have very good memories and seldom forgot what we had discussed. Sometimes when I asked my centenarian friend Roberto a question that I had previously asked, he would answer it patiently but remind me that we had already discussed the matter two or three years ago.

Old people and most women spoke Quechua exclusively. Young and middle-aged men, as well as a few young women (particularly those with more schooling, who did not adhere as much to tradition as the older women did), often spoke in Spanish during interviews. I taped all interviews and music, as well as our *chansanakuy* (joking sessions), which would crop up occasionally during our conversations. Because Chillihuani is very remote and most people have never seen a foreigner, it was surprising to me that our sense of humor was so much the same. As an outsider, I found it difficult at first to understand their myths and metaphors, but when it came to joking or having a good time, I never experienced a gap in understanding and I soon began to feel as though I had grown up in this village under the clouds.

Chillihuani herders, especially the elders, are well versed in oral history and often talked about the Incas and those ancestors who lived before the Incas. Sabine MacCormack's (1991:179) historical research supports the notion that Andeans' memories go back to pre-Inca times; she found that even though imperial rituals had been introduced by the great Inca Pachacuti as early as the mid-fifteenth century, aged Andeans who were living around the time of the conquest remembered how their region had been administered before the advent of the Inca. Oral history is extremely important to any effort to piece together a coherent picture of Andean society.

In order to shed more light on specific issues revealed to me by the people of Chillihuani, and to analyze them more thoroughly, I have compared their accounts, where applicable, with those written in early documents by Incas who learned to write in Spanish and by Spanish soldiers and missionaries. Analyses of more recent investigations have been helpful in defining specific issues and circumstances more precisely. When reading early Spanish documents, one must be careful with regard to the interpretation of the conquerors and early chroniclers since few of them understood the customs and the religion of the people they conquered. This situation has hardly changed. The *mistikuna,* people of usually mixed descent who live in towns and cities, rarely understand the realities lived by the *runakuna*—"the people," as the Indians of the high regions refer to themselves, who speak predominantly Quechua (or *runasimi,* "the language of the people"), wear homespun clothes, and chew *coca* leaves. Although the Indians of the Andes use two last names, their father's and their mother's, I have sometimes used only the first of the two last names, since both are not always given.

Because Quechua was not a written language in Inca times, we find tremendous variation in orthography. My spelling of Quechua is based on the Quechua-Spanish-Quechua dictionary prepared in 1995 by the Academia Mayor de la Lengua Quechua. For an occasional clarification of concepts I used the *Diccionario Quechua Cuzo-Collao* by Antonio Cusihuaman and the *Diccionario Kkechuwa-Español* by Jorge A. Lira. As is common among most investigators of the Quechua language and culture, I have used the English -*s* to designate the plural, since Quechua does not have an equivalent suffix. The Quechua suffix -*kuna* (as in *wasikuna,* houses) cannot be used in all cases where the plural is warranted. Quechua quotes from documents have been left in their original spelling. Names of people and places have, for the most part, been left in the customary spelling, as it appears in many documents and maps. Wherever possible I have tried to identify the Latin names of the plants and animals to which I refer. The sources to which I had access were, however, not always consistent. The principal source for Latin names of plants is Daniel Gade (1975). The Latin names of plants not mentioned in Gade's book were taken from Weberbauer (1945), Yachasun (Pantigozo de Esquivel, 1995), and Franquemont et al. (1990). The Latin names of animals are as given in the dictionary of the Academia Mayor de la Lengua Quechua.

I am responsible for the translations of all documents or communications that required translating. Spanish-speaking herders, friends, and experts of the Quechua language assisted in translations from Quechua to Spanish and/or in the clarification of complex ideas expressed in Quechua. Possible errors in facts and interpretation, of course, remain mine.

This book does not overlook the everyday lives of the people of Chillihuani, but it focuses primarily on fiestas and special occasions. This is because rituals are at their most diverse and their most explicit during fiestas. They are performed not only at the level of the individual but also at the level of the family and the community. Fiestas also mark those times which are of special importance for people's herds and fields and act as specific markers of the seasons of the year. In fact, people orient themselves and their activities predominantly with respect to fiestas rather than to the months of the year. The interactions among people, their animals, the earth, and the entire cosmos, as well as the respect they pay to all, are most pronounced in the rituals of a fiesta.

Since I lived in Chillihuani off and on between 1988 and 1996 (1988, 1990, 1991, 1992, 1994, 1996), I have participated in the fiestas discussed in this book on several occasions. Thus, the descriptions of a given fiesta or event contain my accumulated observations and experiences over the years. Fiestas are discussed in chronological order as they occur in the course of the year, starting with Pukllay in February.

The herders of Chillihuani are excited about the prospect of having a book published about their customs, including the rituals which are normally performed within the confines of the family. Most villagers want to see their names in the book. I have thus used pseudonyms only for those who were not sure whether their names should appear.

Central Ideas of the Book

In Chapter 1 we ascend to Chillihuani, where people eke out an existence from the land and their animals. As we climb higher through the beautiful yet dangerous landscape, it assumes an increasingly spiritual personality. Ancestral worship in *machu mach'ay,* the cave of the ancient one, introduces us to the beliefs that pervade this society of herders—beliefs that center on respect for ancestors and all of life.

In Chapter 2, which describes the first night of Pukllay, we begin to see these beliefs in action. Secret rites are held in honor of the great deities to assure that *enqa,* the eternal life force, is replenished and will flow throughout the year in order to promote fertility and harmony.

The dual forces that reside in all matter imbued with life come to light in a frightening manner in Chapter 3 as Illapa, the god of thunder and lightning, approaches the small Mamani house. Fear and awe, inspired by the thunder god, are written on people's faces and are expressed in every gesture. Later, with the danger gone and the lives of the family spared, three black animals are sacrificed in honor of the thunder god and the great mountains where this deity resides. The rituals of the sacrifice take us back to the religious ideology of pre-Columbian people and reflect a deep respect for the powers of nature and for the animals offered.

The ritual demonstration of love and respect for animals continues in Chapter 4, which culminates in *irpay,* a marking ceremony and a ritual wedding of two young alpacas.

Solidarity among villagers and ties to the deities are reconfirmed in Chapter 5 with intricate rituals and ancient ceremonial songs and dances. Chillihuani comes alive as this radiant society in exquisite attire strides proudly to Capillapampa, also called Ch'urumarka, a promontory high above the village and site of ancestral ceremonies. These people are masters within their mountain world. They have nothing in common with any image of downtrodden, introverted, hopeless mountain Indians as they are sometimes ignorantly portrayed by outsiders.

In the evening groups of young people come to the homes of their elders to sing and dance, to recite poems, and to wish their elders well, as did their ancestors long ago. *Warak'anakuy,* also known as *soq'anakuy,* an ancient dance, takes us back to Inca times when blood had to flow to restore fertility to the earth and when borders between the *suyus* (regions) had to be defined for religious, social, and strategic purposes.

Most of the rituals in this remote region are rooted in the Inca and pre-Inca past, though the meaning of many may be dimmed. Roberto Yupanqui Qoa, a respected elder of Chillihuani, sheds light on some of these mysteries in Chapter 6. Although he has seen a century go by, he retains charm, humor, and much memory of the strong oral tradition of his ancestors. Far from the mainstream of modern Peru, his views are little tainted by the ideology of the conquerors and their successors.

During Pukllay, the ideals of pre-Columbian life are brought together in a holistic way. Fertility and procreation, reciprocity, solidarity, and respect are imbued with love. Chapter 7 focuses on the fourth day of Pukllay, when groups of young dancers come to the Mamani house to honor their elders. They tell how they fell in love and how and why they got married. Romantic yet practical, they relate that they chose their partners according to ancient practices. On this night and during the days and nights to come, young people flock to one or more of the Tusuna Q'asa Pata, the high places located between mountain peaks right on the borders between *suyus,* where ritual dances, pentatonic music, libations to Pachamama and the Apus, scenes of jealousy, and the final pull of a partner across the border of the *suyu* characterize their rites of love. Lovers may join for life as they disappear dancing into the night.

The dance at Tusuna Q'asa Pata is the first part of a series of ceremonies leading to marriage in Chillihuani. Chapter 8 focuses on *rimanakuy*—the traditional wedding—which may occur at any time after Pukllay. During *rimanakuy,* the parents of the young people meet and talk about all aspects of married life. This is not a trial marriage—referred to as *sirvinakuy* by people in the valley and by many Andean investigators. Within the community it is legal and binding, and it is consummated with rituals of respect between the young people, their parents, and in the presence of the Andean gods.

Sometimes *rimanakuy* is followed by *casarakuy,* a "Catholic" marriage. In Chapter 9 we accompany a couple as they take the blessings of the priest and then engage in a week full of ancient rituals. These rituals focus on the deep Andean concern of the reconciliation of opposing but complementary forces. Male and female are united into *warmi-qhari* (a couple, literally woman and man), a unit of dual forces which, during the time of transformation to married life, is surrounded by a multitude of other forces, both beneficial and malignant. These forces must be dealt with during the long and dangerous journey the wedding party must undertake to reach their home and during the eight days that follow their marriage vows.

Although the rituals of Pukllay have few, if any, Christian elements, the Fiesta de Santiago described in Chapter 10 has been superimposed on an ancient Andean celebration held in honor of Illapa, the thunder god. For the people of Chillihuani, however, the Fiesta de Santiago is the "Day of the Horse." The thundering hooves of horses remind them of their thunder god. During this horse race, close to the eternal snow on what may be the highest racetrack in the world, the riders appeal to their thunder god and other feared and respected deities to bring rain and protection from lightning. The race is spectacular. At its conclusion, out of respect for the participants, no winner is announced.

Ancestral elements that predate the conquest are also central to the festivities of July 28, Peru's Day of Independence. While Peru commemorates this important political event in its history, the people of Chillihuani engage in age-old rituals that give meaning to their lives and guide them in the ways of their ancestors. During the reign of the Inca Empire, women possessed equal rights and performed rituals and duties parallel to those of men. The splendor of Inca times may be gone, but ancient ideology has remained intact; as Chapter 11 reveals, the members of separate male and female hierarchies still carry out their respective rituals in Chillihuani. Male and female elders initiate young men and women to the duties they must perform and the respect which they owe others. There are no juvenile delinquents in Chillihuani. Young people are too busy with their apprenticeships in rituals and a variety of other communal duties.

Chillihuani provides glimpses into its past and that of the Inca Empire and pre-Inca life. But many puzzles remain. In Chapter 12, Roberto Yupanqui Qoa, centenarian and custodian of ancient customs, speaks of his *ayllu* (village) and sheds light on some of the central enigmas of Andean ideology. He talks about the days when his grandmother's grandmother was herding her flocks on the high pastures. He remembers his youth when elders kept him awake every night to learn the ways of his ancestors, the Yupanquis. "We belong to the Yupanquis, to the Inca Yupanquis, to those Yupanquis," he told me proudly, referring to the ninth Inca, Pachakuteq Yupanqui, a very successful emperor. Roberto speaks in powerful metaphors—such as the double-headed snake and Llaqtayoq Mach'aqway, the great snake, emblem of the village. These metaphors shed light on his village and, in turn, illuminate concepts that were of great significance in pre-Columbian times.

Some of the most powerful of these metaphors come to life in our ascent to the sacred lagoon Waqraqocha in Chapter 13. As my companions approach Waqraqocha, a pristine mountain lake, we experience the intimate relationship between these people and their powerful gods. Standing in close proximity to the divine lagoon, where life originates and ends, nature presents herself first in the guise of harmonious serenity and later in a terrifying storm; this sequence illustrates the dual aspects of respect and fear which inhere in the gods of the Andes.

Life continues in this village under the clouds, imbued with the joy of living and the sadness that follows death. Chapter 14 brings together these forces, the meeting of which lends coherence to the Andean way of life. The rituals of respect are as instrumental today as they were in the past. They provide a sense of continuity for the Andean people—a feeling of belonging not only to the present, but also to the past and the future. They instill a sense of being one with the village as they stimulate the force of life to flow throughout the cosmos with renewed vigor.

Ascent to the Realm
of the Apus

It is February 1988. The rainy season is in full swing. Pachamama, the great Earth Mother, is satisfied with the continuous rains and drinks the precious liquid that pours from the sky. The peasants in Cusipata in the Vilcanota Valley are happy. The harvest at this altitude should be good. Little children are full of joy. They play in puddles, splashing the muddy water with their tiny feet.

Higher up in the mountains the rains are forcefully accompanied by hail, thunder, and lightning. Lightning has killed many people and their animals in the past and will take its toll again this year—everyone knows it. The herders say that hail always follows lightning; hailstones can reach the size of chicken eggs and destroy crops within minutes. Mountain creeks turn into thundering rivers, and landslides tumble down from steep mountainsides, burying the narrow path that winds up to the dizzying heights of Chillihuani.

Yet, despite nature's torments, the herders of Chillihuani who descend to Cusipata seem as high-spirited as the people in the valley. This is a time for ceremonies and rituals, with Chillihuani's most important fiesta of the year only a few days away. Everyone is preparing for this significant event—which the Quechua speakers call Pukllay, meaning "play" or "game," and the Spanish speakers call Carnavales. During Pukllay ties of love, respect, and reciprocity are renewed among people, their gods, their animals, and all of nature.

Pukllay is a movable fiesta. It can begin on any Sunday within the period from February 2 to March 6 (Urton 1993:125). The people from Cusipata say that Comadres Day always falls on a Thursday, one week after Compadres Day. Pukllay starts on the Sunday following Comadres Day and lasts for eight days. "Pukllay has always been celebrated by our ancestors, the Inca, and even before," I have been told with pride by the people of Chillihuani. Not much has changed in this village which extends up to 5,000 meters (16,404 feet) above sea level, where it meets the line of permanent snow.

On February 12, two days before the rituals start, Juan Mamani, a *curandero* from Chillihuani, arrives in the valley to get provisions for the upcoming celebration. Antolín, a native of Cusipata who has been assisting me for several years in my doctoral and postdoctoral research on the organization of irrigation and other aspects of Andean life in the Vilcanota Valley, meets him in the marketplace in Cusipata. He is *compadre*[1] with the *curandero* and his wife Luisa. Antolín and his wife Pascuala are also my *compadres,* since I was asked to hold their fourth child during baptism. Antolín and the *curandero* come to greet me. At this encounter, and contrary to all expectations, the *curandero* invites me to celebrate the ancient rituals of Pukllay with his family in the heights of Chillihuani.

There is much to prepare. Antolín is also invited. He and his wife Pascuala help me with preparations for the fiesta. We want to contribute with some of the most important ingredients required for the ceremonies. *Coca* leaves (*Erythroxylum coca*) are essential to all rituals, as are *chicha,*[2] a fermented corn beverage; *trago,* a low-grade sugarcane alcohol also referred to as *alcohol* or *licor;* and other mysterious and exotic items of the kind that another *comadre,* Catalina, sells in the marketplace in Cusipata. She has brought some of these items from other regions of the highlands as far away as Lake Titicaca. Still others she has obtained through barter from people who brought them from the coastal and jungle regions of Peru.

Catalina is a herbalist with a profound knowledge of Andean rituals. She inherited this trade from her mother, who is well known in the region. The herders usually buy some of these precious items, but often they can afford only the absolute essentials. I follow the advice of my *comadre* and make a selection of *llonqhetaku,* a powder derived from red earth; *coca* seed; and *wayruru,* which are oval, brilliantly colored poisonous seeds that grow on the tropical tree *wayruru* (*Batesia flori-*

bunda). Catalina asserts that *wayruru* bring good luck and are used for protection. She explains that the solid red bean-like seeds are called "*solteros*" (single ones), seeds with red and black spots are called "*casados*" (married ones), and black seeds are called "*viudos*" (widowed ones). They are used as love charms and may be sold as necklaces (Gade 1975:169). *Huayrur* or *wayrur* (from the Quechua *huayruru*, or *wayruru*) signified "the most beautiful girl" among the Incas, according to Zuidema (1990a:56).

I also buy *coca* leaves, which grow in the humid tropical valleys of Peru. Since *coca* leaves are central to the lives of highland Indians, they require closer attention. *Coca* leaves have religious, social, and physiological significance and are essential in all Andean rituals. They have been sacred to the Andean people since time immemorial and were already present in the graves of pre-Inca cultures. They are used in both curing and divination. Some people say *coca* leaves have wisdom (Bastien 1985:56), and the healers of Chillihuani assert that they have power. They are mediators between people and their gods. It is believed that by blowing onto a *coca k'intu* (three leaves held together in a bouquet, green sides up) in the name of a deity, holding it toward the east in a gesture called *phukuy* (ritual blowing), a person can avert problems—even disaster. At the social level, to exchange *coca* leaves affirms solidarity. *Coca* is a social cement and provides "the context par excellence in which communication takes place."[3]

The physiological effects of *coca* leaves have long been known. *Coca* can be chewed with *llipht'a,* which is compressed ash usually made from any one of the following plants: quinoa (*Chenopodium quinoa*),[4] qañiwa (*Chenopodium pallidicaule*), baccharis stalks (*Baccharis*), amaranth (*Amaranthus*), or cacao pods (*Theobroma cacao* L.), any of which contain substances that help to extract alkaloids from the leaves. When chewed with *llipht'a, coca* may aid in suppressing feelings of hunger, thirst, cold, and fatigue. *Coca* also serves to alleviate several ailments, among them altitude sickness (*soroqch'i* in Quechua; *soroche* in Spanish). Some people consider *coca* a dangerous drug. But the effects of chewing the leaves are very different from those of ingesting cocaine. As Alan Ereira remarked in his 1991 film *From the Heart of the World*: "The toasted leaf that the Kogi chew is as far from refined cocaine as rye bread is from rye whiskey." The chewing of *coca* leaves has also been shown to add many important vitamins, minerals, and other substances to the people's often very simple diet (see also Davis 1996).[5]

In addition to the above items, I have yet another surprise for the Mamani family—*phallcha* flowers (*Gentiana primuloides*) from the high village of Ocongate where I was visiting a few days earlier. *Phallcha* flowers grow in the highest zones of the Andes, close to the perpetual snows. It is commonly stated that they bloom only in February. They have vivid colors—orange, various shades of red, yellow, white, and gray. I once found a blue *phallcha* flower in July, but my high-altitude companions confirmed that this is rare. These flowers are believed to have fertilizing power and are therefore required for some of the most important rituals during Pukllay. They are used as gifts of love and are central to love songs. They also serve as medicine against coughs, pneumonia, and other illnesses. Although the people of Chillihuani find these flowers within their village, specimens from other regions are much welcomed for the offerings.

We also buy rice, sugar, and tea and take along a jar of *chicha* that my *comadre* Pascuala has brewed for the occasion. We know that the ascent will be long and steep, but Antolín, although he has never been to Chillihuani, is confident that he can find the way and carry most of the goods. For many years he has conversed with the people from the snowy heights whenever they come to the valley and has been *compadre* with the *curandero* Juan and his wife Luisa for several years. Still, for him, too, this is a trip into the unknown.

We leave early on the morning of February 13. It is the height of the rainy season. Clouds obscure the mountain peaks and emit a constant drizzle. Few people from the valley have ever ventured to Chillihuani, which is located between 16 and 31 kilometers beyond Cusipata. "*Está lejos*" (it is far), people warn me as they look with concern toward the precipitous mountain ranges. But I am not willing to forfeit an opportunity for which I have waited so long. I am prepared to take a risk in the same way the *curandero* and his family are taking risks by inviting Antolín, an outsider, and me, a foreigner, to this most sacred of all ceremonies. So, off we go toward the towering mountain ranges in the distance.

Pukllay or Carnavales is celebrated throughout the Andes. The details of the fiesta, however, differ from region to region and even between villages. Since the sacred rituals during the first night of this week of celebration are confined to the intimacy of each family, there are certain differences at the family level as well. But the way in which Carnavales is celebrated in lower lying regions among primarily agricultural societies where Christian elements mingle with the ancient belief systems differs considerably from the Pukllay celebrations of high-altitude herding societies. In Chillihuani we will participate in ceremonies among people who cultivate some tubers—potatoes (*Solanum* spp), *oqa* or *oca* (*Oxalis tuberosa*), *ulluku* or *lisas* (*Ullucus tuberosus*), and *mashwa,* also called *añu* or *isaño* (*Tropaeolum tuberosum*)—but who rely heavily for their subsistence on their herds of animals—mainly alpacas, llamas, and sheep. If the animals perish, survival is threatened.

Walking an Ancient Trail

To reach our destination, we must traverse three major ecological zones: the *keshwa* or *quechua* (2,400 to 3,300 m), the *suni* (3,300 to 3,910 m), and the *puna* (3,910 to 4,340 m).[6] Families here own small fields in different microregions or even ecological zones to assure a high degree of self-sufficiency and at the same time to minimize the risk of crop failure due to frost, hail, and disease. The village of Cusipata is located at 3,300 meters in the upper limit of the *keshwa* zone. As we leave the village we pass through extensive fields of corn (*Zea mays* L.), the most treasured crop along the Vilcanota Valley, and one which must be planted on fertile ground. Potatoes, wheat, vegetables, and fruit trees are also cultivated in the *keshwa* zone.

Because we started our ascent at the upper limits of the *keshwa* zone, we soon enter the *suni* zone, where wheat, barley, potatoes, broad beans, carrots, onions, and cabbage are common crops.[7] Tubers such as *oqa, ulluku,* and *mashwa* are grown in the upper ranges of this ecological zone, as well as the cereals *quinoa* (*Chenopodium quinoa*) and *qañiwa* (*Chenopodium pallidicaule*) and the legume *tarwi* (*Lupinus mutabilis*). Efforts are being made to bring back *kiwicha* (*Amaranthus caudatus*), another native Andean cultigen, to this region. Due to the great nutritional value of this plant, it was highly esteemed during Inca times and was central to many rituals. The conquerors therefore forbade its cultivation and the plant fell into oblivion until efforts were made in the 1980s to reintroduce it. (Luis Sumar Kalinowski [1993] was a leader in these efforts.)

Capulí trees (*Prunus serotina*), which bear small, cherry-like fruits, grow here and extend to the lower parts of Chillihuani, where, however, they do not bear fruit. Eucalyptus trees (*Eucalyptus globulus*), native to Australia, continue into the *suni* zone, as do the native *kishwar* trees (*Buddleia incana*) and *kehuiña* (*keuña* or *qewña*) trees (*Polylepis incana*). *Kehuiña* trees grow between 3,000 and 4,800 meters above sea level (Tupayachi Herrera 1993). In addition, a vast array of medicinal plants reach up the sides of the mountains from the valley to the snow line.

The crops in the fields look good as we traverse the different ecological zones on our way to the *puna*. In the absence of plant diseases or major meteorological disasters, the people will likely have good harvests. But few families achieve surplus and none will become rich, since the fields are small—too small, in fact, to be further divided equally among their offspring. Many young people must search for work in the overcrowded cities or work as landless peasants. This situation has led to abject poverty and increasing theft. Fields must be watched by day and night during harvest time. Population pressure and land degradation are the major reasons for poverty and theft. Until 1985 people in many rural areas had little or no access to family planning. During my 1984/1985 anthropological research in this region, many people sought advice, but had nowhere to go for assistance. The situation is slowly improving, but the population already exceeds the carrying capacity of the land. Seventy percent of the children in the Peruvian highlands are malnourished. Those who are forced to move to the cities, where work is scarce, are often faced with three alternatives: to beg, to steal, or to die. This is a sad reality in a country where in Inca times people had enough to eat and where the greeting "Ama suwa, ama llulla, ama qella" (Don't steal, don't lie, don't be lazy) articulated and reinforced their most important values.

Parents often cry as they tell me about the prospects for the survival of their children. The people of the Andes show much honesty, dignity, and respect. But the conquerors and their successors have placed many obstacles in their way and have transformed their lives to a constant struggle against hunger, domination, and exploitation (see Wright 1992.)

In both the *keshwa* and *suni* zones, animal breeding is secondary to agricultural activities. Only a few families have herds of sheep; some have cows, horses, donkeys, pigs, and chickens. Almost every family keeps guinea pigs, referred to as *cuy* or *cuye* in Spanish and *qowe* or *qowi* in Quechua (*Cavia porcellus*), which provide the meat for virtually every festive meal. Cattle used to graze on pastures far from house and corral, but due to increasing theft, families can now keep only a few head—and those must be kept close to their homes.

We have been on our way for several hours, moving steadily under the persistent drizzle. People greet us with shy friendliness as we pass through Tintinco, a marginal agricultural village. We now enter higher country where shrubs are predominant. Up the hillside to the right we can discern a vast terrain studded with a great variety of ruins, with both round and rectangular stone-walled buildings and stone fences placed around many perfectly leveled plazas. Archeological studies have not yet been carried out at this intriguing pre-Inca site, which may have been occupied by the Wari, whose reign in the highlands was short-lived (Schaedel 1985:507; Julinho Zapata, personal communication). The path leads past Pukara Punku (Quechua for "gate of the fortress"). As we climb a slope adjacent to the path, we see blocks of rosy granite meticulously worked to a shiny luster strewn across a large, perfectly leveled site. More stones are half hidden in the bushes. The leveled ground and the beautiful rosy-red stones tell that this site must have been important in Inca times. Two of the finely worked stones look like large *mesarumi* (*mesa* is Spanish for "table"; *rumi* is Quechua for "stone"), which are flat stone altars used during sacred ceremonies.

The walls of more ancient buildings come into sight. More perfectly leveled areas appear, overgrown by grass and shrubs. The remains of a once-exquisite Inca irrigation canal can be seen through the vegetation.

Many springs and a sacred high mountain lake nestled between the peaks above add to the magnificence of this region. What was the function of the pre-Inca city and of Pukara Punku in the past? Who built these exquisite sites and why were they abandoned? We do not know. But it is known that the ninth Inca Pachakuteq Yupanqui was responsible for introducing superb Inca stone masonry to Cuzco and other areas. Could this have been one of the emperor's residences? Is it a coincidence that Yupanqui is the most common name among the people of Chillihuani?

Our bags feel heavier as the mountain slopes become steeper and the air becomes thinner. Usually on a day so close to the main festivities, Chillihuani herders descend to the valley with their small shaggy horses and donkeys to obtain provisions. But today no one comes within our sight. The path ends abruptly at the shores of a turbulent stream which flows through the ravine Q'eqarani. The stream is swollen from heavy rains, and the bridge across it has been destroyed. But the tips of slippery stones that stick out of the water are as good as any bridge to the highland people. They seldom lose their balance even on the most precipitous terrain and Antolín has no problems crossing. The water that enters his rubber sandals flows out immediately. Contrary to all expectations, I cross without slipping or getting soaked. Good news, since getting one's clothes wet during the height of the rainy season usually means that they remain wet for days.

The altitude makes itself increasingly felt. Even Antolín, who lives at 3,300 meters (10,827 feet), feels the difference. We put our loads down to rest for a while before entering the *puna* zone (3,910 to 4,340 m; 12,828 to 14,239 feet above sea level). It is a region primarily of wild grasses. The predominant species is *ichu* (*Stipa ichu*), the dietary staple of llamas and alpacas. Sheep, and occasionally cattle, may also graze in this zone, which is at the uppermost limit of crop cultivation. Hardy potatoes grow here and occasionally *qañiwa* (*Chenopodium pallidicaule*); in the lower regions *oqa, ulluku,* and *mashwa* grow. It is a rugged region with its own kind of beauty.

As we scan the valley below us, to our great joy we see two young Chillihuani herders running uphill alongside their horses. They greet us, smiling shyly, and graciously agree to put much of our loads onto their horses. They carry my cameras, tape recorder, and other important things on their own backs. What a relief! At that moment I do not realize, however, that we are dealing with present-day *chaskis*.

Chaskis were runners who, during Inca times, delivered messages and goods swiftly throughout the Andes (see Meneses 1992). To the Indians who live in these highest, almost uninhabitable, zones today, altitude and distance mean nothing. Not only are they used to the daily exercise of running through their mountains, but they also have other advantages: bigger lungs and higher red blood cell counts, as well as the ever-present *coca* leaves when things get tough (re high altitude, see Hochachka et al. 1991, 1992; Monge 1953).

Despite the additional weight which our new companions carry, they are soon out of sight. We call, whereupon they stop, smiling in disbelief as we huff and puff uphill. "No," they say with a concerned expression on their faces, "we cannot walk slower because we must reach Chillihuani before night," when the *uraña wayra,* the cold malevolent wind, starts to blow.[8] More than nighttime spirits, the mere thought of stumbling in the dark along a rocky path in these dizzying heights tells me that it is better to keep up with our charming but determined *chaskis*.

We arrive at a place where the path becomes very narrow, winding along a precipice on our left. On the right a steep field of rubble, boulders, and thorny bushes reaches up into the low-hanging clouds. I try to keep my eyes on the wet, slippery path and avoid looking down. We cross freshly accumulated rubble. "*Lloqlla*" (landslide), Antolín cautions, urging me to hurry across this area. I recall the first time I saw a landslide in action. Preceded by the thundering noise of rocks, earth, and mud, it tumbled directly in front of us, depositing piles of debris on the path and leaving us momentarily stunned. My companions tell me that some decades ago a mighty landslide tore away the path and part of the mountainside close to this place. We are now walking on the new path that was subsequently carved into the hill.

The young horsemen remove the rocks that have come to rest on the path and we continue on our way, more alert than before, passing the sites of several previous landslides. The rain has stopped and the sun now peeks through the clouds, bathing the landscape in radiant green hues that blend into the grays of the rocky inclines and the white snow-covered peaks above. A spectacular sight. As I stand in awe, my companions assure me that it will be far more beautiful higher up and closer to the Apus, the great mountain deities. I wonder how much farther we must ascend before we see the first signs of habitation. "Chillihuani is close now," one of our companions assures us. "Right behind the mountain range in the distance."

But soon the path disappears in the flood of the Chillihuani river. Its waters beat against cliffs which we cannot climb. To continue we must return a short distance and then ascend the steep side of the mountain, which is covered by bromeliads of the genus *Puya* and other spiny vegetation. We climb up by holding on to the wet *ichu* grass. Hours pass before we get back onto the path. From here we see a cluster of three tiny huts perched against the mountainside in the distance. These are the outskirts of Chillihuani.

A horse comes running toward us. It greets our companions' horses with tremendous energy. Running back and forth on the narrow ledge along which we walk, it rears up on its hind legs and engages in what seems to be a vigorous game with our much more docile horses. Stimulated by the exuberant visitor or perhaps aggravated by him, the two horses with our equipment on their backs become increasingly animated and race back and forth along the ledge. I climb onto a promontory higher up in the cliff to avoid being tossed into the abyss. The young men do their best to calm their horses and finally succeed in sending the intruder off. We are relieved as it gallops into the distance.

I was later told that some horses are very territorial and can be quite aggressive at the sight of others of their kind.

Llamas and alpacas now appear everywhere, feeding on the hard grasses that predominate at higher altitudes. As we approach, the animals lift their heads and look at us with curiosity. They have an air of innate sophistication about them as they walk gracefully through the meadows.

The Cave of the Ancestors

We take another rest before the final steep ascent. Across the river, the entrance to a cave can be seen in the sheer rock. "Machu Mach'ay," our companions whisper. These are the caves of the ancestors. Two men in brown ponchos, homespun black pants, and rubber sandals come to greet us. Alfonso Choqque and Agustín Yupanqui are members of the village council. Antolín has met them at various times when they came to the valley. They welcome us to their village and sit down with us on the rocks. Stirred by our interest they begin to tell us about Machu Mach'ay, the cave of the ancestors.

In a solemn voice Alfonso takes us back to the beginning of time. "The *machukuna,* the ancient ones, were not part of the world of our God, but of the God Yaya in another world and another life. They were ancient human beings because they did not know the sun. They lived by the light of the moon. And when our present God created the sun," Alfonso hesitates for a moment, and then resumes, "I think he created two suns of strange color—and when the suns rose for the first time, the *machus* tried to hide. Many went to hide in the jungle. Others threw themselves into the mountain lakes and others hid in caves in groups, sometimes two or three together, where they died. Those who escaped to the jungle also died and their spirits are still around." Our companions nod their heads. Alfonso continues: "Then one of the suns became extinct and with only one sun a different kind of people arose, the way we know them today. We are now in the time of the God Churi." (Some people say Jesus Christ is the son of the God Churi.) Alfonso takes a deep breath. There is silence before he resumes: "Soon this time will come to an end. We will see war, conflict, and famine. The Earth will be tired when we come to the end of the time of the God Churi."

"Perhaps we will end up like the *machutullu*" (the old bones), Agustín interjects. Alfonso continues: "Another time will come through the power of a god we do not know. An all-powerful god. *Curanderos* will communicate with this god. This will be the 'Time of the Sacred Spirit.' A different kind of human will arise, perhaps with wings."[9]

"We can go into the cave," Agustín suggests with calm reassurance. Our trail companions no longer seem to be worried about a delay, but refuse to come along. They agree to wait by the path while we descend to the river, cross it on protruding rocks, and ascend another steep slope to reach the rock outcrop at the entrance to the cave. Alfonso and Agustín take off their hats and proceed in silence. From an elevated place we can see depressions in the cave walls stacked with bones. "Machutullu!" (bones of the ancestors), Agustín whispers. Further inside the cave, Alfonso and Agustín fall to their knees. In the dim light of the cave I can discern an *uma hanq'ara* (skull) placed on a flat *mesarumi* under an overhanging rock. Candle wax on the *mesarumi* testifies to the offerings that take place here. Prayers are murmured and *k'intus* are blown in honor of the ancestors and the gods. Alfonso sprays alcohol from a small bottle onto the four corners of the *mesarumi* while he implores Pachamama, the Apus, and the ancestral spirits for forgiveness. Antolín hands me a *k'intu,* indicating that we, too, should join in this ritual of respect for the ancestors.

As Alfonso pulls back his hands, which have been placed over the skull in a gesture of appeasement, a trepanation is revealed on its left side.[10] The edges of the square opening that constitute the trepanation show regeneration of the bone tissue, which indicates that the patient survived the operation. The considerable number of such skulls from Inca times suggests that operations on the skull were common. Several years earlier I had seen three skulls together in a cave in the heights above the Urubamba Valley. One of the two skulls showed a trepanation with sharp edges, suggesting that the patient had died during or shortly after the operation (see Hrdlicka 1978).

The spirit of the skull before us does not rest in peace, but is believed to act as an intermediary between the people and their gods. Outside the cave Agustín explains: "People ask the *machu* who speaks through the ancestral skull to assist them in certain endeavors, or they come to thank the *machu* for help received. But *machus* can also be dangerous. They can appear in different forms. They walk in the night of the full moon. When one hears noises that sound similar to those of humans, these are the *machus. Machus* can affect animals in the same way as humans. They become thin and die. To counteract the malevolent spirits of *machus,* one must make an offering on a yellow paper. If the *machu* receives the offering, people as well as animals may recover."

I leave the site impressed by this encounter. My companions insist that as long as there is still a trace of blood or fat inside the skull, even if it is not visible to the eye, the *machu* is able to communicate, to act as intermediary between the living and their gods and to guard the cave. Alfonso notes with sadness: "Formerly we had our mummies in this cave. Since anyone can remember, they sat in the cave with their knees bent against their chests, their heads supported in their hands, their elbows resting on their knees. But then they took them away." He did not explain who "they" were.[11]

We express our gratitude to Alfonso and Agustín for having allowed us to share this very special experience with them, and we agree to meet again during the forthcoming celebrations. We hurry back to our travel companions, who wait by the path, and off we go toward our destination.

Chillihuani at Last

Shortly before dusk we climb onto another ridge and there it is, the central area of Chillihuani, surrounded by spectacular mountain peaks. The village center consists of a few small huts, a school, and the municipal building, all constructed of adobe and built by members of this community in *ayni* (reciprocal exchange of labor) or *faena* (communal work). From here the dispersed village stretches in all directions about another 16 kilometers (10 miles) toward the eternal snow (see photo 1).

Communities in the Andes are usually divided into two or four parts which are referred to as *sectores, parcialidades,* or *ayllus.* Chillihuani calls its four sectors *suyus.* Chullu, which means "earthen ridge that ends where two streams join," is the name of one *suyu,* and streams do join at several locations within it. Qayara Chimpu is named for its once-abundant supply of *qayara* (*Puyu herrerae*), a wild plant with stiff leaves that reaches a height of 1.5 meters and grows on steep inclines. Laqto (Llaqto or Lakkt'o) means "masticated maize," which is used to make chicha. Finally, *ch'illka,* a resinous species of the genus *Baccharis* with a strong aroma, is the root word for Chillihuani. *Ch'illka* grows in the center of this *suyu.* Chillihuani is the name for both the community and one of its *suyus.*

Suyu is the Quechua word for region, part, or quarter. The Inca Empire was called Tawantinsuyu. *Tawa* is the number four and *ntin* implies "a unit of things that are inherently complementary or indivisible"

Photo 1. View from the hilltop Capillapampa onto the central plaza of Chilli-huani, showing the schoolhouse, village council building, health clinic, and house of the Women's Committee. Individual homes are distributed across the mountainsides and reach into all directions beyond the peaks in the distance.

(Wright 1984:51). Tawantinsuyu, the Four Quarters of the World, consisted of Qollasuyu, Kuntisuyu, Chinchaysuyu, and Antisuyu. Gade (1975:2) explained:

> Collasuyu, the southern division, was the largest in area and included the Titicaca Basin and most of present-day Bolivia, northwest Argentina and the northern half of Chile. Cuntisuyu covered much of the semiarid and arid central highlands west of Cuzco reaching the coast. Chinchaysuyu was the northern part of the realm, and extended along the coast, west of Cuntisuyu, to about the site now occupied by Ica. Antisuyu was the eastern division, taking in the middle and lower eastern Andean slopes; its north-south extent was not well defined.

Cuzco, derived from the Quechua word *qosqo* (navel), was the Inca capital and center of the empire, holding the four parts together. It was considered the navel of the world (see also Guillet 1994:168 for quadripartite division).

"This is our *ayllu*," our companions emphasize in a tone of pride, pointing to the four directions. They turn toward the highest cliffs to the north while one of them whispers, "Waqraqocha knows." Antolín explains that Waqraqocha is a high mountain lake held sacred by the villagers.

The four *suyus* of Chillihuani constitute the community which was officially recognized as a peasant community on March 21, 1957. People often refer to it as their *ayllu,* which is an ancient Quechua term that cannot be defined in the same way throughout the Peruvian Andes. Tom Zuidema (1973:19–20) explained that an *ayllu* can be perceived as any political group with a local boundary and it also refers to the kin relatives of a person. Catherine Allen (1988:257) defined *ayllu* as "indigenous community or other social group whose members share a common focus." The people of Chillihuani generally agree with these definitions (see also Webster 1977:29).

Chillihuani is inhabited by 350 families and approximately 1,500 people. Most are illiterate and monolingual Quechua speakers. Virtually all last names are Quechua except for four people whose compound family names include one Spanish name. A school building has been in existence since 1938, but instruction has been sporadic given its remoteness. Still, the young people who have had a chance to attend school in the valley have done very well. In 1995, for example, Alicia Mamani Illatinco, the third daughter of the *curandero* Juan Mamani and his wife Luisa Illatinco, transferred to seventh grade in Cuzco after six years of schooling in Chillihuani. At the end of her first year of schooling in Cuzco, she received second prize for scholastic achievement among all the students in her grade. Why should this be, given the fact that one rarely finds a book in Chillihuani, there are no newspapers, and only a few radios? I was to discover the reason for this apparent paradox.

For centuries the Indians of the high Andes have been despised by many town and city dwellers in the valley for their simple lifestyle and their customs, such as wearing homespun clothes, chewing *coca* leaves, speaking Quechua, and adhering to ancient belief systems. Yet, some people of the valley admit that the *comuneros* (villagers) of Chillihuani are well organized, cooperate at the community level, and always look neat and well groomed when seen in the valley. There has never been a *hacienda* in Chillihuani, and the herders have not experienced the kind of direct servitude which has been devastating to so many lower lying communities.

As we look at this picturesque village, the sun disappears behind the mountain peaks and the cold wind starts to chill us as we arrive near the *curandero*'s house. Our companions take their leave, since they still have an hour's walk ahead. We thank them, and they return the thanks for what they considered a good trip together. It was a calm day, they remark with contentment. If crossing a turbulent river by jumping from rock to rock, wondering where and when the next landslide might happen, or trying to avoid being playfully kicked into an abyss by overly exuberant horses is considered calm, what does an eventful day look like? I ask. They smile and remain silent. *"Ch'aki qhaqya wayra, chikchi, qhaqya"* (dry thunder winds, hail, and thunderbolt), Antolín responds. He explains that the Apus, those sacred mountain peaks, and Qhaqya, the thunder god, meant well toward us. They had not sent torrential storms, hail, or lightning—common phenomena during the rainy season. I would meet these phenomena soon enough. We walk to the *curandero*'s house (see photo 2) while our two traveling companions hurry toward the snow-covered peaks that stand out starkly against the darkening night sky.

Juan Mamani waits for us in front of his modest adobe house, together with his wife and three of their four daughters. Their dogs, alpacas, llamas, and sheep look on. We greet one another by touching shoulders in a loose embrace according to Chillihuani custom (see photo 3). Luisa and her daughters welcome us after initial looks of curiosity and some apprehension.

We bend down to enter through a tiny door into an adobe house of about three by five meters. A fire in an earthen stove at the far end lights and warms the house and simultaneously heats a pot full of steaming potato soup. At the other end of the house a wooden structure above the ground adjacent to a table with medical supplies serves to store our belongings. Beams along the ceiling and the walls hold most of the household items needed for daily use. There is no room for any other furniture. The house has only one small window with no glass. Two wooden doors, low, narrow, and drafty, squeak as they open and close (see photo 4).

Despite its complete simplicity and diminutive size, there is a very special coziness in this place, which would, on and off for many years

Photo 2. The adobe house of the Mamani/Illatinco family is typical of Chillihuani. Three families reside within this compound of three houses.

Photo 3. The *curandero* Juan Mamani greets a fellow villager with a loose embrace in Chillihuani fashion.

to come, become my home away from home. Beneath the somber black beams holding the thatched roof, I was to witness fascinating rituals, hear songs and legends from times long gone, and participate in age-old dances.

Exhausted, I fall onto the alpaca furs spread out on the adobe floor. Juan's brother enters. He is invited to participate in the Ch'allaska ceremony this very evening with his brother's family. Luisa offers tea with a smile. She then proceeds to fill dishes with steaming soup. Juan brings the dishes to us holding them with both hands. I come to learn that this gesture means, "I offer this food to you with all my heart." In appreciation, the gift of food is also meant to be received with both hands.

The healer and his wife whisper animatedly in Quechua. Luisa searches through her pots and pans. Both look at me with apprehension. I wonder whether something is wrong. Finally, Juan says in an apologetic tone of voice: *"Doctora, disculpe, no tenemos ni cuchara ni tenedor"* (I am sorry, *doctora,* we have neither a spoon nor a fork). Relieved that this was all that was wrong, I assure my hosts that every-

Photo 4. The Mamani/Illatinco family in their one-room adobe house. From left to right: Luisa, Juan, Luisa's mother, and three of their four daughters— Teresa, Alicia, and Libia.

thing is just fine and proceed to drink my soup and eat the potatoes with my fingers in Chillihuani fashion. I accept a second helping while commenting on the delicious meal. Through the flickering light of a candle I can see their faces light up with relief.

The soup consists of fresh and freeze-dried potatoes, *oqa, ulluku,* and *mashwa,* plants which grow in the lower part of the village. Further up, only limited varieties of potatoes can be grown. We are at the limits of agriculture, and the people of Chillihuani depend largely on their herds for subsistence. During this night and in the days to follow, the alpacas and llamas play significant roles in the ancient ceremonies whereby these herders of the high Andes enter into dialogue with their gods on behalf of their animals and whereby the bonds between people, animals, and the spirits of nature are renewed to assure that respect, love, and harmony prevail among all forms of life.

Suyay Ch'isin—
a Night of Secret Rituals

Rituals and ceremonies in the high Andes are a vital part of life and are considered as important for the well-being of the people as economic activities such as herding, agriculture, and gathering.

Ancient belief systems mingle with Christian beliefs along the valleys, but in the heights of the Andes, traditional beliefs have remained strong, leaving little room for Christian elements. As a general rule, the more inaccessible a region, the purer the precolonial components. In the remote mountains of Chillihuani, neither Christmas nor Easter is celebrated. The ancient Andean belief system considers nature the matrix of all life.

Some Andean scholars, among them Bernard Mishkin (1963:462), argued decades ago that "the Quechua religion today is essentially a special form of Catholicism" and that "Catholic ritual and theology have penetrated the most isolated Quechua communities." This assertion does not hold true in Chillihuani or in some other high-altitude communities.[1] In fact Father Juan Hugues A., director of the Instituto de Pastoral Andina in Cuzco, which publishes the journal *Allpanchis,* remarked on the absence of Catholicism: "All authors of the articles which are published here convince us that under the appearances of a Catholic religious cult we find practically nothing of the essential content of official Christianity despite the presence of preachers and missionaries for four centuries. We must recognize this failure. How can we explain it?" (1974:5).

In Chillihuani the ancient Andean religion is expressed most coherently during Pukllay. A vast array of rituals determines the welfare of the herds and thus the survival of their owners for the year to come. Ties of respect and solidarity are rekindled between villagers, *enqa* (life force) is restored to the sacred *enqaychu* (stone effigies of llamas and alpacas), and dialogues with the gods are established through these powerful intermediaries.

It is often difficult for an outsider to understand the devotion of the indigenous people for Pachamama, the Great Mother, and the Apus who are part of Pachamama. Pachamama, literally "Earth Mother," is the principal deity of Andean religion. Pachamama is the earth itself, sustainer of all life. In the words of one of the villagers, "Pachamama gives us life, she nourishes us throughout our existence on this earth and when we die, we go back to our Pachamama from where we will rise again." Pachamama is powerful. She sustains life for animals and plants alike, but she can also kill with devastating earthquakes and allow lightning to strike. Pachamama and the god of thunder and lightning are considered *compadres.*

The herders explain that Apus, those powerful mountain deities, are part of Pachamama, but they have personalities in their own right. Apus can be male or female. They are the custodians of eternal snow and ice and of the life-sustaining water. They are guardians of wild and domesticated animals, but they also watch over people's actions. As is true for Pachamama, they may chastise or grant requests which people solicit by means of *coca k'intus.*

The powers of Pachamama and the Apus are interconnected with those of Illapa, the mighty god of thunder, as well as lakes, springs, meadows, fields, and other phenomena of nature. These deities are omnipresent; they are always there to watch over people's actions and to remind them of the respect they owe to divine power and to life. The fact that the Andean gods coexist in close proximity with the herding society determines people's actions and their worldview.

The people of Chillihuani acknowledge divine powers in everyday life, but they express their love and respect, in both private and public spheres, in a particularly direct and focused manner during Pukllay. People come together from all corners of the village. Energy flows as they sing, dance, and visit for eight days. The first night of Pukllay, which we are to celebrate, is known as Suyay Ch'isin, or "night of waiting." It is a night of ancient rituals during which an intimate dialogue with the deities takes place, with the Apus who watch over the animals, Pachamama who nurtures them, Illapa, and the spirits of wild animals and sacred places (*wakas*). They all receive offerings in appreciation for their aid in protecting the herds and in the hope that they will not harm the alpacas and llamas in the upcoming year.

During the conquest some Indian and Spanish chroniclers mentioned this important festivity, but the invaders forbade all indigenous religious practices. Yet here, in the high mountain ranges of the Andes, these rituals have survived with little modification. Tonight, there will be a dialogue among the herders, their gods, and their animals.

Now We Will Begin!

"*Kunanqa qallarisun!*" (Now we will begin), Juan Mamani proposes after the evening meal. He coordinates the various rituals while Luisa provides the sacred items. We all sit in a circle on low stools and on alpaca furs and ponchos placed on the adobe floor. Juan brings small earthen jars (*puruña*) filled with water for each person. We dip our fingers into the water in a gesture of ritual cleansing. This water and all the water that will be used during the rituals in the days to come has been collected from specific springs, some from far beyond the village and even beyond the district.[2]

I am excited and most grateful to the Mamani family for allowing me to take part in this private celebration, usually reserved for only the closest family members.[3] I am, however, nervous, hoping to perform the rituals correctly. I am expected to participate in every activity in the same way as my hosts, who learned these rituals from their ancestors and have performed them every year of their lives. Should a family omit to carry out rituals during Pukllay, or execute them incorrectly, it is believed that disaster could strike—even death—for the herds and their owners.

Juan and Gregorio start by playing a pentatonic tune on their flutes. The people of Chillihuani make these flutes out of a variety of wild palm tree from the montane forest (*soqos de la montaña,* genus *Phragmites*). Its stems are like tubes with large knotty points or lumps. Some of the herders use plastic tubes to fashion their flutes. The ancient tune called "Takipukllay" is played during Pukllay and at no other time of the year. In fact, it is the only tune one hears during the entire week. The expressions on the faces of the two men are serious while they play this tune, which announces a night full of rituals for the gods, the spirits, the animate and inanimate *wakas* (sacred sites or beings), and for the animals, above all the alpacas and the llamas.

Luisa brings the *mama q'epe* (*señalu q'epi* in some regions), a bundle that consists of various paraphernalia wrapped into a colorful *lliklla* (a woven shawl with ancient symbols of the type used by Andean women since Inca times). The *mama q'epe* contains the most sacred ritual items that have been handed down from generation to generation. Luisa places it on the floor in the middle of the room by the flickering light that emanates from the candles and the fire in the earthen stove. Then she takes out *pukuchus*, bags made of alpaca fur, normally from the skin of a fetus or an entire infant alpaca that has died a natural death shortly after birth. She puts a handful of *coca* leaves into each *pukuchu* and gives one to every adult. The twelve-year-old daughter Teresa later informed me that children begin to participate in the rituals at around seven years of age, when they learn to take animals to pasture. They do not, however, chew *coca* or drink *chicha* until they are at least eighteen years old and then only during rituals.

With graceful gestures that convey respect, generosity, and reciprocity, the *pukuchus* are exchanged among the participants. Each person selects three perfect *coca* leaves and arranges them green sides up into a small bouquet, a *coca k'intu*. Holding the *k'intu* toward the east, we blow on it in a gesture referred to as *phukuy* while asking Pachamama, the Apus, and other deities to make this celebration successful and harmonious.[4] The pouch is then respectfully handed to the person sitting to the left. In a soft voice Juan whispers, "*Apu Awsanqati, phukurimusayki kukata sutikipi*" (Apu Ausangate, I will blow *coca* in your name).

Luisa holds her *k'intu* to the east, blows, and murmurs: "*Apu Awsanqati, kaytan pagamushayki sutikipi*" (Apu Ausangate, I offer this [*coca k'intu*] to you in your name). Gregorio blows on his *k'intu*, whispering, "*Apu Awsanqati, machula kay k'intuta ñoqa haywarimusayki uyway michirinaykipaq allin purinanpaq sumaqllata kachuntaq qhalilla miraykuchuntaq allinta*" (Apu Ausangate, grandfather, I offer you this *k'intu* and ask you in return to provide food for my animals so they will be calm and healthy and reproduce well).

At 6,384 meters, its peak covered with perpetual snow, Apu Ausangate is the highest and most revered mountain of southern Peru. It stands at the top of a hierarchy of mountain deities, all of which receive offerings during this night. Apu Ausangate is a day's walk from Chillihuani. On a clear day, the sacred mountain can be seen from the higher parts of Chillihuani.[5]

In a solemn tone of voice the *curandero* speaks the words "*Sumaqllata ukyaykusum*" (Let us all drink together in harmony). With an elegant gesture, the person who receives a seashell (*mullu*) full of sugarcane alcohol (*trago*) from Luisa acknowledges the gods and the people present, ingests the drink in one swallow, and hands it back to Luisa, who fills the shell for the next person in the round.

Luisa and Juan's actions are carefully coordinated. They perform each act within a vast array of ritual procedures with elegance and finesse. Rituals such as these require considerable preparation and often proceed in rapid sequence. But there is no sense of rushing. The healer and his family work calmly and skillfully. Juan Mamani's distinguished features reflect the wisdom and deep understanding of a man who has been a healer and a leader of rituals for many decades. His calm, gentle demeanor does not, however, lack powerful determination.

Holding a candle in her left hand, Luisa blows on the *k'intus* in her right hand with profound dedication. Her eloquence in the performance of her tasks matches that of her husband. By the candle's light I see the radiance that emanates from her face, still beautiful despite a life of hardship. Respectfully and with complete confidence she performs the rituals throughout the night. The children seem absorbed by the sacred activities they witness and assist their parents as they can (see photo 5).

Luisa opens the *urpu,* an earthen container of *chicha.* She pours the precious liquid into a *qero,* a vase-shaped container (a *qespe qero* is made of glass, a *k'ullu qero* of wood). This first cup of *chicha,* called *ñawin aqha* (literally, the eye of the *chicha*) is tossed east in the name of the deities to be addressed during the night. From the *mama q'epe* she takes more *qeros* and *purus* (gourds), fills them with *chicha,* and hands one to each person. "*Sumaqllata ukyaykusun*" (We will drink in peace), Luisa whispers. Before drinking, each person takes his or her *qero* or *puru,* pours some drops on the ground for Pachamama, and then, using thumb and forefinger, sprinkles drops of *chicha* into the air in honor of the Apus. Lastly we drink to the health of the people present. "*Sumaqmi aqha kasqa*" (Delicious was the *chicha*), everyone says, smiling and thanking Luisa for brewing such excellent *chicha.*

Juan kneels down beside the *mama q'epe.* No one moves as he spreads it out on the floor. It contains the *unkuña,* a small woven blan-

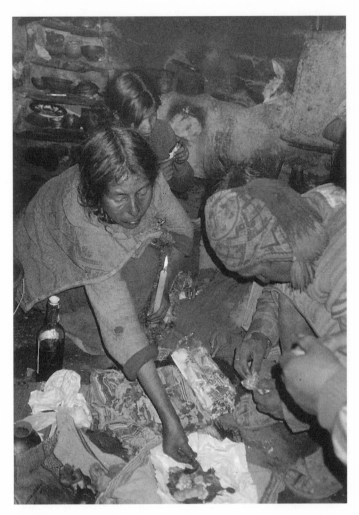

Photo 5. Juan Mamani works in perfect synchrony with his
wife as they prepare an offering.

ket which holds the most sacred of all the ritual items. Everyone focuses on the small blanket with its treasures. There is total silence except for the soft sound of flickering candles and the intermittent shuffling of restless guinea pigs. The healer unfolds the *unkuña*. Two
enqaychu appear.[6] *Enqaychu* are effigies of alpacas and llamas which
are believed to contain *enqa*, the life force. Until now they have never
been seen by anyone outside the family (see Gow and Gow 1975:149

and Flores Ochoa 1977:214 regarding the secrecy of these rituals). *Enqaychu,* sometimes called *illa* or *khuya rumi,* are small, fine-grained stones, usually granite, which resemble alpacas, llamas, or sheep. They come in different shades from white to grayish, brownish, and black. The shapes of these stones resemble, more or less closely, the animal they are supposed to represent. There is general agreement among herders that they contain the most life force (*enqa*) in the form of fertilizing power when left in their natural state, but they are sometimes modified to increase their resemblance to the animal they represent. Under no circumstances may *enqaychu* be bought or exchanged. Later Gregorio explained that an effigy may sometimes be modified so that a hole is formed in its back, which is referred to as *qocha* (mountain lake). Wine, *chicha,* or *trago* may be poured into this hole or *coca k'intus* may be deposited there. Juan affirmed that, little by little, the *enqaychu* consumes *trago* and *coca* leaves (see photo 6).

Photo 6. The *curandero* holds a *pukuchu* in his hand right above an *unkuña* filled with *coca* leaves. The *unkuña* sits on the *mama q'epe.* On the upper-right corner of the *mama q'epe* are gourds (*puru*) used as drinking vessels. Several *enqaychu* sit on the left side of the *mama q'epe* between two seashells (*mullu* or *ch'uru*).

Enqaychu, or gifts of the Apus, can be found only in very high regions and only on June 24 (San Juan Day, the Day of the Sheep) and on August 1, when the earth is believed to open up. Everyone in Chillihuani knows that it is easier for poor people, orphans, and the dispossessed to find *enqaychu.* Sometimes *enqaychu* appear as small concretions in the stomachs of ruminants. Some people in Chillihuani maintain that these are black and refer to them as *hayantilla.* They are also found in the stomachs of vicuñas. Gade (1983:776) was told that these concretions are called *"bezoars."* The herders of Chillihuani believe that the power of the *enqaychu* can be as strong as that of the Apus but that it becomes depleted throughout the year.[7] For this reason rituals must be held every year—during Pukllay for alpacas and llamas, on June 24 for sheep, and on August 1 for male llamas and alpacas to replenish the *enqa* of the *enqaychu* (that is, to revitalize their life force). Gregorio tells me that without rituals, *enqaychu* become *"hambrienta"* (hungry) and thus become dangerous to both people and animals. The herders of Chillihuani believe that people who do not celebrate this ritual are rendered vulnerable to misfortune—they may lose their animals, lightning may strike, the condor may eat the animals, or the animals may get lost or become ill. When the *enqaychu* are not attended in the proper way on their respective days, they become unhappy and bring bad luck. With the appropriate rituals, however, the *enqaychu* make the herds flourish and thereby bring well-being, good luck, and happiness to the family.

Juan places the *enqaychu* beside the *unkuña.* Both face the east. Everyone blows *coca k'intus* to acknowledge their power. We sprinkle the *enqaychu* with *chicha* in a gesture known as Ch'allaska (from *ch'allay,* "to sprinkle"), or sometimes referred to as Ch'uyaska (from *ch'uyay,* "to cleanse"), a cleansing ritual.[8] There is silence, and then the *curandero* whispers: *"Enqa, ñoqa valiyukusayki aswan uywa mirananpaq uñakunapas chinakama kananpaq"* (Enqa, I implore your power that my animals multiply and have many female offspring). *Enqa,* the powerful life force and fertilizing power contained in the *enqaychu,* also represents luck and happiness for the family. (*Sami,* "luck," is also considered a decisive force in the well-being of people and animals.)

Ruphasqa Haywa—an Offering to Burn

We are ready to prepare the offering.[9] Juan places a white sheet of paper on top of the *unkuña* which rests on the *lliklla.* He puts a handful of dark red and some white carnation blossoms in the center of the paper. Red petals are for Pachamama and the Apus, and white petals are for Illapa, or Qhaqya, the god of thunder.

Piles of *coca* leaves are placed on the four corners of the *lliklla,* symbolically stressing the significance of the four cardinal directions. Each adult member of the group arranges *coca* leaves into *k'intus,* dedicating each one to a specific deity, starting with Pachamama, Apu Ausangate, and all the other Apus. I hear them whisper, *"Apu Awsanqati, kaytan pagamushayki sutikipi"* (Apu Ausangate, I serve this to you in your name). *K'intus* are dedicated also to Illapa so that this deity will not strike the animals.

More *k'intus* are offered to Qhapaq Mayu, the mighty river, and to Waqraqocha and Qellwaqocha, high mountain lakes, so the animals will not drown; to mountain paths, so the animals will not get lost; and to condors, pumas, and foxes, so they will not steal young llamas, alpacas, and sheep. Springs and meadows, the grasses the animals eat, and their enclosures (referred to as the *iphiña* [the daily corral] and the *muyukancha* [the sacred corral]) are remembered and are asked to join in protecting and feeding the herds. After each invocation *coca k'intus* are placed side by side facing east on the white sheet on top of the carnation blossoms. As the night continues, several layers are added. Everyone is careful in offering *k'intus* to *all* spirits. To forget one of them might arouse anger in the forgotten spirit, which could bring misfortune to the family.[10]

Luisa serves wine and sugarcane alcohol in a seashell (*mullu, ch'uru,* or *qocha*) which has been stored in the *mama q'epe.* Shells symbolize lakes, and in the vicinity of Apu Ausangate there are various lakes which are associated with the fertility of livestock (see Gow and Gow 1975:149). In a wider context, shells symbolize the sea.[11]

One person after another receives the same shell filled with wine and offers some of the drink to Pachamama and the Apus with great respect, then acknowledges all persons present, drinking to the health and well-being of the alpacas and llamas, which are referred to as *chushllu* and *chullumpi,* respectively, names which are used during festivities and which designate respect for these animals. This ritual symbolically quenches the thirst of the deities, the animals, and the people present and unites them in harmony. The theme of uniting or bringing together is also expressed in symbolic form by means of the ritual items. The *enqaychu* are from the highest zones of the Andes. The *qeros* are from the highlands. The gourds (*purus*) come from the hot lowlands of Peru, and the seashells, known to represent the watery element—the lakes and the sea—come from the coast. The *curandero* told me later that he had brought the water used to cleanse our hands and to perform rituals throughout the eight days from four springs which are far apart within the district of Cusipata. Bringing together four regions, or, symbolically, the four corners of the world (Tawantinsuyu), is a theme that figures significantly in many rituals and offerings.

This theme of uniting objects from different regions is deeply embedded in Andean ideology. Thus, during the pilgrimage to Qoyllur Rit'i, it is common for people to carry rocks from the valley up to the sanctuary of Qoyllur Rit'i, located 20 kilometers from Apu Ausangate, and to bring ice down to the valley. Joseph Bastien, in his book *Mountain of the Condor* (1985:55), remarked that the people from Mt. Kaata in Bolivia "attribute magical properties to objects which combine, or are combined with, different elements. *Coca* from the eastern tropics and shellfish from the Pacific Ocean, both from the peripheries of the central Andes, are considered exotic foods, fruit of the gods, and fine offerings for the earth." Bastien (1985:136) further stated: "Marcelino and Carmen spent a month gathering all the necessary ritual items from the different communities and ecological zones of their *ayllu* and province." This custom must be ancient. Robert Randall (1987:84) noted that "the *wak'a* (sacred site) Qalla Qonchu was an enormous rock which was said to have been brought from Quito by the Inka Urgun to serve as the last stone to be placed in the fortress of Saqsaywaman."

Other ingredients are added to the offering that Juan and Luisa are preparing. *Coca mukllu,* the seeds of the *coca* plant, must be placed onto the offering in even numbers (2, 4, 6, 8, 10, or 12) to bring luck. *Qorilibro* (*qori* means "gold") and *qolqelibro* (*qolqe* means "silver"), thin gold- and silver-colored paper, as well as *qorilazo* and *qolqelazo,* threads of gold and silver colored yarns, symbolize prosperity. *Wayrurus,* colored beans, are added, as well as grains of *quinoa,* in the hope that the alpacas and llamas will multiply to reflect the abundance seen in the tiny quinoa grains. *Qañiwa* (*Chenopodium pallidicaule*), a cereal consisting of many tiny grains, also symbolizes countless llamas and alpacas. Garbanzos (*Cicer arietinum*), which are nutritious yellow fruits with bulky husks, incense,[12] and sweets are finally added.

The body parts of llamas, alpacas, and vicuñas are very important ingredients in an offering. The fur or the foot of an animal, or an entire fetus, can be added to the offering. The body part of an animal represents the respective animal of the same species. A whole fetus is most significant since it represents that particular animal to the fullest. Most parts are from llamas and alpacas, with very few from vicuñas, since they are strictly protected. I was told that whenever vicuña parts are used in offerings, they have been in the possession of the family for a long time.

At last *untu* (the pure fat from the chests of alpacas and llamas) is added to the offering. "*Untu* is like butter," Juan says, smiling with satisfaction. It is very significant because it so thoroughly represents the life force. Randall (1987:72–73) stated that "in the Andes the blood and the fat of animals (as well as of humans) are considered the substance of life where the life force resides." He asserts that the importance of the fat is reflected in the fact that no ritual offering to the deities is considered complete unless it includes alpaca or llama fat, because the camelid is the symbol of a human being, with whom it stands in a symbiotic relationship. Randall further noted that the llama and the alpaca cannot live without humans, but neither can Andeans live without them (especially before the arrival of the domesticated European animals). Randall (1987:72) offered another reason for the use of fat in offerings: fat is highly flammable and thus assures that the offering burns completely and will reach the mountain gods.

The more precious the ingredients, the more powerful the offering. It is therefore preferable to add as many valuable ingredients as possible. The basic, most essential ingredients, however, are *coca* leaves, carnation petals, and *trago.* Without these, no offering can be made.

Juan sprinkles more *trago* onto the offering.[13] Then he folds the paper which holds the gift for the deities into a rectangular package. He again sprinkles *trago* on its four corners and places it in the *unkuña.* He folds it in such a way that two ears form; these must face east in the same way as the *coca k'intus* wrapped in the paper. *Trago* is now sprinkled on the four corners of the *unkuña.* The seashell, refilled with *trago,* makes its round again as we drink in honor of the deities, to the welfare of the alpacas and llamas, and in respect for the people present.

It is midnight. Teresa and her uncle Gregorio take the offering to the *muyukancha,* the ceremonial corral, to burn it in a small cave, a recess in a rocky wall, referred to as *q'oyana* or *markachana.* I am not allowed to observe the burning. To view it is a dangerous undertaking that could cause serious misfortune. There must be total silence while the offering burns and the smoke rises to the sacred Apus.[14] While we wait, Juan tells me that the fine kindling (*llant'a*) which he used to start the fire is a medicinal plant called *maych'a* (*Senecio pseudotites*), which grows at high altitudes. At this point I learn that this offering is brought to the deities only in the name of the female alpacas.

While Teresa and her uncle burn the offering, Juan explains in an earnest tone of voice that the *enqaychu* establish communication with the fertilizing power of the Apus, who are asked to increase the herds. Antolín adds that *enqaychu* are intermediaries between humans and the Apus and can be as powerful as the Apus themselves.

Teresa and her uncle return, and we prepare another offering dedicated to the male alpacas and llamas. It is similar to the offering for the females, but fewer ingredients are used. Juan explains that female alpacas are given greater importance during these rituals because of their reproductive capacities. On August 1, however, rituals are held for male llamas and alpacas only. During that celebration, referred to as Macho Pagaray, the Apus are implored to give the male animals health and strength both for their own sake and for the humans, who rely on them to carry dung to the fields and to return with potatoes and other tubers.

Juan and Gregorio resume playing the ancient tune of Pukllay on their flutes. We place the *coca* we have been chewing on a small piece of paper. Luisa folds it. When people chew many *coca* leaves in a happy, peaceful atmosphere, it is believed that the animals will eat in the same manner and become strong and healthy. Masticated coca, called *kuka hach'u* (or just *hach'u*), contains the thoughts and wishes of the people who chewed the leaves throughout the evening. In the morning the *kuka hach'u* (sometimes referred to as *khullu*) will be buried in the *muyukancha* in a ritual called *hach'u p'anpay*. This is a "raw offering"—*hanku haywa* or *ofrenda cruda,* Juan explains. It is dedicated to Pachamama, asking her to protect the animals so they will be healthy and procreate. A burnt offering—*ruphasqa haywa* or *ofrenda quemada*—is placed into the fire and is dedicated to either Pachamama or the Apus.

Gregorio and Teresa leave again to burn the second offering for the male llamas and alpacas. They return happy and contented. The first offering has been graciously accepted by the gods, who have ingested it with pleasure. The ashes are as white as silver.[15]

Throughout the night everyone concentrates on the rituals. The atmosphere remains relaxed. Between rituals we talk quietly about everyday affairs—the family, the animals, and the natural environment.

Before dawn creeps into the cozy little house of the Mamani family, Luisa wraps the sacred items back into the *lliklla* and stores them in the secret hiding spot. Everyone disappears under their alpaca furs to get some sleep before sunrise. My mind is still active, overwhelmed by this night's events. While listening to the rhythmic breathing that comes from beneath the various alpaca furs, I reflect on this night full of ceremonies.

These ancient rites reconfirm a close interdependence among humans, animals, and nature. This night, through a dialogue with gods and spirits, we entered the realm of the sacred. We wove threads which symbolically bound us to our physical, social, and spiritual worlds. We reinforced ties with the past, with the Apus, with those ancestral spirits living in mountain peaks, and we looked toward the future, hoping for the aid and compassion of the deities from whom we requested health, prosperity, and peaceful coexistence. We engaged in reciprocity, the hallmark of Andean life; we were offering and asking, giving and taking.

Every gesture and movement was performed with great dignity and elegance. Every ritual carried an expression of respect for others—for gods, humans, animals, plants, and the spirit world. On this night and in the days to follow, the message of the rituals is clear. Only where there is respect can we find a way to live and act together. We must adjust and readjust to accommodate the various benevolent and malevolent forces within the cosmos. Pachamama, the giver of life, is also responsible for earthquakes and other disasters. The Apus are protectors of the herds, but they also send malevolent winds which can bring disease and death. There is no trace of aggression or hostility, domination, or subjugation in any of the rituals. Our offerings, our thoughts, our efforts in dedicating this night to a spiritual dialogue among humans, animals, and the powers of nature are meant to reinforce the positive, to give hope to a life so harmonic and serene, yet so vulnerable in this marginal environment.

The Andean people do not separate the natural from the spiritual environment. They believe that, like animals and people, all elements of nature live, feel, and breathe. Pachamama, the Apus, lakes, rocks and springs, all animate and inanimate beings—all aspects of nature need food and drink, love and consideration. All must be treated with sensitivity and concern. It is an ideology which promotes generosity and hospitality and which profoundly respects all forms of life. It was a night of beauty and wisdom.

Thunder God
and Sacrifice

The rumbling noise of thunder penetrates the Mamani hut. As it comes closer, it increases in intensity, alarming everyone. "Qhaqya," Luisa whispers as she emerges from underneath her alpaca fur, fear written on her face. Contrary to her usual calm demeanor, she now fumbles nervously through her belongings to get to her *unkuña.* She takes three *coca* leaves, places them into a *k'intu,* and disappears through the tiny door. The others listen silently. The children are frightened.

There is another clap of thunder, even louder. Without looking outside, Juan and Gregorio seem to understand every facet of this meteorological phenomenon, which expresses itself with intense force in the heights of the Andes. Through the small window lightning can be seen flashing through the sky in a fiery zigzag line. Thunder follows with a deafening roar. It is still at some distance, but it is coming ever closer.

I have heard much about the dangers thunderstorms pose at these altitudes. Death and destruction by lightning are a constant threat to the people, their herds, and their homes during the rainy season. Less than two months ago, in a neighboring village, lightning struck the house and corral of the Huaman Qoa family, killing both parents and part of their herd. Their three young daughters remained unharmed. Now they are *wakcha* (orphans), living in the tiny hut of their mother's sister, whose husband was also killed by lightning a few years ago. People wonder whether this family neglected to bring offerings to Qhaqya, the thunder god. Yet neighbors, friends, and members of the extended Mamani family also felt its deadly force.

Luisa enters through the squeaking door and takes a seat beside her daughters. Another deafening thunderclap hits with a crashing roar—this time dangerously close. There is a moment of frozen silence. The children tap their ears—horrified. Their father tries to calm them with a movement of his hand. He insists that Qhaqya hit a rock and is still at a distance. Strong gusts of wind whip the rain against the rattling wooden door. Qhaqya seems at its fiercest. Every adult takes *coca* leaves and blows *k'intus* to the east, asking the thunder to retreat. *"Howw! T'oqyaq Wayra, T'oqyaq Qhaqya! Ama astawanqa sipinkichu ñoqaykuq uywaykunataqa"* (Oh raging wind and bursting thunder, do not kill any more of our animals). Luisa whispers, *"Allillanta saqewayku"* (Leave us in good shape). I hear the *curandero* murmur, *"Qhaqya, ñoqan ruwani kay haywakuyta ama uywaykunata ni aylluyman ama dañotapas ruranaykipaq"* (Qhaqya, I make this offering for you; do not hurt my animals or my family). Again everyone blows *k'intus* toward the east, murmuring, *"Kaytan pagayku ñoqayku sutikipi"* (This we offer in your name).

Hail starts to pound onto the thatched roof. Small hailstones penetrate cracks in the thatch and accumulate on the floor. "Hail always comes with lightning, always," Juan comments in a reassuring tone of voice which, however, cannot obscure his great concern. Hail can wipe out entire crops, and hailstones as large as eggs, called *runtu,* can seriously injure and even kill people or animals. As anxiety grows, I begin to understand the tremendous preoccupation of the people of the Andes with their most powerful thunder god. I can also understand the value of rituals at times when people can do nothing but hope and pray.

Luisa's youngest daughter Libia hides her face under her mother's shawl. The name Libia is reminiscent of Libiac, the name used to refer to the god of thunder in the central and north-central Sierra.[1]

The thunder roars again, but it is not quite as loud, a sign that the storm is moving away. Luisa sighs with relief and smiles return to everyone's faces. We blow more *coca k'intus,* asking Qhaqya not to hit the other *suyus* of the village as it retreats.

The thunder god has been, and still is, one of the major deities in the Andes, next only to Pachamama and the Apus. In fact, in some regions of the high Andes, the god of thunder and the Apus, the high mountain peaks where this forceful deity resides, receive offerings more frequently than Pachamama. Some elders of Chillihuani told me that the first *coca k'intu* is always dedicated to the thunder god. The higher people live in a mountain environment, the more important the god of thunder becomes.

In Chillihuani they generally call the thunder god Qhaqya and, less frequently, Illapa. Sometimes the herders of Chillihuani use these terms interchangeably, and sometimes they distinguish between Illapa, which assumes a more figurative meaning, and Qhaqya, the name used to designate the actual striking force.[2]

Qhaqya also shows benevolence and is honored for bringing the much-needed rain. In its capacity to flash through the sky in a golden zigzag line, to strike people and animals on earth, to destroy life and to resurrect it, the thunder god shows both benevolence and malevolence. This most powerful deity is feared and revered, worshiped, and appeased (see Rösing 1990).

Illapa, a Tripartite God

To better understand what the thunder god means to the people of the high Andes, we must look to the past, from which certain elements have survived to the present day.

In Inca times, Illapa[3] was a prominent deity close in importance to Wiraqocha (the creator god), Inti (the sun), and Killa (the moon). The chronicler José de Acosta (1589/1962) maintained that the thunder god was the principal deity for all indigenous people of Peru.

Illapa was viewed in tripartite form as Chuquiilla, Catuilla, and Inti-illapa—lightning, thunder, and thunderbolt (see Cobo 1653/1956:160; Rostworowski de Diez Canseco 1983:39). The Peruvian anthropologist Yaranga Valderrama (1979:719) has suggested that the tripartite concept of Illapa is pre-Inca and has been maintained through Inca times to the present. Legends and ancient documents indicate that the ninth Inca Pachakuteq (sometimes spelled Pachacuti) Yupanqui, a powerful Inca emperor, elevated Illapa to the status of a major deity and adopted him as his *guaoqui* or *wayqe* (brother or alter ego). The Jesuit historian Bernabé Cobo (1653/1956:160) wrote in the seventeenth century:

> They imagined the thunderbolt, provider of the precious water, as a man in the sky whose shape is traced by stars with a mace in his left hand and a sling in his right hand, dressed in bright clothes which gave the sparkle to the lightning flash as he pulled the sling causing thunder when he wanted rain to fall. . . . Apart from being greatly venerated in the *Coricancha* (the temple of the Sun in Cusco), the thunderbolt had a temple of his own in

the section of *Totocacha,* where there was a statue of gold which the Inca Pachakuteq made in honor of him, naming it *Intiillapa* (*Inti* = sun; *Illapa* = lightning). Pachakuteq considered this statue his "brother" and took it to war with him.[4]

Information recorded by the early chronicler Sarmiento de Gamboa (1572/1947:178) is especially revealing:

> Pachacuti made two images of gold. He called one of them Viracocha Pachayachachi. It represented the creator, and he placed it to the right of the image of the Sun. The other he called *Chuquiylla,* representing lightning, and placed it to the left of the Sun. This image was most highly venerated by all. Inca Yupanqui adopted this idol for his "*guaoqui*" (brother), because he said that it had appeared and spoken in a deserted place and had given him a serpent with two heads, to carry about with him always, saying that while he had it with him, nothing sinister could happen in his affairs.

Attesting to its significance, the Incas represented the thunder god as a zigzag line on the wall of the Qoricancha, the Temple of the Sun in Cuzco, together with other cosmological symbols. The chronicler Juan de Santa Cruz Pachacuti Yamqui (1613/1927) made a drawing of the temple wall (see figure 1). (For an interpretation of the symbols, see Bauer 1995:118–125; Earls and Silverblatt 1978; Harrison 1989:66–71; Lehmann-Nitsche 1928; Sharon 1978:94–99; Zuidema and Urton 1976.)

In myths, visions, and in its striking appearance in the sky, the god of thunder was of paramount importance in Inca and pre-Inca times.[5] Throughout my years in Chillihuani I have encountered remnants of Illapa's ancient symbolism in oral tradition and in carved stone. Today as in the past, the thunder god is always on the minds of the people, especially during thunderstorms.

The Thunder God's Dual Forces

As I reflect upon the meaning of the thunder god through time, my companions remain silent, visibly shaken by Qhaqya's terrifying approach. Then, with the imminent danger gone, we begin again to chat about everyday events. Modesto, Alfonso, and Ricardo stop by. They live in the highest parts of Chillihuani and were on their way to visit family members when the storm hit. They greet everyone with a loose embrace and take off their soaked ponchos. Still shaken, but happy to have escaped Qhaqya's fury, they speak in subdued voices. They talk about previous close encounters with lightning.

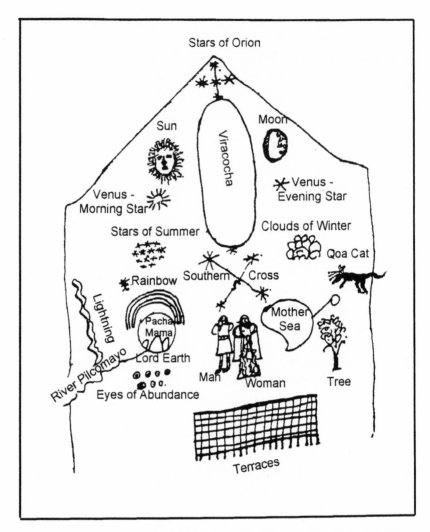

Figure 1. This drawing was made by Juan de Santa Cruz Pachacuti Yamqui, a native chronicler of the early seventeenth century, of a wall above the main altar in the Temple of the Sun (Qorikancha) in Cuzco. His drawing (redrawn by the author with English translations) is important to an understanding of Inca cosmology.

Modesto tells us that he loses several alpacas and llamas every year to the fiery strikes of Qhaqya. "With one stroke of lightning, thirty to fifty animals can die. Often they do not show any wounds because the lightning affects their lungs. An animal that Qhaqya has killed emits a strong burnt metallic smell that contains antimony (*antimonio*), a gas that is bad for the lungs, and by no means may such an animal be eaten.[6] It must be buried at the place where it was hit.[7] Those who bury animals stricken by the lightning must protect their mouths. If they do not obey this rule, they will die while coughing terribly." The others nod silently.

"*Arí*" (yes), Alfonso adds. "If a man eats an animal stricken by lightning, Qhaqya will pursue him. He will become ill. Only a shaman can cure him."

Modesto continues to explain: "When an animal dies from the deadly force of lightning, *coca k'intus* must be blown east in the name of the thunder god. An offering must be made with all ingredients: *coca*, carnations, *untu de vicuña, qorilibro, qolqelibro, qorilazo, qolqelazo*, sweets, wine, and *trago*." Luisa interrupts, "An offering for Qhaqya must contain Qhaqya *sara*." This is maize with split or cracked kernels. Maize cobs with twelve or fourteen rows of kernels are best. Also effective is *misa sara*, an ear of corn that consists of both red and white kernels. Half the cob is red and half is white. It is made by Qhaqya. The others agree that like Qhaqya *sara, misa sara* is hard to find and must be stored with the sacred items in the *mama q'epe* until an offering is made. Modesto resumes: "The offering must be burned in a remote place so the smoke can rise undisturbed to the divinities who consume it." In such a ritual, he would address the thunder god, saying, "Qhaqya, I make this offering to you asking in return that you do not hurt my family and my animals."

Ricardo, who lives in one of the most rugged high regions of Chillihuani, has been listening quietly. Since he lives close to the eternal snow, I ask him whether he has had encounters with Qhaqya. He nods and recounts with sadness: "Two months ago Qhaqya killed my best alpaca. Its head just disappeared from the tremendous power with which it was hit." He shakes as he continues: "My wife and son stood close by and might have been taken by this deadly force. I am so happy they are alive. Our house was not damaged either." The others explain that when Qhaqya hits a house, the owners must leave. They can never live in it again and can never rebuild a house at that spot. People are not supposed to even touch the spot where lightning has struck, but sometimes they are unaware that this has happened. Gregorio nods, saying, "The spot where Qhaqya hit is dangerous but it is also sacred."[8]

There is silence. Luisa offers more hot herbal tea. Alfonso quietly recounts that the strikes of the lighting affect people's health and may cause deformities even in the unborn child. "If a gestating mother is struck during the first three months of gestation, the child may be deformed. In the past such children have been called 'Illapa *churi*' (son of Illapa or son of the thunder). The thunderbolt can divide twins of the same sex while they are still in the womb."

"But Qhaqya is not always malevolent," Modesto says, breaking the silence with a glimmer of happiness in his eyes. "It can be good; the white Qhaqya (*yuraq* Qhaqya) is good, the yellow one (*q'ello* Qhaqya) is bad." The others agree. "The yellow Qhaqya is stronger and louder; it is devastating. It causes damage, makes people ill, and kills, and it always comes from the left side. Sometimes this Qhaqya brings rains, but they only wet the ground and do not penetrate to the roots."

"*Yuraq* Qhaqya, the good, white Qhaqya, also referred to as Qhaqya *munayniyoq* (the loving Qhaqya), arrives from the right side," Juan explains. "It is good and helpful; it does not hit with the same force and does not destroy. It is respectful; it brings good luck, it brings rain that penetrates to the roots of the plants and sees to it that everything goes well."

Modesto says that after a lightning storm mushrooms (*qoncha, setas*) (*Agaricus campestris*) grow in very high regions. These are delicious mushrooms and one can even sell them. But he warns that similar-looking poisonous mushrooms grow close by. "One entire family died from these mushrooms last year," he adds with sorrow in his voice.

Qhaqya, Shamans, and Metaphor

Qhaqya is a good example of the duality of forces which lies at the heart of Andean thought.[9] Qhaqya affects everyone. It holds power over life and death, and sometimes resurrects people who have been declared dead.[10] It is therefore no wonder that shamans are closely connected with the powers of Qhaqya. In different parts of the Andes I have heard people talk about the special relationship between lightning and the making of a shaman. When lightning hits a person and nobody sees it, not even an animal or the tiniest bird, Illapa will bring the person back to life.[11] Antolín explains the three steps which are accepted throughout the region in the making of a shaman:

Illapa

1. kills the person and can even destroy the body;
2. puts the body back together;
3. brings the person back to life.

Restored to life in this way, the person can become a shaman, called *paqo, altomesayoq* (the one of the high table), or *pampamesayoq* (the one of the low table). In some regions shamans are called *hampiri* or *yatiri,* or *laiqas* if they are sorcerers (Gade 1983:783). As the stricken person regains consciousness, he or she must look for a special stone which Illapa has left on the ground where it hit (Gade 1983:781; Rösing 1990:34). This heavy, round, metallic stone, called *bala* in Chillihuani (or *moroqhetu* in some regions), is considered of prime importance in helping the new *paqo* with his or her difficult tasks. The stone incorporates the power of an *enqaychu* or an *illa* and must receive offerings. If the new *paqo* becomes an *altomesayoq,* he or she can communicate directly with the Apus and with Illapa, using the stone as an intermediary.

A few years ago the elders of a village above the Sacred Valley of the Incas gave me a very heavy, round, black metallic stone. They advised that I always keep it with me because it is an *enqaychu* that protects a person from Qhaqya's mortal strikes. I accepted it gratefully.[12]

The relationship between the thunder god and shamans is drawn even closer as Modesto tells us that "when a *paqo* dies, *yuraq* Qhaqya, the white Qhaqya, comes and takes his (her) spirit to the house of the hail (*chikchi wasi; casa de la granizada*) inside the highest Apus. *Paqos*—both *altomesayoq* and *pampamesayoq*—perform special rituals honoring and appeasing Qhaqya. An *arariwa*—a person who is elected by the *comuneros* to guard the agricultural fields for the term of one year—can also preside over these rituals. *Arariwas* offer *coca k'intus* to Qhaqya, requesting that lightning neither strike nor kill. *Arariwas* make noise with their slings to keep Qhaqya's malevolent spirit away. Rituals revering and appeasing the thunder god take place at the height of the rainy season—on December 8 in Chillihuani, and on December 4 or 5 in other communities. The people of Chillihuani tell me that any of these days are celebrated in honor of Santa Barbara, a saint who is considered the female counterpart of Santiago. At this time people disguise themselves as condors and perform ritual dances.

Alfonso tells us that Qhaqya is honored with rituals on December 25 as well. This is interesting since the Incas also propitiated the weather god in December at the solstice festival of Qhapaq Raymi (Gade 1983: 776; see also Acosta 1589/1962:268). La Fiesta de Santiago on July 25 and 26 also centers on the thunder god. The weather god has remained strong despite endless efforts by missionaries throughout the colonial period to eradicate indigenous religious beliefs. Illapa affects, incorporates, and is identified with many phenomena; it is connected with hail, which always arrives with lightning, with powerful winds, and with the blizzards which accompany them. It is also perceived as kin or *compadre* of the earth (see Aranguren Paz 1975).

The most powerful metaphors which mask the thunder god include supernatural forms of animals, among them the catlike *qoa,* a mythological creature always found in close association with the watery element. The old people of Chillihuani assert that "*qoa* is a spirit that manifests itself as a cat. It is yellow and sometimes white. Hailstones and lightning fall from its eyes. It appears in springs, clouds, and in *k'uychi,* the rainbow. Whenever it drizzles while the sun shines, a condition which we call *chirapa,* a rainbow originates between two distant springs and stretches across the sky. In the mouth of each spring there appears a human face; from its hair emanate rays in seven colors. These seven rays can penetrate one's body and can cause death. The *k'uychi* is dangerous; whenever it appears, it can bring sickness."

A *curandera* from the valley had explained to me previously that "a gas emanates from the rainbow as it takes shape. One may not breathe without *coca* leaves in one's mouth because the gas can enter the body and make one sick, usually with diarrhea, which turns the same color as the rainbow. People often die under these circumstances." On the other hand, the herders of Chillihuani recount that like Qhaqya, the *k'uychi* also emits energies with healing powers which the *altomesayoq* of neighboring villages use when preparing their medicine.

Alfonso comments: "As soon as clouds conceal the sun, the rainbow and the human face disappear." He specifies that the rainbow always appears with the human face, but the face can rarely be seen. He further explains that *qoa* appears only when the moon takes shape. "It never emerges from the spring when the moon is full or when there is no moon at all. *Qoa* comes to steal crops by bringing hail."[13]

As I look around at my companions sitting with me in a circle, I realize that several of them have names that are reminiscent of the thunder god—Alfonso Qoa Yupanqui (the mighty *qoa*), Modesto Quispe Choqque—(*qespe* or *qespi* in the Aymara language means "shining crystal" or "reflections," which could well relate to lightning; see Molina 1575/1916:30), and Gregorio Choqque Mamani (Choqque, sometimes written Chuqqui or Chuki, is another Inca name for thunder). Perhaps the ancestors of my companions considered themselves "sons of the thunder," identified with this deity, and took names that reflected this powerful god. Or, perhaps they also considered the thunder their *guaoqui* (brother or alter ego), like Inca Pachakuteq Yupanqui.

Luisa starts to kindle a fire to prepare food. The rain has stopped. The men and children leave the house while I try, without success, to get my cameras to work. Perhaps a combination of cold and humidity or the static electricity in the air causes both to malfunction (see Reinhard 1992 regarding problems with static electricity). I must leave the house to escape the smoke. Outside, white mist hangs over the mountain peaks. The earth is soft and ready to absorb the sacrifice about to be offered.

Arpay—a Sacrifice to the Gods

Gregoria Choqque Mamani, an elderly neighbor who lives in the uppermost of the three small houses of this compound, calls Juan. Widowed with two grown children, she asks the *curandero* to perform the honorable task of sending her black llama to the realm of the gods as a sacrifice from her to the great Apu Ausangate. I hesitate, but Luisa insists that I attend. "Please come," she says in a calm, determined voice that leaves no doubt that this is a most significant event.

As I walk toward Gregoria's house, I see a black llama lying on its side with its legs tied together. Its head faces east and rests on Gregoria's lap. Sacrifices of animals always take place in the morning, with the head of the animal facing east.

The old woman prepares three *coca k'intus.* She blows over them into the wind to the east while she whispers a prayer. Then she places the *k'intus* into the mouth of her llama, comforting it: "*Hallpaykuy chay kukata samaripunaykipaq*" (Chew this *coca* so you can rest). Tears run down her cheeks. Family members stand close by. They have taken off their hats and blow *k'intus* into the wind. Then there is complete silence.

Using a knife, and with great speed, Juan cuts a round hole into the right side of the llama immediately under its ribs. His right hand and arm enter the body of the animal to get to the *sirk'a,* the vein that leads to the heart. With the fingernails of his thumb and middle finger, he cuts the vein and collects blood in his hand. In a ceremonial gesture he retracts his hand and swings his right arm into the air, offering the blood to the sacred mountain. With great respect he asks: "*Apu Awsanqati, kasqallanta, kutichinpuy chay chullumpita*" (Apu Ausangate, make this llama return). The sacrifice is done with tremendous speed; the animal's suffering is brief. He unties the llama's feet so the spirit of the animal can run toward the great mountain.

Gregoria collects the blood from her llama in a *qero.* She sprinkles some onto the ground in honor of Pachamama. Then, facing the mighty mountain, she whispers "*Apu Awsanqati, kay uywaytaqa kaskanta sayachipuy mirachiya uywaykunata*" (Apu Ausangate, make this beloved animal return [literally, "stand upright again"] and let my herd multiply). Her family stands by watching solemnly, absorbed in the significance of the ritual.[14]

As *enqa,* the life force of the llama, reaches the great Apu Ausangate, the animal stops moving. Juan removes the skin and separates the body parts. Gregoria collects all the blood in a jar. Then she receives the organs and washes them. Sometimes those present share the animal's heart and liver, which they eat raw. The people who take part in the ritual take great care that they spill no further blood and that no part of the animal is wasted. Later all bones are collected and buried together in the *muyukancha,* the sacred corral. Should a bone be missing, it can be replaced by an ear of corn. In respect for the animal it is important to keep every part together so it can be resurrected in the same form (see Flannery, Marcus, and Reynolds 1989:85–86 regarding the use of animal parts).

The Mamani family and Juan's brother's family sacrifice a black ram each. The animals' throats are cut; they die quickly. There is less ritual than with the llama, but the first blood that gushes forth is also offered to the deities, asking for the return of each animal in the form of a newborn.

Again all participants remain silent. Everyone hopes that the great Apu receives the animal spirits with kindness and will reciprocate in due time.

Back in the house Juan explains, "This ritual is ancient; our ancestors have always done it in exactly the same way." I show the Mamani family and their visitors a picture of a llama sacrifice drawn shortly after the conquest by the Inca chronicler Guaman Poma de Ayala (1980: 826; see figure 2).

They look at it for a short moment, then simultaneously exclaim that the picture is wrong because the person in the picture uses his right arm to penetrate the left side of the llama. "The right arm must penetrate the right side of the llama," they assert, agitated by this grave error. Although the chronicler Felipe Guaman Poma de Ayala has left outstanding records of the Inca past, a few mistakes do occur in his drawings. Thus John Hemming (1970:130), for example, remarked that in one of his drawings Guaman showed the Inca Atahualpa seated on a throne platform rather than on a litter.

During a sacrifice, as at almost any other time, people talk about their llamas and alpacas with deep emotion. "They are our brothers and

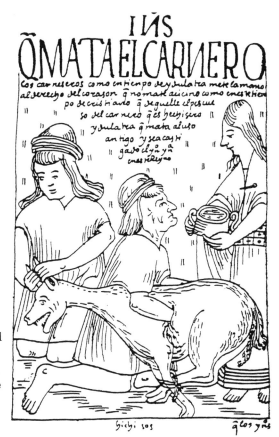

Figure 2. Sacrifice of a llama as it was practiced in Inca times and even after the conquest (from Felipe Guaman Poma de Ayala [1615] 1980:826–827).

sisters," the people of Chillihuani often comment. "We owe our lives to these animals and they owe theirs to us." High-altitude herders have also called llamas and alpacas "our ancestors." In the Andes, humans and their alpacas are part of the same empirical and spiritual world.[15] They are believed to arise from the same source and to be governed by the same supernatural powers (Gow and Gow 1975:141).[16]

Llamas and Alpacas between the Earth and the Sky

I try to come to terms with the deeper significance of this ritual. There is, of course, a practical side to any slaughter. These people need meat occasionally to complement their sparse diet of potatoes and other tubers. Also, animals get old and cannot live through another cold and dry winter, and too many animals overgraze the pastures. But there is also a spiritual side to any killing. In love and respect for the animal, it is not merely slaughtered. It deserves a ritual which will take its spirit to Apu Ausangate, who makes sure it will be reborn and reenter the same corral. Through its death, it also symbolically fulfills the need to feed the gods. As the life force flows toward the mountain and back in perfect reciprocity, the cosmic balance is maintained.

The offering of blood was made to Pachamama and to the Apus. But it was also offered to the mighty Qhaqya, who lives in the highest peaks and whose name was only whispered, perhaps to avoid evoking his fury.

I wonder whether it was a coincidence that all three animals sacrificed were black, and all were male. I suspect that the thunder god's furious approach on the previous night may have obliged the people to make the best sacrifice they could. Some authors maintain that only males are sacrificed to Qhaqya. The people of Chillihuani say that both females and males are sacrificed, usually old and weak animals that will not live through the upcoming dry season.

I ask the *curandero* why only black animals were sacrificed. He tells me that the blood of black animals is the best and that their meat is preferred. White animals, on the other hand, are preferred for the color of their wool, which can be dyed easily. Later I was informed that the sacrifices of the black animals relate directly to Illapa. Illapa brings rain, and water figures prominently throughout the fiesta of Pukllay.

Although I still do not understand the full meaning of the sacrifices of the black llama and sheep on this second day of Pukllay, these rituals are clearly deeply rooted in preconquest cosmology and ideology and are still of great significance for the herders of Chillihuani today. From early documents we know that the color black was important in rituals for major deities (Garcilaso de la Vega 1609/1966:360) and that black llamas were used to bring sacrifices to Illapa. In March the Incas sacrificed black rams to their gods (Guaman Poma de Ayala 1615/1980: 214–215). In October, the beginning of the raining season, black llamas were tied in the main plaza in Cuzco. They were left without water so that they would cry out, asking the creator god Wiraqocha for rain (Guaman Poma de Ayala 1615/1980:228–229).

In the metaphorical world of the Incas, black llamas were perceived as providers of rain. The mythology of Huarochirí is revealing as it explains how Yaqana, the constellation of a giant black llama in the Milky Way (Mayu), was considered instrumental in the fertilization and nourishment of the universe, including all animals, particularly llamas (Randall 1987:75). Yaqana, the black llama, and Wiraqochan, the white alpaca, were responsible for nourishing and fertilizing the universe. Together they made the vital life force move through the universe in the form of water (Randall 1987:76).

Llamas were connected metaphorically with water in still more intricate ways. They were believed to be instrumental in the actual control and stabilization of the cosmological cycle of water. In Inca astronomy, Yaqana, the black constellation of the llama, each night drinks water from springs and the sea to prevent floods (see Sherbondy 1982:20; Zuidema and Urton 1976:60–61).

The belief in the enormous black llama in the Milky Way is still alive in Chillihuani. On a bright moonlit night, Ricardo pointed to the Milky Way and said: "Look at the straight band with small stars in the southern part of the Milky Way. In this cluster of stars one can see many figures. One of them is a giant black llama with a young that is suckling." He pointed to two stars which are believed to be the eyes of the llama. I asked him whether this is the Yaqana. "We simply call it the Llama," Ricardo responded.

Fertility Rites

in the

Muyukancha

The sacrifice of three animals early in the morning of
the second day of Pukllay has left the Mamani family
and their neighbors emotionally drained. Yet they hope
the deities will receive the offerings and grant their
requests to return the spirits of the sacrificed animals
to their corrals. The families return to their respective
homes to prepare the festive meal, a very special soup,
called *t'inpu* in Quechua (*puchero* in Spanish), which
is made with a great variety of ingredients: meat, potatoes, *chuño,* and *moraya* (types of freeze-dried potatoes),
onions, carrots, yucca, sweet potatoes, cabbage, rice,
green chili, dried meat (*ch'arki*), and apples or sometimes pears.

Gestures of generosity, reciprocity, and respect, which
were expressed in a myriad of rituals during the first
night of Pukllay within the family, now start to draw increasingly wider circles to include the neighborhood,
the *suyu,* and eventually the *ayllu,* the entire village.

Luisa prepares many plates of delicious soup. Juan
and the children carry them to their neighbors, wishing
them happiness and prosperity. They, in turn, bring
plates with the food they have prepared, returning the
same good wishes. There is much giving and receiving,
well wishing and rejoicing in this time of plenty, when
nobody may go hungry. It is surprising to see how
much food people can eat on such an occasion, while
during the year they must subsist on so little. I am not
certain whether my own behavior is considered polite,

because after two plates I have to decline the food. I try to explain that I must take it easy due to the altitude. The people smile, I hope with understanding.

It is important that there is joy and well-being during Pukllay because the atmosphere that reigns during this most important fiesta will reflect on the entire year. If people, animals, and deities are content, then they will be so for the coming year. This belief extends back to Inca times. The priest Bernabé Cobo wrote that during fiestas, "they ate and drank the best food and chicha that they could make, because they thought that those who would not be content and eat and drink splendidly, would have bad luck and problems throughout the whole year" (see Zuidema 1982:420).

Cobo (1956) also asserted that during Inca fiestas nobody should be angry or quarrelsome because the same atmosphere that reigns during the time of sacred activities is to be expected for the entire year. This belief remains strongly expressed in Chillihuani today.

A young girl waves from a little house perched high up on the steep promontory, Seqayoq Moqo, across the river. It is Julián Quispe's daughter Bernardina. She announces that she will come to visit. With a big bag full of delicious alpaca *ch'arki* she runs down the mountain. Luisa gives her a bucket of soup to take back to her family. She thanks her and smiles. In this society the women are the household economists; they decide what and how much can be given and who may be invited. Julián's daughter invites us to visit her family. We accept with joy.

We start with a round of short visits to nearby homesteads within *suyu* Chillihuani. In every home we are invited to eat. Then we climb to the promontory Seqayoq Moqo for an extended visit with Julián Quispe Choqque and his wife Facunda Illatinco Yupanqui and their extended family. Julián is an accomplished musician. An esteemed elder, he is much involved in community affairs and is often asked to act as "guide" during weddings, when he leads the wedding party through their activities to the haunting tune of his *antara*. We are welcomed with a loose embrace and a radiant smile. *"Haykuy tiyaykuy"* (Come in and sit), the great-grandmother Placida Yupanqui Yupanqui exclaims with joy. Our host's son Francisco, his wife and baby, and Julián's nephew Leandro Choqque Quispe are also present. As guests they ask us to sit on a small bench covered with ponchos and immediately offer us food and drink. Apart from two benches, there is no furniture in this house, and there are only the most basic household utensils. Here, as in other houses, the very simple living conditions contrast sharply with the great elegance with which these striking people in their festive outfits move and address one another and their guests. Even the little great-grandmother has a radiant smile that enhances her delicate features. With joy she dances to the Pukllay melody that Julián and Leandro play on their flutes. I realize that unlike the other people, who wear sandals made out of the rubber of old tires, she wears sandals of alpaca leather, as did her Inca ancestors. She also wears the *barquilla montera,* a flat hat that was commonly worn in times that are long gone.

Julián takes his flute and plays again. "These are ancient songs from our Incas and their ancestors," Francisco explains. One of the songs is dedicated to Apu Ausangate, one to the alpacas. Then Leandro begins to sing funny songs, songs to tease other people, family, friends, and neighbors. Some songs are invented on the spot. Others are part of the heritage of the community. During Pukllay things are allowed that nobody would dare to say or do at any other time. Leandro, the young herder who lives next to the perpetual snow, jokes relentlessly in spontaneously invented songs. Everyone dances in an atmosphere of harmony and humor, hoping that this will lead to a year full of joy and free from sorrow.

As the afternoon draws near, we thank the charming Yupanqui/Illatinco family for the invitation to their *taki tusuy* (song and dance), for their generosity, and for their friendship. Touching shoulders in a loose embrace, we wish our hosts health, youth, and prosperity for the coming year. They extend the same wishes to us.

It is time to return home to perform rituals for the llamas and alpacas in the *muyukancha,* the ceremonial corral. As we hurry downhill, we see Luisa's daughter Teresa in the distance heading home with the family's herd.

Uywa T'ikarishian—a Flourishing Herd

We arrive at the *muyukancha.* This sacred corral is used only for ritual purposes three times a year—during Pukllay in February, on June 24 during San Juan, when rituals are held for the sheep, and on August 1 when the Apus are asked to provide strength to the male llamas and alpacas who are so important in the transport of goods. Except for these occasions, the animals sleep in the *iphiña*—the daily corral.

The rituals that are about to begin are part of the same overall ideology of Pukllay. They complement the rituals of the previous night and add their own special essence to the great ceremonial realm of this ancient festivity. The alpacas and llamas were central to the rituals of Suyay Ch'isin even though they were not physically present, but were represented by the *enqaychu,* their effigies in stone. Today both the *enqaychu* and the animals themselves will play an active part in the rituals.

Juan prepares the *mesarumi.* Luisa brings the *mama q'epe,* the bundle with the sacred objects—*enqaychu, pukuchus, qeros, ch'urus* (seashells used as drinking vessels), and a *puru* (gourd or calabash). She has brewed enough *chicha* to last throughout the week's ceremonies. She fills the ancient vessels many times to quench the thirst of the gods and the humans alike. During Pukllay the Mamani family uses an *urpu* that contains twenty gallons of *chicha.* The *chicha* is shared with all the guests and is offered to the gods and the animals as a symbolic token of appreciation and reciprocity.

Today, piles of *phallcha* flowers of the genus *Gentiana,* which have been collected in different parts of the high Andes, are offered in the course of the ceremonies. These flowers of many colors—yellow, orange, various shades of red, white, and gray—bloom only in February at altitudes above 3,600 meters. They are believed to bloom specifically for the ceremonies of Pukllay, and it is known that they contribute greatly to the success of the rituals. *Phallcha* flowers are considered female and are symbols of fertility.

Luisa smiles with satisfaction as she mixes the *phallcha* blossoms I have brought from Ocongate with those from other regions around Chillihuani. As is true for the purifying water collected from springs far away in the four cardinal directions, the flowers also must come from four directions, and, if possible, far from the ritual site. Other flowers are mixed into the ever-growing pile—carnations, dahlias, daisies, roses, geraniums, *thurpay* (*Nototriche*), *huamanripa* (a medicinal plant belonging to the genus *Senecio* which cures coughs), and other flowers that bloom in the immediate environment or in the valleys.

We hear the animals on the cliffs above us. Teresa drives the sheep in the direction of the *iphiña,* the daily corral, as they are not a part of today's ceremonies. They will have their day of festivities on June 24. It takes considerable skill and the help of other family members to lead the alpacas and llamas into the *muyukancha,* the ceremonial corral. Every alpaca and llama must be present for the ceremony. Not one may be missing. The animals are nervous in this enclosure, where they meet only two or three times a year. Finally they settle down (see photo 7).

Photo 7. Llamas and alpacas waiting for the rituals to begin.

Juan starts to prepare the offering in much the same way as the night before. He places a white sheet of paper onto the sacred *unkuña* which, in turn, rests on the festive *lliklla*. He places red and white carnations onto the sheet and many *coca k'intus* are blown in respect for the Apus and Pachamama—the meadows, lakes, springs, rocks, trails—and wild animals (mainly condors, hawks, and pumas, who prey on the alpacas and llamas). The name of the thunder god is whispered frequently into the wind and I notice many white carnations in the offering. White carnation blossoms are offerings to the god of thunder. They are also included in the hope that many white alpacas will be born. Qhaqya cannot be neglected; the power of this deity is still vivid in everyone's mind.

The deities and spirits of all these *wakas* (sacred places) are implored to protect the alpacas and llamas. In the prayers the alpacas are referred to with the respectful name *chushllu* and the llamas with *chullumpi*. All spirits that can potentially affect these camelids in beneficial or disastrous ways must be remembered. I am struck by the thoroughness with which all rites are performed.

The *pukuchus,* with their precious contents of *coca* leaves, pass from one person to another as we sit in a circle around the *mesarumi. Qero, puru,* and *ch'uru* also make the round. The deities are symbolically invited to drink, and we drink to everyone's health, youth, and well-being. The four corners, the four winds, the four cardinal directions are emphasized with each new toast and with every *coca k'intu.* The offering contains the same ingredients as in the previous night. Together with the thoughts of the people present and the spirits from the four corners, the ingredients are wrapped into the white sheet of paper on which they rest. The offering receives another benediction before it disappears in the *unkuña,* folded in such a way that two ears form which point east. In this form, facing east, this significant bundle receives blessings of *coca k'intus* and sugarcane alcohol. In the name of the alpacas and llamas, it is dedicated to all deities and spirits that affect the animals in any way possible.

With great care Juan carries the offering in both hands and slowly walks to the *q'oyana,* a small cave-like depression within a large rock. He smiles with satisfaction as he looks at the result of the previous night's offering to the gods. *"Usphaqa kashian yuraq qolqe hina"* (The ashes are white like silver), he says—a sign that the gods have eaten with contentment. Whenever an offering does not burn well, leaving dark ashes and some rough debris, this is a sign that it has not been well received and that the coming year may be a difficult one. When one offering has burnt well, but the next one is dark and rough, the situation is ambiguous. It is considered most important that the offering be made in a calm and joyful atmosphere.

Juan waits while Gregorio lights a fire in the *q'oyana* (see photo 8). As firewood he uses a thin, gray, and highly flammable plant called *maych'a*[1] (either *Senecio pseudotites* or *Senecio roundbeckiafolius* can be used), which was collected at the very heights of the village. He sprinkles alcohol onto it. Then he uses two hard black stones (*yana rumi*) which have become blackened by the fire, striking one against the other until a spark appears. The spark lights the *maych'a,* which immediately starts to burn. Juan unwraps the *unkuña,* takes out the offering wrapped in white paper, sprinkles *chicha* onto its four corners, and places it into the flames. As the fire begins to consume the offering, we turn our heads away and hurry back to the *mesarumi* out of respect for the deities, who descend to consume the precious gift. There is complete silence as the smoke rises into the air. Will the Apus accept the offering? Will they be pleased? Will they protect the herd for another year? These questions are vivid in everyone's mind.

Photo 8. Gregorio starts a fire in the *q'oyana* within the *muyukancha* in preparation for the burning of the offering.

As the fire dies down, the tension subsides as it is seen that the ashes are again silvery white. Now it is time for exuberant joy. Juan and Gregorio play their flutes. Everyone present takes a turn to shower the animals with handfuls of flowers. "*T'ikata hach'iykuy, t'ikata hach'iykuy hinata uyway t'ikarinan paq*" (Let us throw flowers, let us throw flowers so my animals will flourish), Luisa calls out with joy. Flowers have great significance in the lives of the Andean people. They figure prominently in fiestas and are always found on their hats or on the heads of their animals.

Luisa disappears and returns with a ball of pressed red powder called *llonqhetaku* which she prepared earlier, mixing smooth, ochre-colored earth with cold water until it attained the desired consistency. She places the mixture into a large conch shell and proceeds to add *chicha* and *qañiwa*. The many tiny grains of this cereal symbolize abundance. The herders hope that the alpacas and llamas will multiply until there are as many of them as there are tiny grains of *qañiwa* in the solution. *Llonqhetaku* is used to mark the animals, so that everyone will know that the rituals have taken place.

It is time for *irpay,* Luisa calls out in a cheery voice. *Irpay* is the ritual of marking a pair of one-year-old white alpacas. The animals are tied to each other as they stand side by side facing east. Luisa paints them with *llonqhetaku,* first three times around the neck, and then lines are drawn that cross on their backs and sides three times. This celebrates youth and fertility. Further, everyone can see that these animals are being given their due respect during this ritual. Youth is given great importance in the rituals during Pukllay. People wish one another youth in the ritual greetings, and youth and fertility were central to rituals in the past.[2] Everyone takes a turn to paint the solution on the backs of the animals and to sprinkle them with *chicha* and *phallcha* flowers. The young alpacas, which are now considered newlyweds, are dedicated to Teresa, who is usually responsible for taking the animals to pasture and at this young age is starting to build her own herd.

All sacred items are placed back into the *mama q'epe,* which Luisa now carries into the house. There they remain hidden in a secret spot that only she, her husband, and the older children may know.

Night falls. The ashes have cooled. Juan and Gregorio play the "Song of the Alpaca" on their flutes. Everyone dances through the corral. The musicians dance close to the llamas and alpacas, their flutes almost touching the animals' ears. The flute has sexual connotations, and is therefore appropriate for these rituals, which are believed to affect the powers of procreation of the animals and to bring fertility and abundance. Dancing represents joy. "The more we dance with our animals, the greater will be the chance that they will be content and multiply, the happier will be Pachamama and all the people." This is the unanimous explanation for the sacred act of dancing at these festivities. Everyone is happy that the gods have accepted the offering.

Accompanied by the sounds of the flutes and the joyful laughter of the women, who continue to shower the animals with flowers, the alpacas and llamas leave the *muyukancha* to join the sheep in the *iphiña* for the night. An atmosphere of happiness and love prevails between people and animals in the hope that the bonds renewed between them and the spirit world will continue to be strong, that the animals will remain healthy and multiply under divine protection.

Every ritual is rich in symbolism. The meaning of some is clear, while the significance of others is forgotten. Some people, mostly elders, still know about rituals that are no longer practiced village-wide, and they are afraid that as they die, the knowledge will be gone forever.

Nevertheless, everyone, young and old, is aware that the welfare of the animals determines the people's well-being. Still, there is more to the relationship between the herders and their animals than the economic component. Emotions are strong and so are feelings of love and respect for the alpacas and llamas, which are steady companions, share in the scarce resources, endure the calamities of the high-altitude climate, and participate in the ceremonies, which are meant to bring happiness to people and their animals alike. The way in which the people relate to their animals opens a window into the herders' view of the world and their own role in it.

Comprehending these complex relationships between people and their animals is not easy for outsiders. Alpacas and llamas are not to be dominated and looked upon as mere resources. They must be respected in their own right, and the relationship is built on perfect reciprocity.

An ancient Quechua legend explains most succinctly how the high-altitude herders relate to their llamas and alpacas. Teodosio Huanca Mamani (1990:23) wrote:

> The God Pachacamac took pity on the poverty of the first people who lived on this earth. After a long drought which had eradicated plants and animals they had neither sufficient clothing nor food to survive. To secure their future, he gave them llamas and alpacas. These animals were given in patrimony and not as property under the condition that the people would take care of them, look after their reproduction, protect them from their natural enemies and diseases and enjoy the products they receive in return. Should the people not comply, the God Pachacamac would take his animals away from the face of this earth. At that time the end of the world would have come. For this reason the people take special care of these animals, treat them with love, give them beautiful names and fiestas where they adorn them so they would be satisfied and would not complain to their owner, the God Wiraqocha.

Other writings refer to the close emotional relationship between the people of the high Andes and their llamas and alpacas. Guaman Poma de Ayala made a series of drawings and described how these animals not only helped the people with their daily chores but also joined them in imploring the deities in times of need. In one of his drawings he depicted an Inca singing with a llama asking for rain to fall (see figure 3).

The Quest for Survival

The rituals in the *muyukancha* and elsewhere are marked by precision and thoroughness. One feels the concentration, awe, and total dedication the herders exert in making this a successful event, pleasing the gods, the animals, and the people alike. No one may be neglected; to be negligent can bring revenge and misfortune to the animals and their owners. And in the heights of the Andes, misfortune is likely to occur; herds can be decimated within a short time, leaving their owners impoverished.

The herders of Chillihuani explain that a variety of factors lead to many life-threatening problems. The difference in temperature between day and night can range up to 35°C (e.g., 20°C during the day and -15°C at night). Young alpacas whose fur is still sparse frequently die of

Figure 3. The Inca, the Qoya, princesses, and others sing with a llama during a fiesta in Hawkaypata, the plaza of the fiestas in Cuzco (from Felipe Guaman Poma de Ayala [1615] 1980: 292–293).

the cold. High winds, hail, lightning bolts, drought, floods, and snow that remains on the ground for more than three days also contribute to the deaths that occur within the herds. Further, young animals fall prey to condors, foxes, and sometimes pumas. In April of 1996, relatives of the Mamani family, with whom I was living at the time, lost five of their largest llamas to puma attacks within a few days. In addition to animal attacks, disease can affect animals of all ages. Intestinal diseases are most common among baby alpacas and llamas. Diarrhea, caused by *Clostridium wilchi,* may kill from 50 to 90 percent of llama offspring younger than three months old (Flores Ochoa 1979:95). Variations of external parasitic diseases such as scabies or mange, referred to as *qaracha* or *qarachi* (*sarna* in Spanish), lower the animals' resistance and can cause death if not treated (see Flannery, Marcus, and Reynolds 1989: 102–103; Flores Ochoa 1979:95; Huanca Mamani 1990:151–153; McCorkle 1988: 41–46). *Qaracha* is caused by tiny mites, which according to the herders of Chillihuani look like bread crumbs stuck to the skin of the animal. The disease is highly contagious to other camelids and sheep, and some people say that humans can be affected as well. To cure it, the herders boil the herb *molle* (*Schinus molle*) in water and use the liquid, while it is warm, on the skin of the animal.

Intestinal worms also affect alpacas and llamas in Chillihuani. When camelids eat worm-infested *ichu* grass, referred to as *ichu kuru,* thin threadlike worms of white color invade the trachea of the animal, producing pus and foul-smelling breath. If not treated in time, the animals can die. Herders in some regions say that the death rate of young animals is as high as 50 percent. One of Chillihuani's *curanderos* who lives in the highest region of the village of Chillihuani asserts that young llamas and alpacas would not die at such a rate if they were cared for properly.

Alpacas and llamas have a low birth rate and a long gestation period (11.5 months), and give birth to only one young at a time. In addition, many males are sterile and females are known to abort frequently (Flores Ochoa 1979:90).

Herders also lose their animals to thieves, mainly when thick fog covers the high meadows and makes it impossible to view the entire herd at one time. Animals are also sometimes stolen right out of their enclosures at night. By the time their owners wake up, the thieves are often beyond the hills in the distance or have descended to the valley. Consequently, members of a herding family often sleep in different *ch'ukllas,* small huts or lean-tos placed around the corral, to assure the safety of their animals.

Despite so many dangers, camelids have flourished in the Andes for a long time. Before they were domesticated, they were hunted by aboriginal people for thousands of years. The first evidence of domestication comes from the Pikimach'ay Cave in Ayacucho, and is dated to between 4500 and 3100 B.C., and from the Telarmach'ay Cave near Junin, dated at around 4300 B.C. (Flannery, Marcus, and Reynolds 1989:91). Llamas (*Lama glama*) and probably (but not certainly) alpacas (*Lama pacos*) are derived from the still-extant but endangered species, the guanaco (*Lama glama guanicoe*) (Flannery, Marcus, and Reynolds 1989: 89), and perhaps the *vicuña* (*Vicugna vicugna*). Due to overhunting, few vicuñas are left in the wild. In 1965 a pilot program to reestablish vicuña herds was started in Pampa Galeras, Peru (see also Chapter 13).

Investigators generally agree that the guanaco is the ancestor of the llama and perhaps of the alpaca, although the alpaca may have vicuña genes and/or has been selected for high-quality wool. In the dry coastal region of Peru, cloth made from alpaca wool dating to pre-Inca times has been found.

Alpacas differ from llamas physically in a few minor ways. The herders of Chillihuani state that "llamas are larger than alpacas, have longer necks, bigger and longer ears, a larger snout, nose, and lips, and bigger feet. The eyes of llamas are larger and have a livelier expression while the eyes of alpacas are dreamy. The tail of a llama is lifted while that of an alpaca is shorter and held closer to the body. Overall llamas are stronger than alpacas."

Llama hair is strong, rough, and dry; some herders never cut llama hair during the animal's life. In Chillihuani some people cut the hair of their llamas every three to four years. Alpaca hair is long and abundant on the whole body. In Chillihuani alpacas have their hair cut every year or every second year in December, which marks the beginning of summer and the height of the rainy season. To shear wool, two men hold an animal while one cuts its hair with a sharp knife. While other investigators have reported smaller yields, in the high regions of Chillihuani, herders report a yield from alpaca females of from four to eight pounds of wool; males give eight to ten pounds every two years.

Overall, both llamas and alpacas are well adapted to the rugged heights of the Andes. They can endure cold temperatures, and they can eat short, tough grasses because of their split lip. Unlike other ruminants, camelids do not damage the ground because they have "deeply-cleft feet and walk on horny pads rather than hooves which cause less damage to fragile plants" (Alford Andrews 1982:102). Llamas graze in higher and steeper regions than do alpacas.

The herders of Chillihuani assert that male llamas and alpacas are important for their ability to carry loads of dung to the fields and to bring harvested potatoes, *oqa, ulluku,* and *mashwa* back from the fields to the storage areas. Llamas can carry packs weighing between 35 and 45 kilograms for up to 20 kilometers a day. Llama hair is not sold but is used to make slings, blankets, and carrying cloths.

Juan and Modesto explain that the hybrid of a male llama and a female alpaca, called a *wariso,* is larger than a llama and very strong. A male *wariso* can carry heavier loads, but its wool is not good. *Warisos* can have viable offspring. Ruiz de Castilla Marin (1994:42) wrote that because the vicuña, the guanaco, the alpaca, and the llama have the same number of chromosomes and other coinciding features, crosses can have fertile offspring. The Chillihuani herders assert that when a *wariso* is crossed with a llama, the offspring is a normal llama. When a *wariso* is crossed with an alpaca, the offspring is a normal alpaca (see also Wing 1975).

Alpacas are most precious to the herders of Chillihuani. Of the two existing species of alpacas, 90 percent are *wakaya* and 10 percent are *suri.* The *suri* alpaca is smaller than the *wakaya* and has long silky fur. The fur of the *wakaya* is shorter, curly, and less shiny. Opinions diverge about which species is best adapted to high altitudes. Modesto asserts that although young *suri* alpacas are delicate, they become very well adapted to the cold temperatures at high altitudes because of the long silky fibers of their large, heavy coats.

Any outsider who arrives in a village of llama and alpaca herders close to or above the tree line wonders how people eke out a living from such a rugged and marginal environment. But a closer look at the highly efficient use of the available resources shows that people can, indeed, be largely self-sufficient in their high-altitude abode. Male llamas and alpacas carry loads to and from the fields and sometimes travel with loads between Chillihuani and other high-altitude villages. Alpaca and llama hides are used as mattresses and pillows. Their wool is used for clothing, carrying cloths, blankets, ropes, and slings (*warak'a* or *soq'-ana*). Alpaca hair is spun into wool either in its natural colors of white, brown, gray, or black, or a combination thereof, or it is dyed before being processed into thread. Modesto tells that the *unkusa,* also called *onqo sani,* which is the hair that grows for four or more years on the chest of alpacas, serves to make good slings. People fashion *puruwanas,* which are braided slings made from the tail hair of male llamas (for a detailed account of sling braiding, see Adele Cahlander 1980). People use the alpaca hair they do not need for their own purposes to barter (*trueque*) in the valley in exchange for other goods such as sugar, flour, and bread. Some herders sell their wool in the market at Ocongate or in other regions (see Benjamin Orlove 1977 on the alpaca and sheep wool economy in southern Peru).

Meat is either cooked while fresh or it is manufactured into *ch'arki.* To produce *ch'arki,* salt is rubbed into the fresh meat of a camelid or a sheep. For about ten days the frost of the night freezes the meat while the sun dries it in the daytime. Eventually it assumes a whitish color from the salt and is then kept in the storage area of the house. People periodically cut slices from the big piece of freeze-dried *ch'arki* to use in soups, to give taste to any food, and to eat by itself. The anglicized term *jerky* is derived from the Quechua *ch'arki.*

Each part of the animal is either consumed or used to make things. Various dishes are prepared with blood.[3] The tendons of the animals are used for sewing as well as for strings on stringed instruments and to tie musical instruments together. The liver is eaten fried. The lungs are eaten with vegetables and chilies, and the head is made into broth. Animal fat (*wira* or *sebo*), which is present throughout the animal's body, is used to make candles. *Untu,* fat from the chest of the animal, is a prime ingredient for offerings to the major deities. Bones serve to make a comb-like tool, called a *tullu ruk'i,* used for weaving. The animals also provide much-needed dung to fertilize the fields. Sun-dried dung, called *wayk'una,* also serves as cooking fuel.

The health of the llamas and the quality of the products they supply depends to a large degree on the food available. Llamas and alpacas require fresh food, mainly from humid regions. The herders of Chillihuani agree that some of the best plants for camelids are *kunkuña* (*Distichis muscoides*), *caña caña* (*Lilaeopsis andina* Hill), *qoya* (*Festuca dolichophylla*), *cebadilla* (*Poa candamoana* Pilger), *llapa pasto* (*Muhlenbergia Peruviana*), *polo polulu* (*Plantago lamprophylla*), *miski pilli* (*Hypochoeris stenocephala*), *napa pasto* (*Calamagrostis vicuñarum* Pilger), *grano ichu* (*Stipa brachyphylla* Hitchcock), *orqo ichu* (*Calamagrostis Amoena* Pilger), *grama pasto* (*Distichlis humilis*), *iru ichu* (*Fes-*

tuca ortophylla Pilger), and *ichu* (*Stipa ichu*). (See also Sotomayor Berrio 1990.)

Young animals are born, normally between December and March, in the midst of the rainy season when the above plants and grasses are most plentiful and the pastures are fresh and green. Females can conceive again twenty-four hours after giving birth. Llamas and alpacas are considered mature at around two years of age. Llamas live, on average, twenty years, while alpacas average about ten to fifteen years. Their life span depends largely on the quality of food available to them.

Herder families know every one of their alpacas and llamas by sight and every animal receives a name. The Mamani, Illatinco, and Quispe families tell me that common names for alpacas and llamas are Khunpa (companion), Yuraq (white), Qoyllu (lustre or bright white or light), Yana (black), and Ch'unpi (brown). (See Flores Ochoa 1988a for a classificatory system for llamas and alpacas.) In every herd several animals receive the names of birds, such as Ahuya and Chullumpi, which are birds that do not fly well. People assert that these birds are seen in high mountain lakes and are believed to pass underground to other lakes. The people in Chillihuani wonder whether these birds have two different breathing mechanisms.

Suri alpacas share their name with the terrestrial bird *suri* (*Pterocnemia penata* d'Orbigny), which lives in the highlands. This bird has long feathers that have been compared with the long shiny hair of the *suri* alpaca. In songs and poems, alpacas and llamas are also referred to by the names of birds. Some of these songs are highly emotional.

Llamas and alpacas are playful and sometimes exuberant. They form close friendships within the herd. One day as a herd was ready to leave for the pasture, I saw that one of the alpacas had a sore hind leg. It trailed behind, and as the distance between the injured alpaca and the herd became greater, another alpaca stayed behind and waited for the injured one. The healthy animal walked ahead of the sick one, then waited and again walked ahead and waited. The herd was already out of sight, but the two animals did not separate. Together they eventually made their way slowly to the pasture.

Pukllay Martes—
the Incas Invite

On this night again there was little time to sleep. When Luisa calls everyone for breakfast, it seems as though only minutes have passed since we retired under our alpaca furs. She offers soup with *moraya, chuño,* leftover meat, and off we go—the *curandero,* his daughter Libia, and myself—toward the hills in the distance where the Mamani/Illatinco family maintains one of its potato fields.

We cross the river on two tree trunks placed side by side from one rocky outcrop to another across the gorge. Below us roars the rushing Chillihuani River. First Juan walks across, then his young daughter, both seemingly fearless. I follow, hesitatingly, without looking into the turbulent water below.

On the other side, steep rocky terrain alternates with sparse grass covering. After several hours we reach an area with deeper soil where potatoes can be planted. Many small fields are strewn across the hills. There are areas closer to Juan's house where potatoes can be grown, but fields (*chakras*) must lie fallow for five years, after which they can be used again for two years. There are no written laws regarding the use right of land and the borders of each field, but, by tradition, people know exactly which fields are theirs to use in any given year. After the land has lain fallow, each family plants the *chakras* it has used in earlier years.

As we arrive at the *chakra* that has been planted by the Mamani/Illatinco family, Juan gives me *coca* leaves. We both blow *k'intus* in respect for Pachamama and thank her for the beautiful crop we see before us. On this occasion I discover that Pachamama is not only perceived as the all-encompassing Earth Mother, but there are parts of the earth which are considered Pachamama's daughters. The *chakra* we stand upon is a daughter of Pachamama, and as such is responsible for the specific crop for which she receives offerings in her own name. Each field is named by the owner. We are presently standing on Waka Watana (where one ties a cow). Beside us is K'uchu (the corner) and Leqetani, named after a wild bird called *leqe* (*Vanolus resplendens* Tach.) and Qantuchayoq, the *chakra* where *qantu* flowers (*Cantua buxifolia* Juss.) grow; these are the sacred flowers of the Incas and modern Peru's national flower. Other fields are also known by colorful names such as Khallki (the stony corral), Waylla (the grassy hill), and Amachuyoq (the place where *amachu,* wild poisonous plants, grow).

Juan clears the field of rocks and adds more stones to *apachitas* (also spelled *apachetas*), cairns built up over many years for the spirit guardians of this place. He sprays *chicha* on the field to quench the thirst of Pachamama and her daughter and then selectively harvests potatoes. These potatoes are an early variety, called *maway papa,* and thus can already be harvested in mid-February or even earlier. Potato harvesting is in full swing from the middle of April until the end of May. In June, and sometimes as early as the end of May, people begin to freeze-dry potatoes. The people of Chillihuani recognize about two hundred different varieties of potatoes in this region.[1]

Potatoes, either boiled or freeze-dried as *chuño*[2] and *moraya,*[3] are the staple of the herders' diet. Without potatoes, few families could survive. Often, especially during harvest time, the potato fields receive offerings in the form of *coca k'intus,* and Pachamama is asked that the productivity of these fields be maintained.

During my research in the Vilcanota Valley I observed that most farmers have considerable problems with parasites that affect their potato plants and must use pesticides to be able to get a good harvest. In Chillihuani, however, insecticides and pesticides are not necessary and are never used. There are some advantages to living at high altitudes. Juan smiles with pride as he talks about the precious potatoes that grow in the heights of Chillihuani.

We help Juan to fill his *q'eperina* (also called *q'epina;* both mean "carrying cloth") with potatoes. Again we thank Pachamama and her daughter, the field we stand on, for their generosity. We blow *k'intus* into the wind for Illapa, the god of thunder, thanking him for sending rain and keeping away the feared thunderbolt, hail, and floods.

Ancient Tunes on Capillapampa

As we hurry downhill, the landscape comes alive with color. People dressed in splendid costumes appear from behind hills and ravines. "Pukllay, Pukllay," they call across the mountain peaks and gorges. The women wear the new clothes they have woven throughout the year for this very special fiesta. The huge *niwa* hats the men wear seem to dance through the landscape, undulating like waves in the wind. They are made out of the long-stemmed *niwa* grass that grows in the valley along river shores. The exuberant people swing their *warak'a* through the air as they walk proudly toward Capillapampa (also called Ch'urumarka) high up on a promontory overlooking the central part of the village. An elder told me that formerly this festivity took place in Wakakancha, an ancient sacred site where a small church was built. Then in 1938, a bigger church was built on Capillapampa and surrounded by an adobe wall. People explained that they had to work in *faena* (free of charge) to build the church. Long before the church was built, people congregated at this high place to celebrate Pukllay.

"That's where we will go," Juan exclaims, pointing to a place high above us as he deposits his carrying cloth filled with potatoes in front of his little house. Luisa accepts the potatoes with joy. In a festive mood and full of energy, she calls out to everyone who passes by—near and far—wishing them a wonderful day. "Pukllay, Pukllay," her clear voice echoes against the rocky mountains across the gorge and returns mingled with the exuberant calls of the passers-by. There is a symphony of joy on this radiant day of Pukllay.

Together we ascend the narrow path to Capillapampa. Many more people come in sight. Some arrive from the farthest corners of Chillihuani, more than 15 kilometers away. The panorama is overwhelming as we approach the picturesque adobe wall on the top of the hill. Beautiful people in exquisite outfits receive us with radiant smiles and gestures embodying elegance and self-confidence. The ceremonial melody of the Pukllay tune sounds above the laughter of the people and the greetings by which they welcome everyone who enters the compound. At the far side of the enclosure, the male village elders sit on a bench by a long table faced by a row of young men. The female elders sit on the ground near the wall faced by a row of young women. The young people serve *trago* and *chicha* to their elders in a manner reflecting deep respect. They drink, but there are no drunks. The area is spotlessly clean.

As we enter the enclosure, the village president, Ricardo Illatinco Chino, a man around forty years of age in an especially striking outfit, hurries toward us, half curious, half surprised to see such an unusual visitor. He introduces himself in a friendly manner, but is anxious to know why I came to attend this fiesta. The *curandero* explains. The village president is satisfied. He smiles and welcomes me. Immediately he walks to the area by the wall where the women sit together. He asks his wife to come and meet me. Lorenza, a charming woman, expresses happiness that I came from so far to attend this very special celebration. Then the village president introduces me to the other village authorities and offers a gift—delicious bread from the bakeries of Oropesa, far away in the valley. Bread is much valued. It must be brought from far since bread is rarely baked in Chillihuani due to the scarcity of fuel.

Groups of women and men begin to dance to the ceremonial tunes of the flutes. Women wear the characteristic homespun outfit of this village, consisting of several skirts (*pollera*), a woven blouse (*aymilla*), a small jacket (*haguna*), a shawl (*lliklla*) held together by a shawl pin (*tupu*), and a flat hat with woolen fringes of different colors (*montera*). Women wear this costume most of the time. New clothes of the same type are worn during fiestas (see photo 9).

The fiesta outfits of the men, called *tusuq p'acha* Pukllay Martes (dance clothes on Carnival Tuesday), consist of a woven shirt (*aymilla*) and a jacket (*haguna*) over which they wear a poncho with another one folded across one shoulder, one or two *llikllas* worn over the shoulders, woven black pants (*wara*) which reach below the knees, the *kantunka*, which is a belt with much colorful wool attached, and the large *niwa* hat worn over the knit hat (*ch'ullu*). Both sexes wear rubber sandals (*usut'a*). Women carry their belongings in the *unkuña* and the larger *q'eperina*. Men also use the *q'eperina* to carry larger items and the *ch'uspa*, a small woven bag, to carry *coca* leaves and money. Although the *unkuña* is considered a "female" item, most men carry an *unkuña* instead of or along with a *ch'uspa* (see photo 10).

Women and men line up in parallel rows for the Pukllay dances, called *qhashwas*, which are performed in a circular pattern. These dances originated in Inca times or before. The more the people dance, the happier the deities will be, the better the harvest will be, and the more numerous the animals in their herds.[4] The thumping sounds of

Photo 9: Women and men dance the Pukllay dances on Capillapampa (Ch'urumarka).

the dancers' feet, the swirling skirts, and the swinging *warak'as* mix with song and laughter, flutes and drums, to produce a vibrant atmosphere in this high mountain wilderness.

Andrés Felipe, one of Chillihuani's most outstanding musicians, stands in the courtyard playing the enchanting Pukllay tune on his flute; people move to his music with graceful dancing steps. Tall and athletic, with handsome features, this young musician emanates an air of royalty in his gorgeous Pukllay garments. In addition to the flute, he also plays the drum, the bass drum, the mandolin, and the *charanga* (a small guitar played by Indians), and he has composed many of the songs he plays.

Throughout the afternoon I meet people from the four *suyus* of Chillihuani, all equally joyous and radiant. The music, the songs, the dances, the drinks—everything is offered to the deities. Every movement and gesture expresses respect for people, the gods, and the very earth upon which they tread.

Photo 10. A young herder in his festive Pukllay attire. During Pukllay men wear a *lliklla,* which is a woman's garment.

I have attended many celebrations in the Andes. They usually begin in an organized fashion. But as they continue, participants often become drunk and the events may end with empty bottles strewn along the roadside and drunken celebrants rolling in the dust. In Chillihuani, the people drink, but drunkenness is never looked upon favorably. Those who do get drunk are still expected to carry out their functions in a dignified manner. Neither was intoxication looked upon favorably by the Incas. It is known that the eleventh Inca Wayna Qhapaq drank great amounts of *chicha,* but was never seen drunk. Irene Silverblatt (1987: 145) quoted the Inca chronicler Guaman Poma de Ayala (1615/1956, 3:98) with regard to this topic: "At present, in this life, more Indian drunks exist than in the old times. In the epoch of the Incas, there were none [to speak of]; for they were immediately subjected to [traditional] justice. The Inca ordered that those who were terrible drunks, who spoke in an evil way, who slapped women in the face, who fought with anyone or with their wives, be brought to justice."

Contrary to the common belief that all highland Indians are drunk much of the time, the herders of Chillihuani only drink in their village when they carry out rituals. Those who drink within village boundaries outside the framework of religious activities are looked upon with contempt. When the herders are visiting the valley, however, they do accept a drink when it is offered. Peruvian anthropologist Oscar Núñez del Prado (1984b:113) observed the same attitude toward alcohol in the remote village of Q'ero. He stated: "Courtesy obliges him [the person of Q'ero] to drink the first cup with the person who invites him, but otherwise he openly rejects alcohol outside the three village festivities."

The Pukllay ceremonies on Capillapampa stir an energy that sustains vibrancy and enthusiasm throughout the entire fiesta. The sun disappears behind the mountain range in the west and night starts to fall as we descend the precipitous inclines. Although hundreds of people came to the hilltop to celebrate, in respect for Pachamama nothing is left on the ground, nothing is disturbed. After all are gone, the site remains as it was before the celebration began.

Taki Tusuy—Song and Dance

Back in the Mamani house we settle down on alpaca furs. Already we hear the dogs barking. Sounds of flutes and the laughter of young people penetrate the night. Luisa and her daughters dance with joy. "*Tusuqrunakuna*" (the dancers), they exclaim. Soon a group of young people arrives. To the rhythm of the music they move through the low door into the cozy house. One after another the young people greet their hosts, their respected elders. With a loose embrace they bring their good wishes for happiness, youth, health, and prosperity for the coming year:

Mamay Luisa, Taytay Juan, watukamushiaykiku
Sumaqllata qhawaykusayki wataman
Kunanhina sumaqlla kankichis, qoriyuq, qolqeyuq
T'ikahinalla llanllarinkichis.

"Mama Luisa, Papa Juan," the young people address one host after the other,

We come to visit you,
we wish to see you as beautiful in the coming year
as you are today, with gold and silver
and fresh as flowers.

Luisa and Juan offer drinks to the young people. They, in turn, offer a drink and *coca* leaves to their hosts. Luisa, with more exuberance than ever, encourages the young people to eat and drink, to sing and dance. "*Taki tusuy!*"[5] she exclaims as she dances on the earthen floor in perfect synchrony with the music. The young men start to play the Pukllay tune on their flutes, and the young women sing with high-pitched voices both ancient songs and new ones, invented on the spot. The same tune is played over and again. Tempo and pitch, however, differ with every song. Between the songs the young people talk about things of special interest. After some time, they express their curiosity about me, the stranger. They finally dare to ask where I come from, from what place in the world. Leandro turns to me and pleads, half joking, half serious, "Steal me and take me to the distant country from where you came." This stimulates considerable conversation. The young people wonder how it would be to live in a foreign country. They get excited about the thought of seeing other lands. But Luis cautions that this would be difficult since they do not know the language or the customs. "We hardly know Spanish," Alicia interjects. They laugh in agreement, but the idea of seeing other countries is planted.

There is a moment of silence. "*Taki, taki, takisunchis* (Let's sing)," Luisa exclaims again. "Picha Picha Anillochayta," Pascuala suggests. The others agree. The men play the flutes, and Pascuala sings with Leandro:

Pascuala:

Picha picha anillochayta tarikunqa,
Chaycha chaycha yanachay kanqa.

(Who, who will find my ring,
He, he will be my love.)

Leandro:

Ñoqan, ñoqan tarikuni
ñoqan ñoqan tarikuni
ñoqa punicha yanachayki kasaq.

(I, I will find it
I, I will find it
I will be your love.)

We talk about the *suyus* from which the young people come. Leandro tells about his home, close to the great Apu Ausangate, next to the eternal snow. *"Takisunchis 'Awsanqati Qoyllur Punchu'"* (Let's sing "Ausangate with Your Poncho as Bright as a Star"), Alicia suggests. The men play the tune on their flutes, and Alicia sings:

> Awsanqati qoyllur punchu
> Punchuchaykita wikch'urikuy (bis)
> Punchuchaykita wikch'urikuspayki
> Punchuchaykiwan haku kuskalla puririsun (bis)
> Ch'urumarkapi cargo ruwaq
> Amalla amalla macharachiwaychu
> Ch'illkapampapi cargo ruwaq
> Amalla amalla macharachiwaychu.

> (Ausangate with your poncho as bright as a star,
> Throw your poncho from one of your shoulders,
> With your poncho over our shoulders
> We will always walk together,
> To do the cargo in Ch'urumarka,
> Don't don't make me drunk,
> To do the cargo in the pampa of Ch'illka,
> Don't don't make me drunk.)

Other songs follow—sad songs, happy songs, and songs full of mischief. Pukllay is the time to let off steam, to tease and to express what cannot be said at any other time. "Boy losing girl songs" are just as common in the Andes as elsewhere. Many songs refer to the beauty of flowers and birds. Then there is a song of sadness. Everyone joins in singing "Tawantinsuyu," which recounts the end of the Inca Empire. The people hum in a slow, sad, solemn way, followed by the word *Tawantinsuyu*. This is repeated several times. The tragedy of the end of Tawantinsuyu, the Inca Empire, is lamented.

No one speaks for some time. Then joy resumes. As is customary, Luisa, the hostess, asks the young herders to dance, and Juan, the host, asks the young ladies, who are normally the young men's wives or sisters, to dance. Then one of the young men asks me to dance. Luisa watches intently. As she realizes that I know the Pukllay dances, she asks me in a friendly but insistent way to share the role of the hostess and to dance for the rest of the night. I love to dance, but I envision another night without rest. I try to figure out when I had my last good night's sleep. It seems long ago. I was already exhausted by the time I had made the ascent to Chillihuani, but Pukllay is not a time for the weary. Rituals and sacred ceremonies continue throughout the days and most of the nights. It does not really matter anyway, because there is neither time nor place to sleep in this tiny house full of happy people.

Yawar Mayu—Why Must the Blood Flow?

The music resumes. Julio asks me to dance. With a mischievous grin, the *curandero* hands me the *soq'ana,* a woven sling, smaller than the *warak'a.* The *soq'ana* is used to dance; the *warak'a* is used for games and to throw stones to retrieve llamas and alpacas. Sometimes the terms are used interchangeably.

The *warak'a* is an Inca insignia, one of the chief hunting weapons in Inca times (Rowe 1963:217). I know that the herders use the *warak'a* to hurl stones into the far distance to bring back llamas and alpacas, but I am not certain how to use the sling in a dance. "This is the *soq'anakuy* (some say *warak'anakuy*), you must whip your partner, whip him, whip him hard," the young people exclaim joyfully. Julio laughs in anticipation. Juan explains that I must whip my partner's exposed lower legs.

Julio starts to dance, bobbing back and forth rhythmically. With vigor and elegance he moves in a semicircular pattern.[6] I adjust my steps to the music as we dance to the clapping of the enthusiastic crowd. "*Waqtaq! waqtaq!*" (Whip! Whip!), the young people exclaim. I swing the *soq'ana;* it touches his calves. "*Yapaway astawan, yapaway hoqtawan!*" (More, more, another one!), they cheer. "*Yapaya hoqtawan!*" (Give another one). The *soq'ana* again sweeps his calves, this time more forcefully. "*Yapay! Yapay!*" the whole crowd exclaims, trying to get more energy into this dance. I wonder whether this is a performance of strength, courage, or resistance to pain. I lash out another time, more forcefully. But the crowd is not satisfied, nor is my partner. "*Por favor, Señorita*" (Please, Señorita), Julio implores now in Spanish with much charm and enthusiasm, "*con más fuerza*" (harder). "I cannot do it any harder; it must hurt," I respond. "*Manan nanachinchu! Yapamuy aswanta!*" (It does not hurt, do it again much stronger!) my partner responds, laughing. He falls to his knees and pleads with enthusiasm to make the dance a success.

We continue to dance and to laugh and occasionally I whip my partner's legs, persuaded by him and the young couples around us. The music stops. I return the *soq'ana* to Juan. "Well, these are our customs," the young people affirm proudly. I ask the healer about the meaning of the dance. "It is to animate lazy dancers and to warm up in a cold night," he answers with a joking intonation in his voice. I know there is more to the story. A showing of strength and courage is certainly part of it. I know I must wait to be able to find out about the deeper meaning of this ancient custom.[7]

We continue to chat and to joke. Men play their flutes, and women sing. The dogs bark ferociously. The Pukllay tune coming from outside mingles with the songs inside the house. Another group of young people arrives. There is no room to enter, so the group that came first has to leave. Each member of the groups that enter and leave embraces the hosts, wishing them eternal youth, health, and happiness.

Playing, singing, dancing, eating, and drinking continue. One group follows the other. The last group of young visitors leaves just before dawn. The haunting melodies emanating from their flutes echo in the remote mountain world as they disappear in the haze of the new day.

For the next five days, groups of young people continue to visit families in the various parts of the four *suyus* of Chillihuani. The young people show their respect for the elders of the village by bringing them their good wishes, playing the sacred tunes for them, singing ancient songs, and inventing new ones. Their visits reconfirm friendship and solidarity within the entire community. Throughout most of the night, the house echoes with laughter, songs, and music, with humor and a vibrating energy. Luisa, usually soft-spoken, has been transformed into an outgoing person whose enthusiasm seems boundless. She makes sure that joy and energy will continue to flow throughout the festivity.

We put on more clothes, spread out the alpaca furs, and lie down to sleep. The early hours of the day seem colder than usual. It is so cold that I wish we could have continued to dance. But instead the guinea pigs dance around us, happy that the floor is theirs for a few hours.

6 ◈ Survival Today and a Look into the Past

It is dark and cold in the early morning on this fourth day of Pukllay. I hear the creaking door open and then close with caution. Juan and Luisa are preparing for *señalupampay,*[1] the marking of the young alpacas and llamas.

Every family knows its alpacas and llamas well and closely follows their development from birth. However, the animals are also marked so they can be distinguished from the animals of other herds when they mingle in the pasture. Even animals within the family herd are marked differently when sons and daughters start to build their own herds, which usually begins with their first hair-cutting ceremony.

Señalupampay is an ancient custom practiced among high-altitude herding communities in the Andes. Prehistoric evidence about the marking of alpacas and llamas comes from the ceramics of the Candelaria culture, which depict male llamas with tassels in their ears (Ryden 1934:158). This find suggests that the breeding of llamas and the ritual of ear marking occurred in pre-Inca cultures. The custom of cutting specific parts from the ears of the animals, however, is believed to be a Spanish custom that was taken over by the herders of the Andes following the conquest of Peru (Nachtigall 1975:135).

Today as in the past, *señalupampay* is considered very important among herding communities. For the Aymara of Bolivia, "The marking of the ears of domestic animals is the most important ritual of the year that involves animals" (West 1988:195). The rituals associated with *señalu-pampay,* however, differ to some extent among regions and even among villages as to their practice and the time of the year they take place.

Within Chillihuani, a variety of methods are used to mark animals. The *curandero* from Llaqto paints his animals with *llonqhetaku.* Juan Mamani and his family, like most herders, make distinctive incisions in the animals' ears. Some people put tassels of different colors into the ears of their llamas and alpacas. The Mamani family adorns male llamas and alpacas with tassels on August 1.

As dawn starts to creep through the cracks of the wooden door, Juan calls his family to come and witness the ceremony. Three alpacas and two llamas, all approximately one year old, are led into the *muyukan-cha.* They look around nervously before they finally settle down. The family assembles around the *mesarumi,* blows *coca k'intus,* and asks the deities to watch over the animals so they will remain healthy and grow strong. All the ingredients necessary for an offering are placed on a white sheet of paper that sits on the *unkuña.* We toast to Pachamama, the Apus, Qhaqya, and all sacred places these animals will encounter in their daily excursions. *Trago* is sprinkled onto the offering.

Cups full of *chicha* spray through the air in the ritual of Ch'allaska and land on the llamas and alpacas. Luisa and her daughters tie red wool around the necks of the two males and around the flanks of the three females. While Gregorio holds each animal as though in an embrace, Juan makes a tiny incision in the right ear of each animal, then wipes the drops of blood with a piece of cloth. Luisa places the ear pieces of the female animals around her *unkuña,* while the pieces from the male animals are placed around Juan's *ch'uspa.* Then she picks them up and adds them to the ingredients in the offering, which includes *coca* leaves, *coca* seeds, petals of carnations, *qañiwa,* maize, *chuño, garbanzo,* sweets, and so on. Juan explains that this is a *hanku haywa (pago crudo),* a raw offering, which in Chillihuani is buried in the *muyukancha* either the same day or the next morning, in contrast to a *rupha haywa (pago quemado),* a burnt offering, which is most often ignited in the *muyukancha.* Angelica Aranguren Paz (1975:126) wrote that in the region of Puno, pieces cut from the ears of sheep and alpacas are collected for three years, after which time they are buried in August under the *mesarumi* in the center of the corral.

Gregorio walks to the far end of the *muyukancha.* He digs a shallow hole into the soft moist earth and buries the offering while he implores the deities to let the herd prosper. More *coca k'intus* are offered by all people present; more *chicha* is showered upon the animals. Juan and Gregorio play tunes on their flutes to honor and appease the deities and for the pleasure of the animals and the people present. One female alpaca is dedicated to Teresa, who is beginning to build her herd, and one to little Libia, who helps her sister take the animals to the high pasture.

It starts to rain. Dark clouds obscure the sky. The five marked animals join the herd in the *iphiña*. Teresa pulls her *lliklla* over her head as she takes the animals higher up to the pasture. We hurry into the house away from the gusts of wind and pouring rain. Frozen, we wait for Luisa to light a fire in the earthen stove to cook the first meal of the day. The crackling noise of the fire soon absorbs the sound of our shivering bodies. Everyone welcomes the warmth that slowly seeps from the earthen stove through the tiny house. But soon the place fills with smoke, which comes from the smoldering roots of the *qayara* plants (*Puya herrerae*) and which leaves us coughing. My eyes start to burn like fire. As I bend down to move through the door, Juan hands me his poncho. I put it over my shoulders but continue to shiver as I press myself against the wall of the house to get some protection from the rain under the slight overhang of the roof. The wind beats the rain against the side of the house and onto the muddy ground. Cold and miserable, I yearn for the sun to appear. Yet this is the height of the rainy season when the sun may hide for days.

Qayara and *achupalla,* both of the genus *Puya* and belonging to the family of bromeliads, have stiff leaves; the roots are important as fuel. The green parts serve as food for llamas, alpacas, donkeys, and guinea pigs. *Qayara* roots are piled up in front of the Mamani house. They cause this irritating smoke as they burn, but eventually they give us warmth and a meal. Every year the *qayara* plant that grows on the precipitous slopes of the mountains becomes scarcer (see photo 11).

Each time Juan returns from a dangerous precipice where he hacks this plant from its steep rocky substrate, he looks concerned. His wife Luisa smiles with relief when he arrives safely with the essential fuel to cook more meals. Luisa and Juan, like most villagers, worry about the decrease of this plant. Few trees and bushes grow at this altitude, and the only alternative for making a fire is to use the dried dung of the animals. But dung is needed to fertilize the fields, without which harvests of potatoes and other tubers will be meager at best. I shudder at the thought that some time in the future, perhaps soon, there will be no fuel

Photo 11. *Qayara* growing on steep cliffs.

with which to cook or to warm one's frozen limbs. I wonder whether this could eventually mean the end of the pastoralists' way of life, a life that despite its hardships has a fascination of a very special kind and values unknown to most.

I feel both sad and angry that these people must engage in such difficult struggles to survive. There is no money to buy a stove and no kerosene to feed it.[2] The tiny income from an occasional sale of alpaca wool, some meat, *chuño,* or *moraya* is scarcely enough to buy the most urgent necessities—sugar, salt, tea, and sometimes medicine. Most herders own few animals and have little or no surplus at all.

I think of the herder Teresa, who passes the whole day within the moist clouds, exposed to the elements, watching the herd attentively to detect disruptive behavior. She must see to it that the animals eat well and that the males do not fight. She must use her *warak'a* to bring back straying animals and to chase away predators such as condors, pumas, and foxes. She must also watch out for thieves who sometimes come from far away and steal animals hidden by the thick fog and clouds. It is challenging work that requires considerable strength of body and mind.

Juan Mamani and his family own few animals—on average thirty llamas, alpacas, and sheep—and Juan cannot work in his fields as much as other men because the *curandero* must spend a lot of his time with his patients. People who come to the house to be cured are always invited by Luisa to eat and drink, and to sleep if they come from far away. I have often seen Juan leave his house during the day and again in the middle of the night, sometimes in pouring rain, hail, and thunderstorms to attend patients who live at distances up to 16 kilometers and who are too sick to come to his house. There is never any charge, although, in a gesture of reciprocity, he sometimes receives potatoes and other tubers in recognition of his much-esteemed services.

The rain has soaked my clothes. I scoot through the door to exchange rain and wind for the smoky hut. Thanking Juan for his poncho, I hang it over the poles above us in the hope that it will eventually dry. Luisa smiles at me as I sit by the earthen stove in the rising smoke that emanates from the life-sustaining fire. I must be a pitiful sight—shivering, coughing, with my burning eyes half shut.

"Doctorita," Juan says in an encouraging tone of voice, "Roberto Yupanqui Qoa will come to visit after his *señalupampay.* You wanted to know of times long past. He is the one who can tell you what happened in Chillihuani when his grandmother's grandmother was herding her flocks on the high pastures. He is very old and knows all about Pukllay as it was celebrated long ago."

The dogs bark, and the sound of hurried steps comes closer. Roberto Yupanqui Qoa enters through the low door with a big smile on his face and a surprisingly energetic gait for a man of his age. His brown face, deeply wrinkled by the scorching sun and icy winds, reveals a life of hard work, yet of satisfaction. The old man's eyes are alert and reveal a twinkle of good humor and self-confidence. Age has not erased the air of elegance and sophistication that characterizes Roberto's features and every gesture of his body. *"Imaynallan kashanki?"* (How are you?), he calls out with joy, while he places his hands on everyone's shoulders in a loose embrace. I thank him for his visit, touched by the fact that he walked far through the cold wind and pouring rain. He looks at me, surprised. "Señorita, doctora, I always come when I promise, even when a storm breaks loose and hail thunders from the sky."

Luisa dishes out soup. Don Roberto accepts with grace, using both hands to receive the dish. We eat silently. Every bite is much appreciated and recognition is given to Mother Earth, to the hostess, and to all people present. Then we drink herbal tea together. Roberto opens his *ch'uspa,* which is filled with *coca* leaves, and offers some to every adult. "Let us start with a *k'intu,"* he suggests in an animated tone of voice. Everyone puts three leaves together, blows to the east, and asks for the blessings of the gods, inviting them to attend. This is a custom that precedes every meeting in the hope that the dialogue will be dignified and harmonious.

There is silence. Then Roberto turns to me and begins to speak. "Pukllay was good when I was young. It was really good. Pukllay has always been a time of happiness, a time of song and dance." I ask him about the songs people sang in the past. He smiles. "Señorita, my voice is no longer good, but I will sing a song for you, a song that my grandmother learned from her grandmother and taught me. It is 'Paqocha Taki', the 'Song of the Alpaca'; I will dedicate it to you." He sings with deep emotion:

Ñan patay ch'illka tapurikusayki,
Kaytachus maytachus pasarunman karan,
Sut'in reqsiy mantosa sut'in reqsiy paqochachay,
Ñan patay ch'illka tapurikusayki,
Kaytachus maytachus pasarunman karan,
Sut'in reqsiychallan wik'uña hina pasarunman karan,
Chushlluy maqchisuri karqan,
Mantusakunawan kanman karqan,
Sut'in reqsiylla kanman karqan.
Nigrinpas karqan k'intuy k'intuy,
Qhasqonpi ch'ulla sapallan unkusaqniyoq,
Unkusananwanpas, millmachanwanpas
Ñoqañan pagasqayki ñan patay ch'illka,

Willarillaway ñan pata ch'illka, (bis)
Ñawinpas murmuntuy murmuntuy, karqan
Wik'uña hina pasarunman karan,
Jayentayuspa.
Willarillaway runa masillay, (bis)
Pagasqaykicha millmallantapas.
Vuelta rimullay mamay, kutirimullay mamay
May orqomanpas mikhureq hina,
May qochamanpas wayt'areq hina.
Ñoqapas sonqoykita qatispa,
Flautachayta toka tokayuspa,
Qhepaykita puririmusaq
Waya, waya, waya,
Waya, waya, waya.

(*Ch'illka* [a plant] by the high path, I want to ask you,
If along here or there would have passed,
My alpaca, so easy to recognize, my *paqocha* [same as alpaca], so easy to
    recognize.
Ch'illka alongside the high path, I want to ask you,
If along here or there she would have passed
like a vicuña, she would have passed easy to recognize,
She was my alpaca, her wool was clean, smooth, and shiny,
If she would have stayed together with the other alpacas,
She would have been easily recognized,
Her ears were standing straight like *k'intus,*
On her chest she had a strand of long wool,
With the strand on her chest and her wool,
I will pay you, *ch'illka* by the high path,
Advise me [tell me], *ch'illka,* you who grow by the side of the high path!
Advise me, *ch'illka,* you who grow by the side of the high path! [bis]
She had black eyes, black like the *murmuntu* [a kind of algae],
She would have passed by, like a vicuña,
Crying softly,
Advise me, my friend, advise me my friend,
I will pay you at least with her wool,
Come back *mamita,* return *mamita* [*mamita* is a term of endearment]
To any hill to eat,
To any lake to swim,
I follow your heart
playing my flute all along,
Behind you I will walk,
Waya, waya, waya,
Waya, waya, waya.)

Other songs follow, old songs Roberto's grandmother taught him: "Song of the *Warak'a*," "Rumichikchipi" ("Hail of Stones"), and others. Roberto's voice improves with each song, as his enthusiasm increases. "I like to sing these songs," he says, smiling apologetically, "but my grandchildren get bored. They are good children but when I sing old songs, they say, 'Awkicha (grandpa), these songs are no longer of any use, forget them.' But I will not forget them, I want them to be remembered always; they may not die." In a melancholic tone of voice he continues: "I sang them with my wife, when she was still here on *kay pacha* (this earth), before she left me." He looks at the floor sadly. Roberto's wife died when she gave birth to their fifth child. Roberto raised the children by himself. He is proud of his accomplishment, but his grief about the early death of his beloved wife has never left him.

Then a sparkle returns to Roberto's eyes. "Let me tell you about Pukllay, the way we used to celebrate it. On the fifth day of this fiesta, young people came from all directions across the mountain ranges. Men played the flutes and women sang beautifully. They sang so loud that one could hear the songs throughout the mountains in every house. Now they don't sing as loud and lively as they did then. Formerly only *solteras* (unmarried women) went from one house to the next to visit. They drank sweet white *chicha* made from *quinoa*. We wore the *kantunka* (a belt with much wool) in front and not in the back as they do now. When the people came from *suyu* Llaqto with their big *warak'as*, they looked like *suri* alpacas with so much wool. The hats were flat, black and white and with a big rim, somewhat like *monteras* (the type of hats worn now), but without the dangling threads of wool. Both women and men wore these hats. They looked very attractive. The costumes were different as well. Everybody wore completely white costumes and the slings they carried were purely white, too."[3]

With increasing enthusiasm Roberto continues: "Let me tell you about the first night when we celebrated Ch'uyaska (the cleansing ritual at Suyay Ch'isin, the Night of Waiting)." He sighs with a nostalgic look in his eyes. "In the night we brought out our *enqaychu*. They were good *enqaychu*. We prepared the offering and burned it in the *q'oyana* without the *unkuña*. We put it into the fire with two clean hands. Paper was never used for the offerings."

He pauses, smiling with contentment, and continues: "Good *enqaychu* we had. I still have the *enqaychu* that my grandfather found. He was digging far into the ground to build an earthen stove. There he found the *enqaychu* of an alpaca. It is beautiful; it has its little ears and everything. I have it in my house." Roberto goes on: "And then we made *k'intuska* for Pachamama, for the *laguna* and for each Apu—for each sacred mountain in its own name. All Apus have names. Most important are the peaks Waqraqocha (bullhorn lake peak) and Qellwaqocha (gull lake peak), which surround the sacred mountain lake Waqraqocha (bullhorn lake). Then there is Wawayoq Orqo (the peak with a baby) and Condorenqaychuyoq (the peak that looks like the effigy of a condor). At its side above the lagoon is Puka Q'asa, the red gorge. Higher still is Cruzniyoq, the mountain with a cross." Roberto continues to talk about the entire landscape that lives and breathes. There is a name for each geographical point. Each is recognized and honored with a *k'intuska.*

The old man takes a sip of his herbal tea. "It is getting late, but I must tell you more. Yes, Pukllay was a good fiesta. Everyone treated everyone else with respect. But we also teased one another when the dances were on and everyone had fun. We had nicknames for one another. There was the *machu atoq,* the old fox." He laughs mischievously. "Those from Cusipata we called 'Cusipata *q'oto*' (Cusipata goiter) when we met them in the valley. Those from Tintinco we called '*vaca ñuñu*' (cow's udder). Those from Llampe were the *qhoro chuño* (mutilated *chuño*). Those from Hurin Cuzco (the lower part of Cuzco) we called *aya maki* (dead hands—it seems they did not work as hard); those from Pampacolca we called *qaraq maki* (itching hand). And they called us *uchu kachi* (chili pepper and salt) as we bought these items every time we came to the valley."

He laughs heartily. "And then on one side of the bridge of Quiquijana there were the *simpas cadenas* (chain braids), on the other side the *iskay simpas palominas* (two braids of pigeon dung).[4] Roberto shakes with laughter. Then he calms down, looks at me, and says somewhat apologetically: "Don't worry, it was all done with love, there were no bad feelings."

The dogs bark. Nicacio Huaman, an old man from a neighboring village, comes to greet the Mamani family. Juan places a poncho on a low stool, inviting the guest to sit. Libia brings more herbal tea. Luisa lights another candle. The children sit and listen in the middle of the room. Roberto sighs. His face takes on a worried look as he continues: "And then the fiesta was over. Not a single flute could be heard in the mountains."

Nicacio Huaman nods and adds: "*Arí,* for seven weeks until Easter everyone had to worship the saints. If someone still played the flute and the authorities in the valley heard about it, they took him to church, asked him about his religion, and he had to pray. Therefore, people had to pray, and they prayed sadly; sad, because they could no longer play the flute. They could not put flowers on their hats either, because if they did, the priests who heard about it would punish them."

With sadness in his voice Roberto tells us: "Yes, things have changed. People have forgotten the times when we played the panpipes. Now we only use them at weddings. In the past women played drums. Now one sees only men with drums; women hardly ever play" (see figure 4).

Figure 4. Women played drums during Inca fiestas such as Inca Raymi Killa, held in April at the end of the harvest (from Felipe Guaman Poma de Ayala [1615] 1980: 216–217).

Tinkuy—Confirming the Rules of Life

Joy and excitement return to Roberto's voice as he talks about *tinkus,* encounters between the *suyus.* "These were fair games. Everyone showed courage as we fought between the *suyus* with our *warak'a.* Now we use the *warak'a* when we dance the *qhashwa.*"

I realize that Roberto is talking about the *tinkuy,* a significant ritual encounter and get-together. Catherine Allen (1988:205) described it well:

> Through *tinkuy,* social unity is created dialectically and expressed in terms of complementary opposition. Although *tinkuy* refers to ritual dance-battles, the word has wider applications. It is not easily translated into English. . . . When streams converge in foaming eddies to produce a single, larger stream they are said to *tinkuy,* and their convergence is called *tinku* (or *tingu*). *Tinkus* are powerful, dangerous places full of liberated and uncontrollable forces.

This is an opportune time to find out about the meaning of yesterday's puzzling dance, a sort of *tinkuy* with the *warak'a.* Roberto's eyes light up as I ask him to lead us back through time to his youth, to the *tinkus* at the borderlines between the *suyus.*

We wait in silence. Excitement shows on the old man's face as it twitches from time to time with deep emotion. In a proud voice he begins to relive some of the most exciting events of his life: "Yes, at Pukllay we had to prepare well for the *warak'anakuy* (*juego de la honda,* the game of the whip), the *tinkuy* that took place on the Tuesday of Pukllay. It was a fair battle between the *suyus.* One suyu fought against the others to assure everyone knew where they belonged. Our weapons were the *warak'a* and the unripe fruits of the *qayara* plants. We cut the tip of the plant so it can no longer grow. On the tip a ball forms, the *qayara uma,* the head of the *qayara,* which is as heavy as a rock. If one hurls the *qayara uma* at a person who is not protected, it can injure him, so we protected ourselves well."[5]

I ask about the kind of protection used. "*Allinta, willasqayki*" (Good, I will tell you), Roberto agrees. "To protect ourselves we used hats made from the skin of our llamas. The hats covered the head and the face; only the eyes showed. We put a layer of alpaca hide of various colors stuffed with dried *ichu* grass around our necks. This we called '*pillu.*'[6] Dressed in our ponchos, we took our *warak'a* and *qayara* balls and went to the borderlines of the *suyus.*"

Roberto shows increasing excitement as he continues: "Now we men formed two lines opposite one another. It was one *suyu* against another. We swung the *warak'a* with the *qayara* heads so they would hit the men who formed the line across from us. The women of each *suyu* went along; they stood together in a group and they sang loud. The louder they sang, the more enthusiastic the men became in this battle dance. More and more women came to cheer us on in our game. With clear loud voices they sang: '*Ama turachay, mancharinkichu, yawar mayupe rikukuspaike*' (My little brother, do not be afraid when you find yourself in a river of blood)."

Roberto smiles proudly as he explains that he too was a brave warrior who engaged in this fair but ferocious game. "Blood had to flow," Roberto emphasizes after a time of silence. "The young men are proud of their scars." During conversations with other people throughout the years I have learned that at least a little blood should be released in the whipping game. One person explains: "Pachamama needs a few drops of blood and we all come together to provide this offering. So we meet as opponents and end in solidarity."[7]

Roberto reiterates that this game, the *yawar mayu,* has the potential to cause harm, but that it is not done in a mood of hostility. Instead it causes solidarity. It brings fertility for all. *Enqa,* the eternal life force, must flow. I ask Roberto why the ritual battle takes place right at the boundaries between the *suyus.* "We must respect the borderlines," he stresses. "Only then can we live together in harmony; rules must be obeyed." The four *suyus* are separate, yet they are part of the same *ayllu,* Chillihuani. Later I witness how the whole village cooperates in *faenas,* community work projects. Yet within this overall cooperation, there are divisions in terms of where people from the different *suyus* are supposed to work. In the excavation to establish a drinking water system, for example, the people from *suyu* Llaqto work at the uppermost part of the system, the people from Chillihuani work at the lower part, and the people from the other two *suyus* work in between. Within the social realm, the reaffirmation of boundaries is most significant in relation to the rule of exogamy. Young people should marry outside of their own *suyu,* an important marriage rule that is not always obeyed but that is recognized during the dances at the borderlines of the *suyus* (see Chapter 7).

In a disillusioned tone of voice, Nicacio Huaman laments that everything changed when Christianity arrived. Roberto's eyes start to twinkle again as he affirms this emphatically, nodding his head: "We still continue to dance the *warak'anakuy* on Tusuna Q'asa Pata. You *must* go there."

It is almost five o'clock. Roberto has been talking since noon without signs of fatigue. When he arrived, he announced that he would have to leave at five to make sure his animals would be all right for the night and to get ready for the visits of the *tusuqrunakuna,* the dancers who come to visit. He has no watch, but he always knows the time. I give Roberto gifts for himself and his family. He is touched. "I have a gift for you, too," he says. An ancient *unkuña* from my grandmother's grandmother. I will give it to you when you return." I have noticed that people are very much concerned about one's return. They often talk about what we will do when we meet again, what we will talk about or what they would like to bring. They seldom forget.

We go out into the dusk; it still rains slightly. Roberto thanks the Mamani family for their hospitality. He picks up a sack of potatoes that he left outside the house and throws it over his shoulder. I express my hope that he will be home before night falls. "Don't worry," he says smiling. "I have always arrived safely at my little home below Waqraqocha." I ask him about his secret, why he keeps so young and alert, physically and mentally. He laughs. "I never drink hard liquor, only a small amount of *chicha* during fiestas, and I always have hope, whatever happens." As Roberto disappears in the dense fog behind the mountain ridge above, I feel as though I just had a conversation with an old friend. Roberto told me that he had never seen a foreigner in his life, and he has had little exposure to the mainstream of Peruvian society. Yet, in an atmosphere of warmth and respect he has told me about the ancient customs of his ancestors with frankness and honesty, with charm and a mixture of humor and sadness. A great old man, and a respected elder of a society that is still intact.

Opposition or Solidarity? What Lies behind the Yawar Mayu?

I was intrigued by the *yawar mayu,* this ritual battle and *warak'a* dance that takes place during Pukllay and during certain other events, and that allows us insight into central aspects of ancient Andean culture and ideology. In the historical literature we find reference to ritual battles in different parts of the Andes and during different periods. The chronicler and priest Bernabé Cobo ([1653] 1956:212–213) wrote:

When the moon was new, those who had been knighted came to the plaza with new clothes, black tunics, beige mantles and white plumage, and with their slings in their hands they divided into two bands, one composed of those from Hanan Cuzco (Upper Cuzco), and the other of those from Hurin Cuzco (Lower Cuzco). They hurled a certain fruit like *Tunas* that we called *Pitahayas*. They came to prove their strength until the Inca rose and calmed them. They did this to become known as the bravest and strongest. Then they sat down in friendship and offered a sheep to the new moon. . . .

As was true in Inca times, this ritual, although harsh, occurs in an atmosphere of solidarity and is without hostility. My first impression during the dance in the Mamani house agrees with Cobo's description of people who prove strength and bravery. However, it is more than that. *Yawar mayu* has strong connotations about initiation; it seems to have been a cleansing ritual. During Inca times whipping was done in an attempt to "civilize" young people during initiation ceremonies. Tom Zuidema (1992:264) found that each time initiated boys returned from the mountains, "their fathers, mothers' brothers, and lords 'civilized' them by whipping their legs and commemorating the ancestors (*huari*) in songs (also called *huari*)." Zuidema further noted that during the celebration of Qhapaq Raymi, one of the last acts was that "the boys bathed, received new tunics, and were 'stoned' (Betanzos [1551] 1987: 69) by their relatives with green *tunas* (cactus fruits). Each uncle gave his nephew a shield, a sling, and a club. Then, on the first day after the new moon in the month of Capac Raymi Camay Quilla, the boys divided themselves according to their moieties and battled each other with the green tunas."

In other parts of the Andes it has been observed that apparent ferocity leads to reconciliation and opposition to solidarity during this whipping game. In Pacariqtambo during a ritual battle in 1982 between the headmen of two *ayllus* (Nayhua and San Miguel), Gary Urton (1993:127) observed:

After a good deal of posturing and gesticulating, the fight between the headmen began. The two men stood within a few paces of each other and began lashing at each other's legs with their *warak'as.* Every time one or the other of the headmen landed a good blow on his opponent, an excited cry went up from the people crowding the intersection. After several minutes of this, the headmen stopped and embraced each other in an exaggerated, almost theatrical display of comradeship and began serving each other cups of *chicha* provided by their respective female allies. The two headmen then stepped out of the intersection, and their places were taken by the head dancers of the two dance troupes. These two young men squared off against each other and began hurling unripened peaches at each other across the intersection. . . . This fight went on for a few minutes (with no winner being declared) and then the dance troupes alternately danced in the intersection.

Urton (1993:129) explained that the ritual battles are staged as tension begins to build before the redistribution of potato lands. He argued that

the fight between what may be termed "the heads of the moieties" (i.e., the headmen of the first *ayllu* of each moiety) as well as the symbolic reassertions of moiety complementarity during the *kashwa* dances of Carnival and Mardi Gras represent collective means of realigning political identities, and reestablishing hierarchical relations of authority within the community in anticipation of the tensions and potential conflicts that may arise during the redistribution of the communally owned potato lands.

Whipping in the context of initiation, symbolizing regeneration and renewal, as well as fertility, was observed in the 1600s by Bernabé Cobo and other investigators (see also Hopkins 1982, Randall 1987:87, Sallnow 1987:136–146). It still takes place today during Qoyllur Rit'i, a pilgrimage to the Sinakara mountain range in the high Andes, where at night in the glacier above 5,000 meters young initiates undergo rituals to become *ukukus* (bear dancers who perform a multitude of tasks during Qoyllur Rit'i). Whipping releases blood that appeases the mountain, feeds the earth, and grants the initiate membership into the ranks of the *ukukus.* The idea of bringing a sacrifice to the mountain is prominent during Qoyllur Rit'i. The *ukukus* are not the only ones who are ready to bring a sacrifice in return for health, luck, fertility, and other requests. Most of the tens of thousands of people who climb to the mountain, sleep outdoors in subzero temperatures, and carry heavy loads (including rocks from the valley to give to the glacier) are motivated by the desire to bring a sacrifice. For example, some members of the Mamani family, along with others from Chillihuani, leave for the site of Qoyllur Rit'i at 4:00 P.M. and walk without sleeping for the twenty-seven hours required by the journey.

At Qoyllur Rit'i and other significant sites, people bring a sacrifice to Pachamama and the Apus in return for the fertility of the land and the health and reproduction of animals and people. Deborah Poole (1991:

320), in her studies of the meaning of the dance, found that "the *yawar mayu* dance carries marked connotations of fertility, initiation, and renewal. The *yawar mayu* song which accompanies this *paso,* in contrast to all other *pasos* which are without lyrics, is the same as that sung for ritual battles." In these battles, the blood shed on the battlefield is said to "feed" the earth mother, thus increasing her fertility and generosity.[8]

Yet, a good harvest depends not only on Pachamama's benevolence, but also on Qhaqya's cooperation. One of Roberto's songs, called "Chikchiparape" ("Rain of Hailstones"), alludes to white and yellow maize kernels as metaphors of the white and yellow Qhaqya. As the men fight with their *warak'a,* they symbolically transform the evil forces of the destructive yellow Qhaqya into the benevolent, rain-producing white Qhaqya. The same symbolic transformation was accomplished as Roberto and his men reconciled following the *yawar mayu* battle.

The well-known ethnohistorian Luis Millones (1993:275) wrote that understanding the Andean past is not easy since there have been only a handful of indigenous chroniclers, and iconographical studies are only in their beginnings. His ethnohistorical research showed that we get an idea of how past events were perceived through an analysis of indigenous historical and contemporaneous festivals. Nevertheless, he cautioned that extant indigenous music and dance, although they may retain some ancient elements, have also taken on new significance. In the context of the historical and wider geographical and contextual frameworks, Roberto's explanations about the *yawar mayu*[9] as a ritual battle and the actual dance with the *warak'a* in the Mamani house became more meaningful to me. The dance expresses many central concerns of the Quechua people, both past and present. It is a show of strength, bravery, and endurance by the men and women who today, as in Inca times, are proud of these attributes. Opposition and solidarity, complementarity and transformation, fertility and the idea of sacrifice are all part of the game. It is a dance held in an atmosphere of enthusiasm and love. Whipping one's partner is not meant to harm him. In a ritual context, a person wants to make a sacrifice by shedding a drop of blood onto the sacred earth, which will reciprocate by providing fertile fields for everyone. I realized that my performance during the *yawar mayu* dance on the Tuesday of Pukllay was weak; not a drop of blood hit the sacred earth.

Ritual fighting during Pukllay was banned by Peruvian authorities in colonial times, as were many other indigenous practices which did not fit the ideology of the conquerors or conflicted with their idea of who held the power. I must admit that I, too, found myself in a difficult situation as I was handed the *soq'ana* during the *qhashwa* dance. Yet, within the cultural context of the Andean people these ritual dances and formerly ritual battles were certainly as important to them as are many rituals and/or sports events around the world which have the potential to cause injury or even death to the participants.[10]

Catherine Allen (1988:210), during her study in the Andean village of Sonqo, found that "ritual recognizes that potential for violent conflict is inherent in every opposition and puts the violence to use within a limiting and controlling frame." *Yawar mayu* is based on this Andean principle, which asserts that opposing forces must join; out of their opposition comes complementarity.

The concept of the joining of complementary forces will be brought to life tonight in Tusuna Q'asa Pata at the borderlines between the *suyus* of the village. Here young people fall in love, and some take the first step toward marriage by pulling their partners into their own *suyu*. It is a playful battle with the *warak'a* where opposing forces—male and female—unite to the sounds of the flute and the movements of ancient dance steps under the night sky of their village.

Munanakuy—

Falling in Love

The rituals for alpacas and llamas, especially the marriage ritual for the animals during Pukllay, set the stage for people to engage in games with romantic and sexual connotations which end in energetic dances in high places between the *suyus* and often lead to love, permanent relationships, and new life. Of all of Chillihuani's annual fiestas, Pukllay is most vividly associated with youth and love; it provides cherished opportunities for young people from the four *suyus* to find partners (see photo 12).

"Young people always fall in love during Pukllay as they dance between the *suyus*," the *curandero* tells me. "It is an ancient custom; our ancestors danced there long ago. Sometimes people fall in love right there on Tusuna Q'asa Pata (*tusuy* = dance; *q'asa* = gorge; *pata* = high place), the place between the high mountain peaks at the borderlines between the *suyus* where the dances take place. But sometimes they have been in love before secretly," he adds with a mischievous smile. "Tonight you will hear how we people of the *puna* fall in love."

This is the fifth day of Pukllay. From afar we hear the haunting Pukllay tune. Luisa hastily removes dishes, pots, and other household articles from the floor to make room for the visitors. Dogs bark, and within an instant the house is full of people, laughing with joy and wishing their hosts health, youth, happiness, and prosperity. Some of the guests are married. Others are ready to announce their secret loves, or hope to fall in love perhaps tonight, at Tusuna Q'asa Pata.

Everyone is in a festive mood, ready to talk, to sing, to joke. Juan knows that this is the most opportune time to bring up the subject, to hear how it happens, this most exciting event of falling in love. He asks, whereupon the young people laugh and the women smile shyly, not ready to volunteer. So the *curandero* tells his story. When he was very young, he fell in love with a girl from the high *suyu* Llaqto. She was also very young. He tried to forget her and went to work far away in the valley. But eventually he was drawn back to his towering mountains and to her. He points to his wife Luisa, who responds with an amused laugh. Everyone else joins, laughing contentedly. "This is the best place of all," the *curandero* affirms, and the young people nod in agreement.

There is silence again. Luisa insists that it is my turn to speak since I am a quasi-hostess living with the Mamani/Illatinco family. Everyone listens with curiosity. There are sighs of relief as I disclose that I met my husband and fell in love during a dance outdoors, amidst trees and grass, in plain nature. In the Andes, nature, especially the high pastures, is considered "uncivilized" and "wild" while *llaqta,* the village, is perceived as "civilized."[1]

Among herders, most young people meet and fall in love while taking their llamas and alpacas to pasture. One sometimes hears people whisper, "*Waynapas munayukuran michisqanpi*" (This young man fell in love while herding on the high pasture). But the young people do not like to admit this, given the high *puna*'s connotation of "wild and uncivilized" and the assumption that love scenes take place in the mountain wilderness before marriage.[2]

"What *suyu* is your husband from?" a young herder asks. I explain that my husband came from a different continent, separated by a large body of water. Everyone nods with apparent understanding. Since I fell in love surrounded by nature and my husband is not from the same *suyu,* the young people consider my situation close enough to the way things are in their own society. Excited whispers and animated smiles show that they are ready to tell their stories.

Lidio Yupanqui Quispe steps forward with a big smile. An outstandingly good-looking, vigorous young man, he met Julia Illatinco Qoa, a charming young woman, just over a year ago. While Lidio tells of their encounter, Julia smiles shyly, and at times pulls her *lliklla* over her face.

"We fell in love in the high *puna* where we take our llamas and alpacas to graze. We talked every day. Sometimes I forgot to watch my family's alpacas. One day condors flew low and one came down to

Photo 12. Young people assemble by the church on Capillapampa, where they start the round of dances on the boundary between the *suyus.*

snatch a young alpaca. I took my *warak'a* and hurled a stone into the distance. But I could not save her. Some time later I lost two adult llamas in dense fog. My father got angry. My sister took over the herding and I left to find work in the jungles of Madre de Dios where it is hot and humid. I was washing gold and made some money. But I was homesick for the mountains and for . . ." He looks at Julia, his dark eyes full of love. "After a year I returned. We often met in the pasture. One day Julia took me to her parents' house. Nobody was home. When her father came, he took the whip and started to beat me hard. 'Papá, papá!' I called out. 'I want to marry your daughter, I promise.' So he stopped beating me."

Everyone bursts out in laughter. I discover that it is common for a young man to get the whip from the girl's father when he finds them together. "All of us get the whip when we try to steal someone's daughter," the young men tell me, laughing. "The girls' parents are very strict, always. We must respect women, or else." All young men agree that the parents care much about their daughters and demand utmost respect.[3]

Animated, Julia steps forward to continue their story. "The next day I came home from the pasture without my *lliklla*. My mother asked where it was and wanted to know whose *unkuña* lay in my sleeping corner. I told her the *unkuña* was Lidio's and it was he who had my *lliklla*. She advised me to give much thought to our decision."

The group affirms that an exchange of clothing or other personal items is a custom from long ago. It is a firm commitment, a sign that the young people have serious intentions to stay together. At this time they promise not to be with any other partner.

Formerly parents had a say or even decided who their son or daughter was to marry, but no longer, though parents sometimes introduce their daughter or son to a young man or woman they think might be a good match. Everyone in this round agrees, affirming that "now we always choose our own partners."

The young people become eager to tell their stories, to tell how they found one another. Juana and Felipe met while walking to the Sunday market in the valley; Andrés and Irene found their love during the dance following the horse race during the Fiesta de Santiago. Libia and Francisco fell in love while they were working outside the village. But most young people fall in love on the high mountains as they take their animals to pasture, away from the village and close to their Apus, in the wilds of the *puna.*

Feelings of love and romance are strong but do not alone determine the choice of a partner for life. Neither is physical beauty a decisive characteristic, although both sexes agree that a good-looking partner with a charming personality who dances and sings well and plays an instrument is nice to have around.

The characteristic most cherished in a mate is compatibility at work. "We must work well together," the young people emphasize over and again during this night and on other occasions. A good character, honesty, reliability, responsibility, and a good family background are also desired in a mate. A partner should have a happy disposition and not be jealous, must be a good mother or father, and know how to raise animals. Weaving skills are considered particularly desirable in women.

Apart from the fiestas that bring young people together, it is not easy to find a spouse in the village. To provide a setting for eligible young men and women to meet regularly, an organization was created several decades ago with the objective of bringing young people together in a group where they could exchange ideas, participate in recreational activities, dance, sing, and play music. This organization, called Qhashwa, is structured politically much like the village. It has a president, vice president, secretary, treasurer, and members at large. While getting a chance to know one another, the young people simultaneously learn about the formal tasks involved in an organization.[4]

One of the reasons why it is difficult to find a partner is that marriage is considered appropriate only with partners who are four generations removed. In other words, only cousins of the fourth degree, offspring from great-great-grandparents, can marry. Age, however, is not that important. People marry on the average between eighteen and thirty years of age. Age differences between partners vary and a bride may be several years older than the groom.

Luisa comes to offer herbal tea, *chicha,* and hot potatoes. "*Taki tusuy*" (Let's sing and dance), she calls out (see photo 13). The young men take their flutes and play the Pukllay tune. The young girls sing songs; some are sad, but most are happy. Then it is time for "teasing songs," which are often invented on the spot. As noted, Pukllay is the time when everyone may be teased. In fact people whom one would not dare to tease except during Pukllay are prime targets in these songs. One never knows what will be exposed at this time of Pukllay, when inhibitions are least pronounced.

Juana, known village-wide for her good voice and inventive mind, announces with a mischievous grin on her face that she will sing the "Song of the *Gringa.*" She and the others are amused as she sings that I may remain forever in the heights of Chillihuani herding llamas and alpacas. Except for some young people during Pukllay, the people of Chillihuani do not refer to me as "*gringa*" (nickname for a foreigner).

Leandro takes over. He is known for composing the most daring songs. In his song I am taken to the high mountains, where I am herding alpacas close to the eternal snow around the sacred lagoon Waqraqocha. He wonders whether I will be sad and crying to be so far from my home or whether I will be happy to herd animals so close to the sacred Apus. He refers to the unusual color of my eyes and hair, which so closely resemble the green lagoons Waqraqocha and Mama Waqraqocha and the *ichu* grass around them. He wonders whether I really belong to the mountain whose colors I display.

In the next song I find myself locked in a rock *carcelrumi* (a prison of

Photo 13. A young man offers his hat to a young lady, asking for a dance and perhaps hoping she will keep it in return for a piece of her clothing; such an exchange would mean a firm commitment.

stone) which can be opened and closed with a key so I will never leave. To be locked inside or transformed into a rock is an ancient, pre-Columbian theme that is clearly represented in the Inca myth of origin and other myths and stories.

Everyone cheers and laughs, affirming that I will stay forever, herding alpacas close to the snowy Apus. In these songs people express freely what they think and thus reveal what is most significant to them. I have often noticed that they wonder how an outsider feels about their customs, about their beliefs, and about living in their village. They always ask how long I will stay and when I will return to their village. Here and in other villages I often hear people say, "This is a good person who always returns." But they are never certain that I really will return, and locking me into a rock removes the uncertainty. I discover that I am intrigued not only about the way my friends in the high mountains think and feel, but also about what they think about me and how they envision my actions, which in turn reflects their worldview.

Now the songs revolve around the *curandero* and his wife. They are respected elders of the community, but do not escape the teasing mood of the young people. This is Pukllay; laughter and joy must continue throughout the fiesta.

We hear music in the distance, coming nearer. More people arrive, crowding into the tiny house. The first group must leave to make room for the others. "You *must* come to Tusuna Q'asa Pata," Lidio insists; the others nod. I ask for the meaning of the site. "You will see," they say, smiling in anticipation.

The Dance of Love at Tusuna Q'asa Pata

On a narrow path Julia, Lidio, and their companions move along the steep mountainsides to the rhythm of the Pukllay tune. The high, clear voices of the women who sing the Pukllay songs pierce the silence of the night. Usually clouds hang low during the rainy season, but tonight the stars of the Milky Way sparkle and shine, making it much easier to distinguish the path from the precipice.

As the group approaches the border between *suyu* Llaqto and *suyu* Chillihuani, music and laughter echo between the rocky walls. In the distance figures dance against the night sky, and there it is—Tusuna Q'asa Pata—the site where the dance takes place, between mountain peaks right on the borderline of two *suyus*. (There are several Tusuna Q'asa Pata, designated sites within the village where dances take place on the borders between *suyus*. The event is also referred to as Tusuna Q'asa Pata.)

Young people cluster around a *mesarumi*, holding *qeros* in their hands and hoping that they will fall in love or make the one they secretly love accept them. A young man in a striking poncho sprinkles *chicha* from his *qero* onto the four corners of the sacred table of stone while he confides, "*Pachamama, ñoqan anchata wayllukushani kay sipas tarinokusqaywan. Pacha mamallay yanapayway kay sipaspa munakuwananpaq*" (I very much love this young woman with whom I meet. Pachamama, please help to make her love me too). At this *mesarumi*, Pachamama is asked for permission to dance on her ground.

Every young man brings at least one flute. Some use as many as four different flutes. Female companions help carry the flutes while the men play. The men of each group or *suyu* play together, using flutes that emit the same tones.

The music stops and starts often. Couples dance to the haunting sounds of the flutes. The echoes resound against the rocky sides of the surrounding peaks. The music becomes faster, and two young dancers swing their *warak'a.* They seem determined to leave a few drops of blood for Pachamama. As they dance on the borderline, the young man pulls the girl into his *suyu.* They continue to dance as they disappear into the night.

Julia and Lidio have been standing by the *mesarumi* sprinkling *chicha* onto its four corners, blowing *coca k'intus* into the wind. They start to dance to the tunes of the flutes. They are still on the border between the two *suyus,* but Lidio starts to pull Julia toward his *suyu, suyu* Llaqto, the place of his ancestors. A young man approaches the dancing couple. He takes Julia's hand and tries to pull her away from Lidio. Lidio gets her back. The other man insists on holding Julia to keep her from moving toward *suyu* Llaqto. Lidio pushes him away but he follows them as they dance speedily toward Llaqto.[5] Lidio's companions try to convince the intruder to give up. He finally leaves. Julia and Lidio cross the borderline. They have confirmed their choice. If their parents agree and the gods are not against their union, they will join for life.

Other dancers are less serious. A few young people push and pull, but do not insist. Two girls try to pull a young man in different directions; they seem to have fun but there are no final results. The games of love continue all night—some serious, others less so. A few married couples dance, reliving the thrill of their courtship. Being pulled into a man's *suyu* does not necessarily mean that the couple will eventually live there. A young couple may live with the parents of either spouse, depending on where there is space for them; or they may construct their own adobe hut in either the wife's or the husband's *suyu.*

This night and the days and nights that follow are dedicated to this joyous and for the most part serious game, where love may win, but where doubt and jealousy also play a part. During the week of Pukllay, young people who are anxious to find a partner for life sleep and eat little. In groups they move from one Tusuna Q'asa Pata, a specific site situated on a *suyu* boundary, to the next designated site between two other *suyus* to meet people from the four *suyus* of their village and from other high-lying villages. The encounters on the different boundaries follow a general sequence. On Pukllay Martes (Tuesday of Carnival), the dances start at Capillapampa, the high place where the church stands. On Wednesday they continue at Roq'a Q'asa, the gorge where many *roq'a* plants grow. Here young people join from distant high-altitude villages. On Thursday the encounter is at Muhunmayu (the river that serves as seed bed). The dance at Antapata Q'asa (the high place east of the gorge) attracts people from Pitumarca as well. On Saturday, the four sectors of Chillihuani dance together at Oqheq'asa Pata (the high gray gorge), with people from Pitumarca and Hayune. From here the whole group walks on Sunday to Qollpamoqo Q'asa (the gorge of the salty hill), and on Monday, after a dance at Pukamayu Pampa (the place of the red river), they celebrate *kacharpari* (the farewell).

The dances at Tusuna Q'asa Pata have their roots in the ritual battles of the *yawar mayu*. Just like the combatants in any ritual battle, the couples recognize established borderlines as they dance across them, joining for life with the one they love from another *suyu* or another high-altitude village. But sometimes young people choose to engage in the ancient practice of *suwanakuy*, stealing the bride. I have never seen this, but I have heard much about it and learned more about this ancient custom one stormy afternoon when I ventured to the house of Doña Luciana high up in the *suyu* Qayara Chimpu.

Suwanakuy—a Nostalgic Tale

Doña Luciana is a woman in her nineties—with delicate, intelligent features and an outgoing, enthusiastic temperament. With joy she tells me about her life as we sit in the windy patio outside her adobe home. "I always danced at Tusuna Q'asa Pata," she says with a nostalgic smile. "We young people took our *warak'a* to dance and occasionally we beat our partners' legs. We danced at the borderlines and met young people from the four *suyus* of Chillihuani and from other high villages—Sachaq and Hayune in the district of Quiquijana. We met at Muhunmayo and Oqheq'asa Pata. Some young people used the heads of the *qayara* plant as weapons in the friendly fights at the borderlines. They whipped one another so strongly that sometimes they almost fell over. But they continued whipping and singing with joy. When we met in Qhatawuy with those from Pataqolqa on the Saturday of Pukllay, the whipping and dancing were fierce and joyful as well."

With a nostalgic expression, Doña Luciana continues: "In Tusuna Q'asa Pata the young people fell in love. Sometimes a young man abducted a girl from another group, an opposing group, and took her to a Tusuna Q'asa Pata at a different borderline. Then it could happen that the group to which the girl originally belonged stole her back. This occurred often. A man could only abduct a girl with the help of the group of his own *suyu*."[6]

Doña Luciana leans forward and vigorously pats my arm. With a flicker of adventure and excitement in her eyes she confesses, "*Arí* (yes), I too was abducted at Tusuna Q'asa Pata. The chase went from one *suyu* to the next during *suwanakuy.* There was always great excitement. Finally, with the whole group from his *suyu,* the one I loved carried me to his home. And he became my husband. He came to live in my *suyu* and here we settled in this house around this windy patio." She smiles with satisfaction. Looking around, I can see that this compound has been inhabited for a long time. The doors of the various small adobe buildings built around the open patio where we sit have intricate wooden locks of a type that is no longer used.

Suwanakuy is a vigorous game of love. In cases of actual jealousy between individuals or problems between *suyus* or whole villages, people are given a chance to deal with them in the open.[7] In courtship, *suwanakuy* helps to establish and consolidate ties. Doña Luciana confirms that at Tusuna Q'asa Pata, young men sometimes stole a piece of clothing from a girl so that they could meet her later to return it. In this way these young people established relationships. If the girl accepted his approach, the young man had to tell her parents that he loved her and had to ask for her hand.

The old lady continues to speak with great dignity of the exciting games of Pukllay—dancing, loving, and "abducting" a beloved. Her account matches that of Don Roberto, who spoke about Pukllay with the same enthusiasm. But their stories also reveal that there is more to it than love, jealousy, and bride theft. Both asserted that the young men had to defend their *suyus* in symbolic ways that reconfirmed borders; the women joined the men, singing loudly to encourage them. After these confrontations all four *suyus* came together to celebrate in solidarity.

The dances continue until the eighth day of Pukllay and end with the *kacharpari,* the farewell. It is during Pukllay, more than at any other time of the year, that Chillihuani resembles an Inca *ayllu,* and its four *suyus* share definite similarities with the four *suyus* of the ancient Inca Empire, Tawantinsuyu. During Pukllay people feel very close to their ancestors. They speak only Quechua and make sure that only pre-Columbian musical instruments are played. There are few if any Christian symbols throughout Pukllay. Games that define the borders remind their inhabitants about proper interactions within and among *suyus.*

Pukllay is a celebration of life, love, fertility, procreation, and *enqa,* the very life force itself. The gods are honored and appeased for giving life to the animals and providing nutrition on the pastures. They are implored to protect the herds and make them flourish. Burnt and buried offerings in the sacred corral and rituals that consummate the marriage of young alpacas with *llonqhetaku* and *quinoa* symbolize the much-desired multiplication of these animals.

During Pukllay people expend enormous energy during the days and throughout much of the nights. Their joy of living and the exuberance they display seem to have no limits. The energy that is generated must linger until the next fiesta begins. Despite the boundless vigor and zest, however, all activities are channeled. All actions are bound by the respect owed to everything imbued by the newly animated life force. Thus, the exuberant dances at Tusuna Q'asa Pata give way to long-established rules, as young people in love go on to join in *rimanakuy,* the Andean marriage.

Rimanakuy—
a Wedding
Andean Style

In the heights of Chillihuani people fall in love and marry as they have for hundreds of years, perhaps even before the Incas imposed their laws. The Peruvian civil law and Christian religion have affected the marital process on the surface, but ancient traditions as they have existed between the people and their Andean gods are at the heart of all events that lead to marriage.

The dance at Tusuna Q'asa Pata in Chillihuani is the first part of an Andean marriage process that goes far back in time. When Pukllay is over, much talk about what happened continues and young people are asked: "*Pukllaypi* (or *Carnavalpi*) *atikurankichu solterata?*" (Could you find a partner during Pukllay?)

Before we follow Julia and Lidio to *rimanakuy*,[1] as the traditional Andean marriage ceremony is called in Chillihuani, perceptions about the marriage process in the Andes must be clarified. It is necessary to understand the principles underlying marriage and its meaning within the framework of the Andean mind.

Not much is known about the traditional Andean marriage. Carter (1977:212) stated: "Until we have more detailed reports of rituals sealing the marriage contract in the Andes, we will be forced to continue in the realm of conjecture." There is much dispute among investigators about whether there is such a thing as a trial marriage, generally referred to as "*sirvinakuy*," whether it is a proper marriage within the Andean frame of mind, or whether it is one of several steps within a multistage marriage process. The question has also been raised regarding whether *sirvinakuy* is an ancient custom that dates from pre-Inca days (Maclean y Esteños 1952) and has survived despite continued opposition by Hispanic authorities, or whether it was, in fact, devised by the Spanish invaders.

Ralph Bolton (1973:148), who worked in a Quechua-speaking village near Lake Titicaca, argued that "while most Andean studies refer to 'trial marriage', it would be more appropriate to speak of consecutive states of marital development." Carter (1977:212) quoted Albó (1972), who agreed that it is incorrect to speak of trial marriage. Instead Albó asserted that what really occurs "is a long series of stages which seal, ever more firmly, the mutual commitment of a couple to one another and which provide recognition by members of the community that there is a new autonomous family unit." Similarly, Carter (1977) suggested that Andean marriage may involve an entire process of transition, a process that accounts for the traditional stability of Andean unions. He does not believe that Andean marriage can be equated with *sirvinakuy*, usually believed to be a trial marriage.

My observations about Andean marriage agree with those of the above researchers and Oscar Núñez del Prado (1984b:126), who in his research observed that the concept of *sirvinakuy* which is used by sociologists does not exist in Q'ero. As is true for Q'ero, in Chillihuani the traditional Andean marriage fully legalizes the union between a woman and a man. In Chillihuani trial marriage does not exist.

To shed more light on *rimanakuy,* as the herders of Chillihuani refer to marriage Andean style, it is necessary to consider historical evidence about the marriage process. Accounts of early investigators show that Andean marriage has remained essentially the same for centuries. Bernabé Cobo ([1653] 1956:248), a Spanish priest who studied Andean customs in the seventeenth century, described marriage among commoners:

> In the province of Cuzco the parents of both persons who contract the marriage meet. The bridegroom goes together with his parents to the house of the bride's parents or of her closest relative. In testimony that he received her as a wife, he puts a woolen sandal on her right foot if she was a virgin, or else a sandal of *ichu.* He takes her by the hand and together with both sets of parents they walk to the house of the groom's parents. There the bride takes a shirt of fine wool from under her belt and gives it to her husband who puts it on. Until late at night the oldest relatives of the bride remain with her to instruct her about her obligations as a wife. The older relatives of the bridegroom instruct him about his duties as a husband.

They offer gifts and they drink throughout the night. This the Incas called marriage.

This marriage of commoners as it was observed by Cobo in the seventeenth century shares important elements with the present-day marriage process in Chillihuani—*munanakuy, rimanakuy,* and *casarakuy*—which involves elements such as the exchange of clothing, meetings with the parents, and the couple's instruction by relatives. In Chillihuani people seldom use the term *sirvinakuy.* Trial marriage is not a part of social reality. Instead, *munanakuy* is followed by *rimanakuy,* a ceremony in which the young couple and their parents come together to talk about all the issues considered important to married life and give their consent to the union of the young people in the presence of the Andean gods (see also Escalante and Valderrama 1992:xxii–xxiii).

Even before Pukllay, Julia and Lidio's parents knew that these young people were serious about each other, since they had exchanged clothing and Lidio had proclaimed his serious intentions to Julia's father when the latter confronted him with the whip. During Pukllay Julia and Lidio announced their love to the village at large while dancing on Tusuna Q'asa Pata. Yet, custom demands that the parents be officially asked for the hand of their daughter by the prospective son-in-law and that the young people meet with their parents to discuss the moral, social, and economic issues they will face as a married couple. The parents are the witnesses in the marriage ceremony.

Night falls as Lidio and his parents walk to the house of Julia's parents. As is the custom, his parents bring *coca* leaves, a bottle of wine, *trago,* and food. Julia's parents receive Lidio and his parents in their small adobe house, which is lighted by candles. In a gesture of respect for the guests, Julia's parents politely invite them to take a seat on a couple of small stools while they themselves sit on the ponchos and blankets spread out on the adobe floor. Lidio falls to his knees, praying to Pachamama and the Apus, asking for their permission to join Julia for life.[2]

Then his parents unfold their *unkuñas* and offer *coca* leaves to Julia's parents. Everyone blows *coca k'intus,* asking Pachamama and the Apus to be witnesses in this event and to give their blessings. Soft-spoken and somewhat nervous, Lidio talks to Julia's parents about his love for their daughter and asks for their permission to marry her. "*Hallpayukusun, ukyayukusun!*" (Let's chew *coca* leaves, let's have a drink!), they respond.

They chew *coca* leaves and drink in respect for one another. Both sets of parents then speak to the young people about their responsibilities as a married couple, about their rights and duties. "You must get up early, work hard, and be always respectful toward one another, toward your elders, and other fellow humans," they advise the young people.

In the high Andes, survival and some degree of economic stability can be achieved only by means of hard work. The economic future of the young couple is an important aspect of *rimanakuy* and must be given considerable thought. As the night goes on, Julia, Lidio, and their parents agree that the young couple will reside for one year with Julia's parents, then for another year with Lidio's parents before they construct their own adobe house. In this way both sets of parents benefit from the presence of their children, and the young couple has a chance to accumulate more animals before establishing their own neolocal household. The household is considered the most important social and economic unit in the high Andes (Bolin 1987:53; Bolton 1977:220; Brush 1977: 138).

Lidio and Julia started to accumulate their own alpacas, llamas, and sheep when they were about two years old. They received animals at their first hair-cutting ceremony.[3] Julia and Lidio are both twenty-five years old and have a sizable herd of alpacas and llamas, as well as some sheep: Julia has eleven alpacas, two llamas, and three sheep; Lidio has nine alpacas, four llamas, and five sheep.

Bride and groom will each receive a small parcel of land along the steep mountainsides on which to plant their own potatoes (see photo 14). All families have use rights to land to grow tubers. They retain the same *chakras* through the generations, and traditional law prescribes that land be divided equally among offspring. There is, however, no more undivided arable land in Chillihuani, and for this reason young people receive only small plots from their parents. Given the poor condition of the soil, a plot can be worked for only two years and then must lie fallow for five years before it can be used again. Families return to their own plots after the fallow years (see also Mayer 1985:59).

After lengthy discussions, reflections, and instructions, the parents of Lidio and Julia agree to the conditions under which the young people will live and consent to the marriage. They offer more *coca* leaves to one another and pour drinks. A new network of reciprocal rights and obligations is established. They toast the gods and one another. As they pour wine, they make sure that the last glass is filled without leaving a

Photo 14. Young people harvesting potatoes on their steep *chakras*.

remainder in the bottle, since this could mean bad luck for the couple. This belief is also present in other parts of the Andes, where a residue can mean the separation of the couple at a later date (see Aranguren Paz 1975). This custom also prevails in Cusipata.

The path to *rimanakuy* is not as smooth for all couples as it was for Julia and Lidio. Sometimes the parents of either or both young people do not consent to a union. If the young people are not willing to forfeit their love for each other, they may leave the village for some time, live together elsewhere, and return to their village later.

When people fall in love, as they do at Tusuna Q'asa Pata, they communicate with the divine about their relationship. Exchanges of clothes are socially significant rituals of reciprocity that symbolize equality and further solidify the relationship. These rites, together with the consent of the parents and their discussion about the future of their son and daughter during *rimanakuy,* place the marriage into moral, religious, social, and economic contexts. Children who are born from this union are considered legitimate by the people of Chillihuani.

When married in *rimanakuy,* young people start to take over increasingly more responsibilities within the community. Until approximately 1987, an unmarried person could not take over any *cargo* (an office in the political-religious hierarchy of the community).[4] Now this is possible. However, everyone still prefers village authorities and anyone working toward these *cargos* to be married. Among the Incas young people started to pay tribute and to help the community with public works at marriage. They received fields (*chakras*), built their houses, and lived by themselves (Cobo [1653] 1956:248).

Names and Kinship Rules

As night gives way to the dawn of the approaching new day, all issues are settled. Julia and Lidio are now a married couple. It is common among herding societies of the Andes that neither of the partners will relinquish his or her surname, which consists of the name of the father followed by the name of the mother; nor will either partner add any of the other partner's names. The children of Lidio Yupanqui Quispe and Julia Illatinco Qoa will carry the surname Yupanqui Illatinco. In the second generation (the grandchildren of Julia and Lidio), the surname of Julia's father will be lost while Lidio's father's surname can continue indefinitely.

In some regions of the Andes, people who share last names are not allowed to marry. In Chillihuani the sharing of a common last name by bride and groom does not present an obstacle to marriage, since this does not necessarily mean that the people are related. The surname Yupanqui, for example, is very common in Chillihuani and some people have the surnames Yupanqui Yupanqui. Nevertheless, it can usually be proven that the lines of the partners who join in marriage have been separate for four generations. The people of Chillihuani affirm that "only the grandchildren of their grandchildren are allowed to marry." In other words, a man can marry a descendant of his great-great-grandfather's wife or any woman further removed (Zuidema 1973:19).[5] To disobey these rules would mean committing incest, which is considered a most shameful act (see Núñez del Prado 1984b:119).

Thus, the people of Chillihuani obey the same kinship rules that the Incas followed, restricting marriage to people who are unrelated over a distance of four generations. Zuidema (1977:250) reported on the *ayllu* of an Inca descent group that consisted of an apical male ancestor and four generations of descendants. The males descended from their fathers in the paternal line and the females from their mothers in the maternal line.

It is not known precisely how names were acquired and transmitted in pre-Columbian times. Zuidema (1977:255) stated that lineage (clan) names were not used in pre-Spanish Peru. Instead parallel transmission of names was of some importance, but this was combined with other rules—for example, cross-transmission from a mother's brother to a sister's son and from a father's sister to a brother's daughter. Also, names were given in response to a person's achievements (see Zuidema 1977 for an in-depth discussion). Another means of name giving was discovered by Irene Silverblatt (1987:94), who wrote that in Inca times "the social category *ñusta,* often translated as 'princess', required that these women who were not full descendants of the Inca royalty be called by the name of their natal land."

Research of colonial marriage, birth, and death records has revealed that during this period most men received their fathers' surnames and women received their mothers' surnames (Zuidema 1977:254). This parallel transmission of names during the colonial period has also been reported by Oscar Núñez del Prado (1984b:118) for most of the people of Q'ero. Billie Jean Isbell (1977:92) wrote that "the data for Chuschi suggest that the principle of parallel transmission was applied to surnames when naming was imposed on the Andean people by the bureaucratic-minded Spanish who enforced an agnatic bias."

Kinship is reckoned differently among the Quechua and the Spanish. In Quechua, for example, different terms are used depending on whether one refers to the sister of a woman, *ñaña,* or the sister of a man, *pana.* The brother of a man is *wayqe;* the brother of a woman is *tura.* Father's brother (uncle) is called father and mother's sister (aunt) is called mother. (For a more detailed description of the Quechua kinship terminology, see Allen 1988: 255–256.)

The terms *mamay* (mother) and *papay* (father) can, however, be used to address a variety of other people within the kinship network as well as outside it. These terms can also be used to express respect and endearment. For example, an old man, or a respected younger man, can be addressed as "*papay.*" The same is true for older or respected younger women who are *mamay. Mamita,* using the Spanish diminutive, is a term of endearment that can be used for a woman or girl of any age, while an adult man and even a little boy can be addressed as "*papito.*"

A grandmother is called "*qoyacha*" (*qoya* was the empress among the Incas), a grandfather is called "*awkicha*" (*awki* is a mountain god or spirit). A grandchild is called "*haway*"; a grandson is called "*qhari haway*," a granddaughter "*warmi haway.*" Hispanicized kinship terms have penetrated communities to various degrees.

The Sharing of Tasks

As the newlyweds start a life together, each will have specific tasks in accordance with Andean custom. As was true in the past, however, the division of labor is never so strict as to prohibit one gender from doing the other's task if the need should arise (Murra 1956:123; Silverblatt 1987:9).

Both men and women spin wool and both sexes weave, although women do the greater part of weaving and they fabricate the intricate patterns found on *ponchos, llikllas, unkuñas,* and *ch'uspas.* Women's weaving skills were also much admired in Inca times, when women wove the finest clothes; in their capacity to weave intricate symbolic patterns into the fabric, they were considered the historians of their society.

Men as well as women weave blankets. Men knit their own *ch'ullus* (hats), which may also involve complex designs, and they may weave their *ch'uspas* and their black pants and simple ponchos. They always fabricate *warak'as* and ropes of all sizes, and also the *kantunka,* the belt used in the festive Pukllay outfit. Women weave skirts, jackets, belts, and sometimes men's pants. Weaving not only provides the family with clothing, carrying bags, tools, and so on, but the designs woven into the fabric also are significant to each family and to society at large. Chillihuani patterns are highly symbolic and reminiscent of Inca designs. Many represent cosmological ideas considered important today as in the distant past. Chillihuani weaving symbols include features such as mountain lakes, snowflakes, and lightning flashes.[6]

Women are primarily responsible for the rearing of the children, although men normally participate in this task. Women do the cooking and the brewing of *chicha,* both of which are honored tasks.

In the fields, men do the heavier tasks such as turning over the earth with the *chakitaklla,* a foot plow used by the Incas. (For a detailed study of this significant tool, see Victor Rivero Luque 1990.) Women must plant the seeds. It is believed that unless women put the seeds into the earth, the plants will not grow; this belief has endured since preconquest times. Irene Silverblatt (1987:29) quoted the priest and chronicler Arriaga ([1621] 1968:22), who wrote, "Like anyone who was going to meet the gods, women had to purify themselves before sowing. They experienced this act as a holy one, the time to consecrate their bond with the Pachamama. Talking to her, invoking her, reverencing her, women placed seeds in the earth." Today women blow *coca k'intus* in honor of Pachamama before sowing. Both sexes participate in the harvesting of potatoes and other tubers and in preparing the fields for sowing.

Men, women, and children participate in herding the flocks, although the young generation is primarily responsible for this task. If no other family members are present, very young children, starting at age five or six, may take the flocks to pasture. Men shear the wool, sacrifice the animals, and cut the meat.

Balance, Harmony, and Equality—Now and in the Past

In Chillihuani the contributions of both marriage partners are considered equally important and complementary (see Harris 1978; Miles and Buechler 1997:2). Partners work at making the household and marriage function properly. The importance of the complementarity of the sexes is the hallmark of Andean ideology. In the pre-Columbian past, "Women's work in the *ayllu*—from weaving, cooking, and sowing to child care—was never considered a private service for husbands. These were the contributions women made toward the continuance of their household and their community" (Silverblatt 1987:9–10).

The equality of the sexes and the complementarity of their work is strongly expressed in Chillihuani, as it is elsewhere in the high Andes. Jorge Flores Ochoa (1988b:240) stated that "the status of the woman is never unequal to that of the man; their roles complement one another harmoniously." The equality of the sexes has its roots in pre-Spanish times. It has been expressed symbolically through ritualized gift giving, such as an exchange of clothes or other items between lovers. A ritual exchange of clothing and formal speech making was part of the marriage of the Inca king and queen and expressed their equality (Silverblatt 1987:8).

Upon their first encounter with Quechua society, some investigators formed the impression that men dominate Andean society since they speak up more frequently and most political positions are held by men. Women tend to sit beside the hearth cooking and caring for children. Such observations have led investigators to ascribe a submissive role to

Quechua women. Closer examination shows, however, that women make many important decisions and critically influence their husbands' views. Prominent investigators such as Jorge Flores Ochoa (1979:68) and Oscar Núñez del Prado (personal communication) consider women to be the power behind the throne.

Household economics are controlled by the wife. She decides how much of the harvest will be consumed, what portion can be exchanged or sold, and what products must be harvested to assure an adequate family diet. She also selects the seed stock to plant in the year ahead. Being in control of the family budget, she decides whether guests can be invited. She organizes *cargo* activities in cooperation with other women and prepares food for major functions. She encourages family members, neighbors, and friends to help in these tasks (Bolin 1990a:12).

Occasionally men travel with their llamas to other regions of the Andes. Flores Ochoa (1988b:240) observed that during the absence of men from home, women take care of the house and fields, tend the flocks, and make valuable weavings for use in barter. He concluded that given these circumstances, "women have higher status than do men."

Work is extremely important to the people of Chillihuani. To do a good job positively affects status. The *curandero* Juan Mamani often re-calls with pride that his people work relentlessly; even while walking they spin wool. It is interesting that in the heights of the Andes people want to be photographed while they are at work and not when at rest. People are proud of being capable of hard work. Young women may show off their strength by carrying enormous loads. When I asked my centenarian friend and teacher Roberto what he considered most im-portant in his life, he answered, "that I do good work each day."

Faena (communal work) is especially significant and is the source of much pride and joy in Chillihuani and other parts of the Andes. "Work is the maximum expression of their values," wrote Flores Ochoa and Fries (1989:21) about the people of Q'ero in the province of Paucar-tambo.

During *faena* the people of Chillihuani express most succinctly their values regarding solidarity, complementarity, and respect. Men and sometimes women work on projects such as cleaning the paths through-out the village, renovating the school building, or installing drinking water. Women always provide food for the people who work and offer *chicha,* which gives a festive glow to communal work parties.

The Spanish invaders consistently misunderstood the Indian concern with work and the pride attached to it. The priest Bernabé Cobo ([1653] 1956:247), in his study of Andean life, remarked that women in ancient Peru lived a life of drudgery due to the hard work they had to perform. Still today it is difficult for non-Indians to understand the tremendous pride that ties the people of the Andes to the hard daily work they do within their community. This pride does not, however, apply to the work imposed on the Indians during the colonial period, when forced labor was common and Indians were not recompensed justly for their work.

Juan Núñez del Prado (1985:250) captured the dichotomy of Indian and non-Indian ideologies very well. He stated: "Hanaqpacha [the Andean heaven] is a place of agricultural activity in which even children work, and its paradisiacal condition lies in the fact that lands are abundant and fertile and harvests are not subject to losses or calamities. This concept contrasts with the occidental concept of paradise, which is presented as a place of eternal leisure." My friend Roberto's idea of an afterlife exemplifies the Andean way. When I asked him what he would wish for if there were any kind of existence after death, he answered: "I would wish for a place with excellent *chakras,* good harvests, many healthy llamas and alpacas, and beautiful weavings."

The equality of the sexes in the high Andes is apparent not only in the mutual appreciation of the work done by both genders and the equal status of men and women, but also in the rules associated with inheritance. In pre-Spanish times, "women obtained access to labor, land and other material resources by virtue of their *ayllu* membership as did men" (Silverblatt 1987:223). The misconception that a family received one *topo* (one third of a hectare) of land for each dependent son and only half a *topo* for each dependent daughter derives from the writings of the early chronicler Garcilaso de la Vega ([1609] 1966:245), who has been shown to be wrong in this instance.

In Chillihuani, as in most other parts of the Andes, children inherit in equal parts. The youngest son or daughter, called *"chanaku,"*[7] is expected to remain with the parents as long as they live. He or she will inherit the house and everything in it as well as his or her share of land and animals in return for the help and care given the parents in their old age. Older sons and daughters may help to provide labor for maintaining the parental property. A very old or widowed parent may move into the household of one of the children, thereby liquidating his or her autonomous household (Bolin 1987:56).

Personal items often pass from mother to daughters and from father to sons. This type of parallel transmission of property, of certain land rights, ritual rights and obligations, and ritual objects also seems to have occurred in the past (Zuidema 1977:255) in different parts of the Andes. An interesting case of parallel transmission of property is described for Ecuador, where, "in pre-Spanish times, both an Indian chief and his sister-wife were independently instituted as chiefs by the Inca at the time of their marriage, when she inherited land and service of certain people from her mother's family" (Zuidema 1977:255–256 quoting Oberem 1968:82–83).

Given this information about the general rule of inheritance, I was surprised when one of the elders of Chillihuani told me that the precious *vara* (staff of office) of his family, which is normally used by the *varayoq* (indigenous mayor),[8] was passed to his granddaughter. Perhaps this elder was referring to an office passed down through women in the past. The chronicler Martín de Murúa ([1590] 1946:427) related a legend about an old woman who owned a staff handed down to her by a female deity. Staffs are symbols of office in the Andes, and in the past may have been passed down through a line of women, from mother to daughter (see Chapter 11 for more on parallel male/female hierarchies).

Thus *rimanakuy* and its associated rights and duties are in many aspects reminiscent of pre-Spanish times. Marriages based on equality between the sexes work well in Chillihuani, where divorce is rare. Still, about 10 percent of the villagers go through a civil wedding, and approximately 30 percent engage in *casarakuy,* which is considered a Catholic wedding. But *casarakuy,* more than any other step toward a consolidation of the wedding bond, exhibits a vast array of traditional rituals. Rather than reflecting Catholic beliefs, it is a ceremony that takes us even more deeply into the realm of ancient Andean beliefs.

It is mid-July. The priest from the small town of Qui-quijana in the Vilcanota Valley looks with concern to-ward the high mountain ranges that rise steeply from the valley floor. He is no longer in the prime of his life, and the annual ascent to Chillihuani becomes increas-ingly more difficult for him. But he must hold mass, a short Catholic service for couples who want to join in *casarakuy*.[1] It is ironic that *casarakuy*, which is consid-ered a Catholic wedding, is followed by eight days and nights of rituals that are based on extremely powerful symbols of the Andean world. These rituals coherently and spectacularly illuminate ancient ideological con-cepts rooted in duality and are expressive of the con-stant struggle of opposing yet complementary forces. These forces achieve equilibrium as they unite and transform.[2]

Like birth and death, marriage is a rite of passage. It is a process of transformation in which dual forces—male and female—are united. This process is integrally related to Andean thought and action and is deeply rooted in the past (see also Randall 1982). Without an understanding of the way the Andean people view the merging of opposite principles and the workings of dual forces in establishing equilibrium, it is difficult to comprehend the marriage process and Andean culture as a whole. "In the Andes almost everything is under-stood in juxtaposition to its opposite" (Bastien 1985:58 quoting Duviols 1974).

Marriage exemplifies the Andean concern for uniting contrasting elements, opposite principles—male and female—and of transforming them into one unit, *warmi-qhari,* literally woman and man (see Allen 1988:72), thereby creating equilibrium, harmony, and new life. Andeans recognize duality in a variety of oppositions, such as vertical and horizontal, upper and lower, civilized and uncivilized—that is—in concepts that have meaning only in relation to each other. Regardless of the type of transformation—birth, marriage, death, or the change from day to night, from one year to the next—these processes do not take place without danger, and they require careful and precise measures of control (see Randall 1982).

As we follow a couple through their wedding festivities, we are held in an atmosphere of serenity and respect, on the one hand, and of rambunctiousness on the other. *Casarakuy* reveals to the fullest the dynamic interplay of opposing forces that exist in the realms of the sacred and the profane. These forces radiate from the newlywed couple in the center via *padrinos* and *madrinas,* to the powerful *yana uyakuna* (blackfaces), sometimes referred to as *negros* (black ones) or *bailarines* (dancers).

These deep symbolic patterns upon which Andean culture is built cannot be erased from the lives of the people in the high mountains. The priest knows this and he must try to make sure that the Christian element represented by the sermon in the church will not be forgotten in the maze of ancient rites and exuberant rituals that follow. So, again, he undertakes the exhausting ascent to perform mass in the old adobe church on Capillapampa above the central area of Chillihuani.

The priest remains in Chillihuani for three days. On the day of his arrival he holds mass, the *misa de salud,* asking God to give health, understanding, and peace to the community. Upon this occasion he reminds the people to pray daily to God, the holy spirit in heaven. On the second day, his *alma misa* is to remember those who have died since his sermon the previous year. On the third day, his *misa de matrimonio* is for the couples to be married. This is followed by the initiation of the new *carguyoq,* the person who will be in charge of the Fiesta de Santiago, which begins several days after the weddings.

One might wonder why the herders of Chillihuani, who are considered married in *rimanakuy,* marriage Andean style, would engage in the lengthy and rather expensive *casarakuy.* There seem to be several explanations. Some of the people of Chillihuani feel that *casarakuy,* with the bride and groom at its center, strengthens the marriage bond created by *rimanakuy,* especially when taken later in life. The Catholic marriage rituals also expand ties to ritual-fictive kin through *compadrazgo* by adding *padrinos* and *madrinas* (godparents) and simplify inter-actions with authorities in the valley, who bestow a higher degree of es-teem on the pastoralists when they have been married by a priest. There is some validity to all these reasons. But, above all, *casarakuy* serves to bind people ever more closely to their ancestral beliefs. The zeal and sincerity with which the underlying structure of Andean thought pat-terns is revealed during this festivity is impressive and shows that the Indians of the high Andes are far from losing their identity or their love for their ancient culture and religion. During *casarakuy* certain rituals surface that are absent or only faintly expressed in other festivities.

Juan Mamani invited me to attend the wedding of the community president Salvador Illatinco Chino and his wife Justa Quispe Choqque when I returned to Chillihuani in June. I accepted with joy, especially since Juan and his wife Luisa, my family away from home, had been asked by bride and groom to be *ara padrino* and *ara madrina*. (*Ara* is Quechua for altar or flat surface; see Bastien 1985:127.) *Ara padrinos* are horizontal *padrinos*. Ricardo Illatinco Chino and his wife Lorenza Yu-panqui Choqque were asked to be *hatun padrino* and *hatun madrina*. (*Hatun* is Quechua for big, vertical, erect, or superior.) (See photo 15.)

In previous years between one and four couples have taken marriage vows each year in July. This year eight couples are ready to add *casara-kuy* to their Andean marriage. Following the sermon, the couples rear-range their lives in accordance with the moral, social, and economic ties that result from the new relationships. In the month of July, the heights of Chillihuani resonate with melodies of flutes and drums and the thumping of the dancers' feet as different wedding parties crisscross the mountains from their homes to the church and back. The jokes of the blackfaces and their shrill, high-pitched voices pierce the thin mountain air and prevent the approach of the evil spirits as they give way to contented laughter and an atmosphere of harmony, warmth, and solidarity.

Justa and Salvador are in their late thirties/early forties. After nine-teen years of *rimanakuy* they decided to take the Catholic marriage vows. Like most people who join in *casarakuy*, the couple has estab-lished a neolocal household separate from either set of parents. They have two sons, ages eighteen and four. They own a small herd of alpa-cas, llamas, and some sheep, and have several potato fields distributed across the steep mountain slopes.

Photo 15. The wedding party lines up in the appropriate sequence. From left to right: *ara padrino* (with his twelve coins on a platter), *hatun padrino,* groom, bride, *hatun madrina,* and *ara madrina;* one of the musicians stands by.

Salvador has been elected community president for two years. He is a strong man, good humored and full of energy. He works with great concern for his family and the community alike. Justa is a joyous and thoughtful woman who does a multitude of chores in a well-organized fashion. She is a talented weaver.

For weeks Justa and Salvador have been busy with preparations for the wedding. They selected *madrinas* and *padrinos* (only people who were married in *casarakuy* themselves qualify as *madrinas* and *padrinos*), and asked friends to be their *yana uyakuna.* They prepared meals with the help of relatives and asked friends to build a *ramada* (also referred to as *toldo* or *apaki*), a hut with no walls and a roof of reeds that will house the wedding party for several days as many important rituals are carried out. The reed used in its construction, called *totora de la la-*

guna or *saylla* (*Festuca dichoclada*), was collected from a high mountain lake close to their *suyu,* Llaqto. The *ramada* is framed using wood-
en poles made of the *Kishwar* tree (*Buddleia incana*).

Ricardo Illatinco Chino and his wife Lorenza Yupanqui Choqque
were asked to be *hatun padrino* and *hatun madrina.* I first met Ricardo
during Pukllay in 1988 when he was the community president. An excellent orator and outstanding organizer, as well as strong, agile, and
self-confident, Ricardo incorporates characteristics that are reminiscent
of those of his Inca ancestors. His wife Lorenza is lively and outgoing.
She organizes the household in a most accomplished way and can
weave intricate designs into the clothes she fabricates.

The bride and her *madrinas* are aware of the importance of their
tasks during this festivity. Since women do not speak up in public as
frequently as men do, one tends to forget the central role they play within the family and community and the decision making they engage in
on all important issues, including much of the organization of the marriage fiesta.

Julián Quispe Choqque was selected by the *hatun padrino* and *hatun
madrina* to be the *runa pusaq,* sometimes referred to as the *postillón*—
the postilion or guide of the wedding party. Julián, a talented musician,
radiates much dignity and moves with great elegance. As a beloved and
most respected elder, he is the perfect choice to be the guide at this
wedding (see photo 16).

It is July 20, the day the wedding ceremonies begin. The sun has not
yet risen, and the air is cold and brisk as Justa and Salvador, the couple
to be married (*yananchakuqkuna,* sometimes called *kasarakuqkuna*)
head for the adobe church on Capillapampa, at a distance of 15 kilometers. Accompanied by *hatun* and *ara madrina* and *hatun* and *ara
padrino,* as well as by close relatives, neighbors, and friends, the couple
hurries along a narrow path that winds its way along the steep mountainsides bordered by expanses of yellow *ichu* grass. Hours pass before
they reach the church on Capillapampa.

Bride and groom wear their best clothing. Justa has for some time
been busy weaving an exquisite poncho covered with significant geo-
metric designs for her husband, a green jacket with designs, and plain
black pants. Justa herself wears a peach-colored blouse and pink jacket,
three black skirts with wide colorful bands around the hem, and a new
lliklla. Peculiar designs resembling flowers with four petals around a
center decorate her *lliklla* and skirt. I have seen this design once before,

Photo 16. The *runa pusaq* (guide) of the wedding party plays his *antara* (pan pipes) in the *ramada* by the light of the full moon.

in an old painting representing the wife of Manqo Qhapaq, the first Inca Emperor (see Stastny 1993:150).

All festive garments are decorated with designs. Women's garments usually have horizontal patterns, while men's garments show predominantly vertical patterns. Bride and groom wear flat hats with large rims (*barquilla montera*). This type of hat is worn only during special festivities and has been handed down through generations. Families who still own this type of hat loan it to couples who no longer own one and need it to engage in an important event such as marriage.

Contrary to her usual footwear, Justa has squeezed her feet into leather boots borrowed from friends for this occasion. Until now her feet have only felt the gentle squeeze of rubber sandals. Salvador wears black leather boots. This type of footwear, used only during *casarakuy,* makes the round in Chillihuani and is lent to anyone who marries.

At midmorning the bridal pair and their entourage arrive at the picturesque adobe compound that encloses the church. Capillapampa already teems with relatives, neighbors, and friends of the various couples to be married. People greet one another with great respect. Bride, groom, *madrinas, padrinos,* and the guide (*runa pusaq*) meet in a small adobe house to discuss last-minute organizational strategies.

Lorenza and Ricardo are proud in their roles as *hatun madrina* and *hatun padrino,* primary guides in the married life of the couple. They will give advice and moral support to the couple throughout their lives. They bring *coca* leaves and wine to the wedding and provide meals for at least one day. They have asked Julián to take over the important role of *runa pusaq* throughout the first three days of the wedding. They also recompense the musicians for their participation in the wedding by lending them their llamas, which will be used to carry dung to the musicians' potato fields later in the year.

Luisa and Juan are equally content to be *ara madrina* and *ara padrino* and to advise the couple in their married life. They also provide meals, rent the *araphoqtoy* (twelve silver coins carried on a silver platter by the *ara padrino*), buy the rings (engraved with the names of bride and groom), and provide *coca* leaves for the wedding party.

Padrinos, madrinas, and the guide are ultimately responsible for the organization of the fiesta that follows the wedding in the church. They will help their *ahijados de matrimonio* (wedding godchildren) for the rest of their lives, giving them moral and economic support throughout difficult times. They will visit frequently when someone falls ill. Bride and groom, in turn, help their four godparents with the work in their fields, pasturing their llamas, alpacas, and sheep, and will visit them when they are ill.

Now it is time for bride and groom, *hatun padrino* and *madrina, ara padrino* and *madrina,* and the *runa pusaq* to meet alone with the priest in the church to confess. They all must be free from sin as they begin to perform their solemn roles in the wedding. Then each member of the bridal group must affirm his or her personal data—place and date of birth, occupation, marital status, and religion—and sign the marriage contract (*acta de matrimonio*). People often do not know their precise date of birth according to the Gregorian calendar and thus their age is estimated.

The six members of the bridal party (*kasarakuq pusaqkuna*) discuss the pattern in which they will move throughout three of the eight days of festivities regardless of whether they walk, stand, or sit. The *runa pusaq* leads the way while playing the *antara* (panpipes). "He is the guide. He opens the path," Justa's brother, Andrés Felipe, whispers as we stand close by.

There was a time in the past when it was forbidden to play the panpipes. In their ingenuity, the people of the high Andes discovered that by placing a cross on this musical instrument, they could bring it into the church and use it throughout the wedding festivity.

Symbolic Configurations and Ritual Transformation

Each wedding party at Capillapampa moves in a precise pattern as it leaves the church in preparation for the return home. In each case, the *runa pusaq* is followed by the *ara padrino,* the *hatun padrino,* the bridegroom, the bride, the *hatun madrina,* and the *ara madrina.* This configuration of the bridal group and the roles of *madrinas* and *padrinos* gives insight into various aspects of duality, and primarily into the curious fact that in Andean ideology male and female elements overlap. Catherine Allen (1988:180) observed that "in Andean relativistic thought, nothing and no one is absolutely male or female." This is demonstrated through profound symbolism and is expressed most prominently in the ritualized configuration which the wedding parties maintain. Thus, on the right side of the bridegroom we find *hatun padrino* and *ara padrino,* who serve the groom. *Hatun madrina* and *ara madrina* serve the bride and stand to her left. At the same time, though, *hatun padrino* and *hatun madrina* both represent the groom, while *ara padrino* and *ara madrina* both represent the bride. This is why the *ara padrino* who lines up on the side of the groom also represents the bride, whose *araphoqtoy* (twelve coins on a platter) he carries with him throughout the wedding. Although the meaning of certain customs is no longer known by the highland people, or is carried out unconsciously by them, these intricate relationships between the couple and their *madrinas* and *padrinos* were pointed out to me several times throughout the wedding. Their importance was stressed over and again.[3]

But the symbolism does not end here. Since *hatun* (tall or big in the sense of erect or vertical) wedding godparents and *ara* (horizontal) wedding godparents, respectively, represent the vertical and the horizontal axes, they can be represented by the symbol of the cross. Distinctions between vertical and horizontal are also common in parts of Bolivia. Joseph Bastien (1985:122 and 127) wrote that on Mt. Kaata in Bolivia, *hatun padrinos* are vertical sponsors; *ara padrinos* are horizontal sponsors. He went on to note that the vertical and horizontal best men serve the groom and both bridesmaids serve the bride.

The symbolic significance of *ara*, horizontal/female, versus *hatun*, vertical/male, finds support in weaving patterns that date from ancient times. Women's clothes are decorated primarily along the horizontal plane on their skirts, *llikllas*, and sleeves. Decorations on men's ponchos are mostly vertical. In her study on the meaning of patterns in woven cloth, Sophie Desrosiers (1992:23) wrote: "What belongs to men is high and vertical, what belongs to women is low and horizontal." Research by Elena Phipps (1992:39–40) and Ann Pollard Rowe (1992: 40–42) agrees with regard to the meaning of the male/female–vertical/ horizontal configuration of designs.

The cross thus symbolizes the union of the vertical and horizontal lineages, the union of husband and wife, which is crosscut by the *hatun* (erect) *padrino/madrina* and *ara* (flat) *padrino/madrina*. The fluidity between male and female, vertical and horizontal, upper and lower, is ever present. Thus, in the same way that male and female elements are symbolically expressed by vertical and horizontal directions, they also seem to have found expression within other areas of the Inca Empire. According to Robert Randall (1982:49), Garcilaso recounted that "Hanan Cuzco was founded by our king and Hurin Cuzco by our queen . . . without the inhabitants of one possessing any superiority over those of the other. . . ." Regarding *hanan* (upper) and *hurin* (lower), Randall found that "the divisions are always relative within themselves: a hill is *hanan* to the valley below, but *hurin* to the mountain above." Yet, in spite of the fact that upper was considered male and lower was considered female, the Inca lineages alternated in belonging to either upper or lower Cuzco. In other words, every ruling Inca lineage of Hanan Cuzco was succeeded by a Hurin Cuzco lineage, which, in turn, was followed by another Hanan ruler. Randall (1982:51) quoted Cieza de Leon, who wrote: "One Inca had to be one of these lineages (*hanan* or *hurin*) and the next of the other." Thus, when a new Inca took over and *hanan* became *hurin* and *hurin* became *hanan*, a *pachakuti*— a minor reversal of the world—occurred. This worldview of the Incas is found in symbolic form in a variety of ways throughout the wedding.

With several wedding parties congregating on Capillapampa, some ready to enter the church and others leaving the church in the strictly prescribed form, we find ourselves in a place bustling with color and sound, with masses of people filling the compound in an apparently random yet internally coordinated fashion.

Taking an Eternal Oath

The bell rings. The plaza becomes silent. The people in our wedding party take off their hats and *ch'ullus* and enter the church, first the bridal groups, followed by their entourages. In Chillihuani marriage takes place simultaneously for two or more couples. Perhaps this is a carryover of an Inca custom "whereby the marriage ceremony was performed simultaneously for an entire group of couples" (Carter 1977: 214).[4]

The bridal groups kneel down opposite the altar, where the priest starts his sermon in Quechua. He talks about present events that affect the church and the community at large. He speaks specifically about the moral, social, and economic responsibilities people must take on as they marry. Then there is silence except for the occasional shuffling of people who sit or squat on the floor of the church and the noises of hungry babies waiting to be fed.

The priest leans forward as he addresses the first bridal pair, Doña Justa and Don Salvador, with the following words:

> Don Salvador Illatinco Chino, munankichu qoyaykita
> Justa Quispe Choqque wiñaypaq tukuy sonqoykiwan?

> (Don Salvador Illatinco Chino, will you love your wife
> Justa Quispe Choqque forever with all your heart?)

Salvador answers:

> Arí, wiñaypaq munakunin.

> (Yes, I will love her forever.)

Then the priest turns to Justa with the words:

> Doña Justa Quispe Choqque, munankichu qosaykita
> Salvadorta Illatinco Chino wiñaypaq tukuy sonqoykiwan?

> (Doña Justa, will you love your husband Salvador
> Illatinco Chino forever with all your heart?)

Justa answers:

Arí, wiñaypaq munakunin.

(Yes, I will love him forever.)

The priest advises the couple to always behave well, to respect each other, to raise their children well, and to work hard.

The *ara padrino* steps forward. He carries a tray covered with a white cloth. The priest lifts the cloth and moves two rings to its edge. He asks Salvador to put the ring with his name engraved in it on the middle finger of Justa's right hand. As Salvador picks up the ring, he speaks with his eyes cast down:

Warmiy, ñoqan kay anilluta churasqayki kay makiykipi
kay sawasqanchis p'unchayta yuyarinanchispaq.

(My wife, I put this ring on your hand so you will
remember the day of our wedding.)

The bride answers:

Sulpayki ancha munakuywanmi chaskiyki.

(Thank you, I receive it with much love.)

Then the priest asks Justa to take the other ring. Justa speaks the same words:

Qosay, ñoqan kay anilluta churasqayki kay makiykipi kay
sawasqanchis p'unchayta yuyarinanchispaq.

(My husband, I put this ring on your hand so you will
remember the day of our wedding.)

The groom answers:

Sulpayki ancha munakuywanmi chaskiyki.

(Thank you, I receive it with much love.)

The priest now moves the twelve coins to the edge of the tray and asks the groom to give them to his wife. The groom takes the coins with both hands and puts them into the hands of his bride with the words:

Warmiy, ñoqan kay ara qolqe phoqtoyta qoyki tukuy sumaq
sonqoywan chaskiwayá kay sawasqanchis p'unchaypi.

(My wife, I give you these *ara* coins with all my heart
on our wedding day.)

As she takes the coins in her hands, Justa answers:

Tukuy sonqoywan kayta chaskiyki.

(I receive this with all my heart.)

She holds the coins in her hands for a few seconds and then places them back onto the tray, which the *ara padrino* will carry with him throughout three days of the wedding.

"Handing the silver coins to the bride is a symbolic gesture of appreciation for her from her husband and a gift to start life together," Andrés Felipe, the bride's brother, tells me in a whisper. The fact that the *ara padrino* carries the coins on a platter also has symbolic significance. *Ara padrino* and *madrina* will always be concerned about the economic well-being of the newlyweds, in particular the bride, who is represented by the *ara padrinos*. Ricardo further explains that the handful of coins that the bride receives from the groom symbolizes the fact that the fruits of the husband's labor belong to the wife, who will be responsible for its administration.

The priest now takes a wafer, places it into his mouth, and drinks wine from a silver beaker. He then places wafers into the mouths of the bride and the groom in confirmation of their vow to be faithful to each other always. He sprinkles holy water onto the hands and heads of bride and groom, who subsequently make the sign of the cross.

In a rapid sequence of actions, the priest takes white tassels from the altar, reaches into an earthen container, and disperses incense over the couple in the name of Jesus Christ. He places the tassels on the groom's head, then on the bride's head; they kiss it. Now Doña Justa Quispe Choqque and Don Salvador Illatinco Chino are married in the name of the Catholic church.

The couple beside Salvador and Justa receives the same blessings. The mass is over. Solemn and dignified, the bridal groups leave the church in the pattern in which they will move about for the next three days. Outside the church family members, friends, neighbors, and many other villagers exclaim with much joy and laughter, "*Iskay kapun, iskay kapunku!*" (Now they are two in one). People hug one another. "These are the embraces of the peace of God," Andrés Felipe tells me with emotion.

In the church, bride and groom were serious. Every movement was strictly controlled. Once outside the church they move with the same solemnity. Justa pulls her *lliklla* higher up over the lower part of the back of her head, her cheeks, and her chin. For two days and nights to come, both bride and groom will be serious, averting their eyes from outside contact, keeping their heads lowered. They will not speak and will not drink alcohol. They will do everything together and will not leave each other's side for the next eight days. I was especially surprised to see Salvador, an exceedingly vigorous and lively man, behave with so much restraint. *Hatun* and *ara madrinas* and *padrinos* and the *runa pusaq* also move along seriously and with great dignity. This is not only a time of joy but also of great danger. In the days to come the future life of bride and groom will be decided. There is no room for mistakes.

A Pilgrimage of Joy and Peril

Don Julián leads the way, playing the *antara;* he is followed by *ara padrino, hatun padrino,* groom, bride, *hatun madrina,* and *ara madrina.* The band follows. Two musicians play the flutes (*pitu*), one plays the small drum (*tinya* or *caja*), and the other plays the large drum (*hatun tinya* or *bombo*). To the ancient tunes and showered by well wishes, the wedding party starts its journey over hills and through gullies, crossing small streams on slippery stones, 15 kilometers back to the distant mountains of Llaqto.

Not far from Capillapampa, before the long hike begins, we stop at the house of Justa's cousin, Norberto Choqque, and his wife, who sponsor the first wedding meal. The bridal party enters the compound, kneels down to pray to Pachamama, walks around the *mesarumi* in counterclockwise direction,[5] and takes a seat on a stone bench by the *mesarumi.* Julián opens the *urpu* and fills a cup with *chicha.* In a gesture of generosity and dedication, he sprinkles *chicha* on the ground for Pachamama and then throws some of the precious liquid into the wind as an offering to Apu Ausangate and other sacred mountains in the region. Then Julián offers *chicha* to the *madrinas* and the *padrinos.* Each of them receives the glass, pretends to take a sip, and then offers it to everyone in the bridal group with great respect. Bride and groom do not receive the glass; they must abstain from drinking any alcohol until the third day of the wedding festivities.

Food is offered generously to everyone—mutton, alpaca meat, potatoes, *chuño* and *moraya,* peeled maize and *llulluch'a* (or *qochayuyu*), which is algae from the mountain lakes. In a symbolic gesture denoting oneness, bride and groom share one plate and alternate in using one spoon. The others eat with their fingers, in Chillihuani fashion.

Julián gives the signal for the band to play "La Diana." The herders explain that "La Diana" is Spanish music played during fiestas that expresses joy and announces that a wedding or a *cargo* fiesta is taking place. During a wedding the musicians play "La Diana" to salute people. It is also played to indicate the beginning of new activities.[6] The bridal group gets up. Everyone falls to their knees, thanking Pachamama for the delicious meal. Together, holding on to the same positions with the guide leading, they move with the band to sheltered places to obey nature's call. Upon their return they again walk counterclockwise around the *mesarumi*.

The wedding party takes the same seats as before. More offerings to the deities follow, as well as toasts to the people present and thanks to our hosts. As we get ready to leave the adobe compound of our hosts and head for Llaqto, the panorama changes abruptly. Laughter, shrill voices, and thumping footsteps come our way in a cloud of dust. The *yana uyakuna,* blackfaced dancers, come running down from the hill across the gully, full of exuberant energy, rambunctious, and joking in high falsetto voices. The band starts to play. Facing the wedding party, the *yana uyakuna* fall to their knees and pray the *"bendito alabado"* (*bendito* means blessed; *alabado* means hymn in praise of the sacrament). The *bendito alabado* prayer is of Spanish origin.[7] Then they mingle with the wedding party, hugging and embracing everyone, dancing clumsily with the crowd to the tunes played by the band and wishing the bride and groom happiness with these words: *"Sumaqllata taytay (sumaqllata mamachay) pasaramunki casarakuynikita, aswan allintaraq yaya taytanchis, yaya mamanchis yanapanasuykipaq"* (In harmony, papa [in harmony, mama], shall you pass your wedding which will be even better with the help of our good father God and our Virgin).

There are ten young male blackfaces, five of whom are disguised as females (see photo 17). Two of the males wear "modern" clothes—black pants, a black jacket, and a black hat (see Poole 1991). One of these "modern" characters carries a make-believe camera and tubes representing binoculars. These young men—*yana runakuna* (black men)—have blackened their faces with the soot that accumulates on the pots over an open fire. Their "wives," *yana warmikuna* (black women), use the red color of the dark red seeds of the cactus-like plant *ayranpu* (*Opuntia soehrensii*) to color their faces.[8] The oldest two male/female blackfaces are the leaders of the group and, under certain circumstances, perform special roles. The group also has its own *runa pusaq,* or guide, who carries small bottles filled with *chicha.* From time to time he gives a drink to the blackfaces to quench their thirst.

Among the *yana uyakuna,* the "modern" males in their black outfits contrast with the "traditional females" in their hand-woven clothing. The clothes, together with their painted faces and their falsetto voices, allow them to be daring, to act contrary to etiquette. They joke and make fun of all the people present, of one another, of the establishment, the priest, the *mistis* (*mestizos*), and especially the former powerful hacienda owners in the valley with their cameras, their binoculars, and their haughty demeanor. They also laugh mischievously as they carry out very sacred Andean rituals.[9]

Don Julián plays his *antara* and the group sets itself in motion in the prescribed order. Improvising creatively, the blackfaces joke and dance relentlessly in a grotesque fashion, stimulated by the laughing crowd. They stand in stark contrast to the serene bridal group, which remains serious, resisting the jokes. Looking inward, the bride and groom do not seem to react in any way to the merrymakers around them. With their

Photo 17. *Yana uyakuna.* The men wear "modern" clothes and carry make-believe cameras. Their "wives" wear traditional clothing. The "wife" to the left carries a doll and a bottle.

eyes cast down to avoid possible contact with evil spirits, they are guided by the steps of the person who walks in front of them.

The blackfaces seem rambunctious, thoughtless, and disorderly. Yet their demeanor takes place within a framework of precise order. As the group moves along, two of the blackfaces walk in front of the bridal group, two walk behind them, and the rest keep to either side. Even where the narrow path leads over streams and through steep terrain, the blackfaces balance like acrobats on the near precipices in order not to forfeit their positions in relation to the bridal group (see photo 18).

One of my *compadres* explains: "The *yana uyakuna* are the protectors of the newlyweds. They always remain close to them to keep the evil spirits away. Black is a strong color. It protects." In a whisper he continues: "Not even Qhaqya hits dark objects. That is why we wear dark ponchos most of the time, not to get hit. (Brown ponchos are worn for work; colorful ones for special occasions.) *Yana uyakuna* can communicate with Pachamama, the Apus, Qhaqya, and all. They protect and they bring joy and happiness. Never mind their wild behavior."

Photo 18. The wedding party crosses a stream. Note that the *yana uyakuna* walk in front of the wedding party, behind it, and to both sides to protect the couple and their *madrinas* and *padrinos*.

It is not only the black color that connotes supernatural strength and energy, but also their high voices proclaim the esteemed place that the *yana uyakuna* hold in the realm of the supernatural. In the same way that *padrinos* and *madrinas* are the bride and groom's guides and protectors on earth, the blackfaces are their protectors in relation to the spirit world. The transformation the newlyweds are undergoing is fraught with spiritual dangers, as are transformations of any kind. The newlyweds are exposed to these dangers until all rituals in the transformation to married life have been completed.[10]

On the long hike to Llaqto I am clearly caught in the middle of a spectacular display of dual forces deeply rooted in Andean ideology. In a wild array of colors, sounds, and gestures, reminiscent of the forces prevalent in this life and in the beyond, the large wedding party moves under a bright blue sky across the treeless heights of the high Andes. Occasional gusts of wind give relief from the penetrating rays of the burning hot sun that beats upon the earth on this cloudless clear winter day.[11]

Duality is expressed not only in the opposition between the "civilized," serene bridal group and the "uncivilized," loud, rambunctious group of blackfaces, but also within each of these groups. As noted, the bridal pair represents the reconciliation of male and female elements. The vertical *padrinos* stand in opposition to the horizontal *madrinas.* The *ara padrino* and *madrina* represent the bride; *hatun padrino* and *madrina* represent the bridegroom.

The group of *yana uyakuna,* in turn, incorporates dual forces, represented by five traditional "females" and five modern males. Their behavior is degrading in its impertinence, as they make indecent jokes, or push and dance grotesquely, yet it is uplifting in its capacity to bring joy, to make people laugh, and to protect the couple from evil spirits. Their disruptive behavior is at the same time clearly not aggressive; it is kept within strict limits. The positive, humorous energy generated by the blackfaces forms a protective wall around the bride and the groom, who walk silently through the precipitous landscape.

The terrain opens. We stop by the side of the path. The bridal group rests while the blackfaces dance to the tunes of the musicians; they continue to amuse and shock, to protect and disturb, to organize and disrupt. "The blackfaces make people laugh so they forget that they are tired and can continue their ascent," Antolín confides. They dance in a circle, in interweaving zigzag lines, as though they were weaving threads. Zigzag lines stand for lightning. Would they dare to mock even the god of thunder? These zigzag dances of the blackfaces remind me of long lines of disguised people skipping down the mountainsides from the glaciers of Qoyllur Rit'i as the sun rises in the east.

Four times the group rests at significant sites on the way to the home of the bridal pair. The first stop is called Qochapata—the high place with the mountain lake. My companions tell me that formerly there must have been a lake; it is no longer there. The second one is Cruz-moqo (the hill with the cross). Supposedly a cross was set up at this place in former times to protect the potato crops from hail. This is also the spot where four paths come together in the form of a cross. One path leads to Qayara Chimpu, one to the school, one to Yuraqwasi and Chi-leq, and the fourth one to Llaqto. The third site where we stop is Qollpa, which designates a heavily mineralized terrain. In fact, we do find a spring where animals come to drink the salty water. Finally we stop at Qollpa Qhata, which means slope of minerals. At every one of the four sites where we stop, everyone except the bridal couple prays, offers alcohol to the deities, and takes a drink in their honor.

As we approach the fourth resting spot, darkness falls and an icy wind starts to blow, making breathing more difficult. We are at about 4,600 meters above sea level. I try to keep up with the large wedding party as we walk over rough terrain with deep crevasses. I am tired and icy cold, and think about the effects of hypothermia, which can hit quickly under these conditions. Luckily the full moon appears from behind the mountain range in the distance. The landscape assumes a silvery hue, making it easier to evade the crevasses as we climb uphill. In the distance a *susuwa* (a steep field of rubble) appears. *Susuwa* are considered extremely dangerous places where the *condenados* (*kukuchi*)—people who have sinned in their lives—are believed to struggle their way uphill every night.

My *compadres* and friends have often discussed with me the significance of a *susuwa*, asserting that people who have sinned during their lives must leave their tombs in the cemetery and go to a *susuwa*. There they must try to ascend the steep, treacherous field of rubble. But instead of advancing, they roll backward with every step they take. Only when their bodies have wasted away, when all flesh and muscle have been torn from their bones in the torturous attempt to ascend the *susuwa,* will their souls be freed. I have often been warned not to go close to a *susuwa,* since a *condenado* can make his presence felt in the form of the *uraña wayra,* a terrible wind that can cause severe stomach pains, vomiting, and *susto* (a state of extreme fear). Whoever is affected by these phenomena loses the ability to speak and often dies within twenty-four hours. (These symptoms are reminiscent of mountain sickness—*soroqch'i* or *soroche.*)

We continue our ascent in the direction of the giant *susuwa* in the distance. Finally we arrive at an elevated promontory where a tall boulder stands by an adobe wall opposite the *susuwa* and in full view of it. This is the home of bride and groom. We enter the adobe walls of Salvador and Justa's living compound. Away from the icy wind I sit down, exhausted, on a pile of *ichu* grass.

The bridal group heads for the *ramada,* a hut built of reeds from a mountain lake in the vicinity. The sides of the hut are left open. The guide, bride and groom, and *padrinos* and *madrinas* enter. They encircle the *mesarumi,* around which the *ramada* has been built, in a counterclockwise direction. All except the guide sit on a bench of stone covered with ponchos and blankets facing the *mesarumi.* The guide positions himself close to the *mesarumi* opposite the bridal pair. In this hut the group is relatively safe from the dangers of the evil spirits that abound during this time of transformation and transition, in a moonlit night so close to the *susuwa.* I can see relief on the people's faces as they settle down in the *ramada* with their backs against the wall facing the *mesarumi* and the full moon, which now appears high in the sky.

After the *yana uyakuna* have accompanied the bridal party to the entrance of the *ramada,* they walk in a straight line to the bright, moonlit center of the compound. There they fall to their knees, forming a straight line opposite the musicians, who also maintain a straight line. They pray to the deities, thanking them for the safe journey to the newlyweds' home. Then they get up, and to the rhythm of the music, they walk in counterclockwise direction to the *mesarumi* where the bridal group sits. Throughout the days and nights of rituals and festivities, the blackfaces follow the same routine.[12] My *compadre* Antolín explains that if they were to encircle the *mesarumi* in a clockwise direction, disaster would strike. Circling a sacred site in a counterclockwise direction, on the other hand, brings luck and happiness to the couple. Juan adds, "The blackfaces trace circles always to the left so the couple will walk on a good path until the end of their lives."[13]

Hospitality on the Roof of the World

I must admit that when I first saw the simple adobe houses of the Andean people I never imagined that great fiestas could take place in and around them with a wide variety of foods and drinks and a host of intriguing ceremonies for days and nights on end. This wedding is another of those events that shows that organization can be at its most perfect and rituals at their most elegant in the simple adobe world of the high Andes. Hundreds of people are to pass through the compound of the Illatinco/Quispe family during the week of wedding festivities. No one will be left hungry, thirsty, bored, or unattended in any way.

After the exhausting journey from the church to Justa and Salvador's home, we are received with kindness and generosity by friends and relatives of the newlyweds. As soon as everyone finds a place to sit, the *ñawin aqha* of the *chicha* sprinkles through the moonlit night in the direction of the mighty Apu Ausangate. Don Julián, the guide, offers *chicha* to every person in the *ramada*. However, the people who receive the drink do not quench their thirst immediately. In a gesture of respect and generosity, each person pretends to drink, then returns the glass to Julián, the *pusaq runa*. Ricardo, the *hatun padrino,* is the first one to receive a drink from Don Julián, with the invitation *tomaykuy* (please drink). Ricardo thanks Julián, accepts the glass, pretends to take a sip, and then turns to Julián, saying, "*Tomanki*" (You drink). Julián then offers the glass to the other members of the wedding party, who engage in the same ritual of respect, one after the other. After everyone has accepted with thanks, pretended to take a sip, and returned the glass to Julián, he draws a cross over its surface and sprinkles *chicha* into the air in the direction of the Apus and onto the four corners of the *mesarumi.* Then he drinks to the wedding party and to the guests, saying, "*Tomakusunchis*" (Let us all drink together; see Allen 1988:142–143).

As the night advances, the air becomes colder, but no one complains. The wedding party remains serene, the invited smile contentedly, and the *yana uyakuna* are still exuberantly singing, dancing, and joking, with no sign of fatigue.

In the *ramada,* the rituals of respect continue as the evening meal (*tardin mikhuna*) is brought by the young male relatives of the sponsors of the meal. Andrés Felipe, Justa's younger brother, places a woven blanket full of maize kernels on the *mesarumi.* Don Julián unfolds it and with his right hand draws the sign of a cross into the pile of maize.[14] Then Andrés Felipe and other young men place stacks of plates full of cold prepared food onto the pile of maize. Justa's godson brings a woven shawl full of *chuño*. Don Julián places it beside the maize, opens the shawl, and proceeds to engrave a cross into the pile of *chuño*.

Andrés Felipe now places three *unkuñas* on the *mesarumi* filled with *chuño phasi*. These are potatoes frozen and dried in the sun, soaked in water, drained, and cooked in steam in an earthen pot.

The cold meal consists of potatoes, corn tortillas, rice, beans, *ch'arki, qochayuyu,* and roasted corn. Don Julián offers a plate to every person in the *ramada,* carefully wiping the bottom of each plate before handing it on. Rituals of respect are also performed before the meal is eaten. Every person offers his or her plate to every other person in the *ramada,* who receives it with gratitude, pretends to take a taste, and returns it to the person who offered it. All the guests outside the *ramada* also receive plates with food offered by young men.

After the cold food is consumed, young men bring hot soup to the bridal group and all the guests in the compound. Everyone enjoys the delicious hot soup, a blessing on a cold winter night. Bride and groom use only one plate and one spoon, sharing the precious food. The soup is *yawar chhallcha,* consisting of boiled blood, onions, salt, garlic, and spices. In the belief that what happens during the wedding festivity will determine the future life of the newlyweds, everyone eats and drinks much during these days of lavish generosity.

Visitors come to greet the couple and the other members of the wedding party. Each person brings a *coca k'intu* containing four to six leaves to offer to the person he or she greets and to start a conversation. "This *k'intu* is given with love and respect directly to the person without imploring the gods," Juan Mamani tells me. Interactions using *coca k'intus* and sometimes *trago* can take place among women, among men, or between both sexes. Some people say that the number of *coca* leaves offered to a person suggests the degree of friendship that exists between the two people. The more *coca* leaves one receives, the greater the friendship.

More *chicha* is poured from the *urpu* into the *qero.* Again and again, Pachamama and the Apus are implored to grant the couple health, youth, prosperity, many animals, and good harvests in return for their offerings. It is a common belief that during weddings and other celebrations in the Andes, drinking and drunkenness prevail. During this wedding, although offering and accepting drinks are important elements in the rituals, apart from the *yana uyakuna* and a few young visitors who looked tipsy, no one was drunk. Throughout the days of ceremonies, the wedding party performed all rituals in full control and with utmost dignity.

Secret Rituals in the Qolqa

Late in the night, the *hatun padrino* tells me in a whisper that it is time to move to the *qolqa,* the place where the food is stored throughout the year. I know that many important rituals are performed in this room that are usually reserved for the intimacy of the family, and I am pleasantly surprised when Don Ricardo asks me to join the party. I follow as the group leaves in the precisely prescribed sequence toward the small adobe house to the left of the compound. We bend to enter through a low, narrow door and take a long step down onto the earthen floor of this most important of all rooms. Here is kept the food that guarantees the survival of the family until the next harvest.

Through the faint light of a candle I can discern hides and dried meat hanging from the ceiling. The wedding party settles down on blankets and ponchos spread out below the hides. Opposite from the entrance stands a large *taqe,* a bin made of reeds where *chuño* is stored. Other smaller bins are placed around the room; some *chuño* and *moraya* are spread out on *ichu* grass on the floor, symbolizing potato fields.

The *ara padrino* walks straight toward the larger bin. He places *coca* leaves and four bottles of *trago* in a row on top of it. One bottle is a gift from the bride and groom, one from the *hatun padrinos,* one from the *ara padrinos,* and one from the parents of the bride. *Coca k'intus* are blown east in honor of Pachamama and the other major deities and are then exchanged among the people present. The deities are asked to grant the couple good harvests and prosperity.

Now the *ara padrino* asks for permission to start serving the *trago.* He begins with the bottle provided by the newlyweds. One person after the other receives a small glass. Each person makes offerings to the deities, sprinkling some alcohol on the ground and into the air, then onto each bin and onto the potatoes, *chuño,* and *moraya* spread out on the floor. Each whispers prayers asking Pachamama for plentiful harvests of potatoes, for prosperity and happiness for the couple. Only a part of the *trago* from each bottle is used.

The deities have received their respect. Now it is time to address the new couple. The *hatun padrino* falls to his knees in front of the bride and groom. He puts his arms around their shoulders while giving them advice for their new life together. The others follow. Each person expresses blessings and specific advice in a different way. They all speak with much love and concern.

Following the *hatun padrino,* the *hatun madrina* falls to her knees, embracing the couple while giving them advice. *Ara padrino* and *ara madrina* follow. Then Andrés Felipe, the bride's brother, expresses his wishes to his sister and brother-in-law. I too am asked to speak to the couple.

The newlyweds thank everyone for the good wishes. Salvador's aunt, a strong elderly woman, enters. With a self-confident smile she offers *sank'ayllo,* which is *chicha* boiled with *coca* leaves, alcohol, and sugar. The *ñawin aqha* is sprinkled east. Then all those present receive a cupful of this delicious drink to warm their chilled bones. But first each person offers some of the drink to the deities, to the *taqe* full of potatoes, and to the people present. One after the other pretends to drink, then returns the cup to the one who offered it. Although these rituals are of utmost importance to the future of the couple, the atmosphere is relaxed and there is a feeling of warmth, kindness, and community among this group of people who will assist one another in every way for the rest of their lives.

The laughter of the *yana uyakuna* penetrates the house but the blackfaces do not enter. In the early morning hours we leave the *qolqa.* Only *hatun madrina* and *hatun padrino* stay longer. They put the newlyweds to bed in this, their most important quarters. This symbolic act supports the idea that the couple starts out a new life accepting the full guidance of their *madrinas* and *padrinos.*

Outside the storehouse the moon illuminates the bleak, barren landscape and the steep *susuwa,* which is so dangerously close. The musicians continue to play ancient tunes while the blackfaces move like ghostly shadows against the night sky—dancing and joking. Their apparently clumsy and thoughtless behavior conceals their deep devotion to the newlyweds. As they exhaust themselves dancing and joking and keeping awake, they ensure that no harm will come to the couple and that happiness and humor will always be with them. With great concern they watch over the couple, the *ramada,* and the entire compound throughout the night and the days and nights to come.

Arpay and Surun Pakay—Sacrifice and Burial of the Enqaychu

The sun begins to lick the frost from the meager meadows as the shrill voices of the blackfaces break through the thin icy air. On the rocky slopes beside the house an alpaca lies on the ground, ready to be sacrificed in honor of the deities and to provide food for the second day of festivities.

The musicians play throughout the sacrifice in respect for this very significant act. With a swift movement, the blackface in charge of the sacrifice sends the spirit of the alpaca to the great Apu Ausangate, asking this mighty deity to return the same animal. The sacrifice is done in the same way as during Pukllay.

"Apu Awsanqati, kasqallanta kutichinpuytaq!" (Apu Ausangate, return the same!), the blackfaces call out in their high voices as the first cup of blood offered to the mountain gods disperses against the rays of the rising sun. They untie the feet of the alpaca so its spirit can run freely to the great Apu from where it will join its herd again later. "Apu Ausangate—great mountain deity and guardian of animals—please return the spirit of this alpaca," the blackfaces entreat. Then they fall to their knees, praying silently.

Together they carry the sacrificed alpaca to the front of the *ramada,* then dance around it in a counterclockwise direction. Everyone helps to prepare the meal. Neighbors and friends bring potatoes, *chuño, moraya,* maize, and *chicha.* This is another day of great joy. All of the animal's bones are collected and buried in the enclosure. Before they are placed into the earth, an offering with the usual ingredients wrapped in white paper enters the ground. Everyone eats silently.

After the meal the blackfaces prepare for *surun pakay,* the burial of the *enqaychu.* It is a powerful ritual, elements of which are found in a variety of ancient and contemporary rites. Eight of the ten *yana uyakuna* get ready to search for *enqaychu,* which are effigies of all kinds of things the couple may want and which will bring them joy, happiness, and prosperity. Before they leave for the riverside, they fall to their knees in the middle of the courtyard, asking the deities to help them in their search. Then the band plays "La Diana" and off go the eight toward the river Llaqto Mayu, dancing and joking in their high-pitched voices.

They return twice empty-handed to make sure the couple is all right and to announce the stage of their search. Then they leave again. I am told by one of my companions that it would mean bad luck for the couple if the blackfaces brought the *enqaychu* before returning twice empty-handed. The reason for this is not given.

The blackfaces scan the landscape, walk along the riverbank, and cross it to find a strategic site between the river and the adjacent steep rocks. There they offer *coca k'intus* to Pachamama, improvise a *mesa-rumi,* and sprinkle alcohol on its four corners, asking the great earth goddess to provide them, in return, with powerful *enqaychu.* Then they leave in all directions in search of the charmed stones that will bring luck, happiness, and prosperity. Wild with joy, they loudly exclaim the wish that will be fulfilled each time they find a stone that resembles any of the items the couple cherishes. They look at it from all sides, admire it, and explode into enthusiastic laughter. Finally they discover the most important *enqaychu,* a large stone that resembles an alpaca. Over-come with joy, they call out *chushllu,* the sacred name for an alpaca, and blow *coca k'intus* toward the east while thanking the gods. They sprinkle alcohol on the *enqaychu,* and then they tie the large effigy of an alpaca with ropes to the back of the chief *yana uyakuna.* The smaller *enqaychu* are hidden in their ponchos and carried triumphantly to the house of the newlyweds.

Laden with these treasures, the group enters the compound in a straight line, kneels down forming a line opposite the musicians, and again thanks the deities for their help. They trace a circle in a counter-clockwise direction and deposit their treasures close to the *mesarumi,* in view of the couple. Everyone receives them with enthusiasm. The couple is content but remains silent, showing no emotion.

On their knees the blackfaces unpack the *enqaychu* and place them on the *mesarumi* in front of the couple. They toss the *ñawin aqha* from a newly opened *urpu* to the east, then spill *chicha* onto the ground to demarcate the four corners where the treasures are to be buried.

Using a hoe and a *chakitaklla* (foot plow), the chief of the *yana uya-kuna* begins to dig a hole in the ground close to the *mesarumi,* in full sight of the wedding party. As soon as the hole is deep enough to ac-commodate the *enqaychu,* the excavator rings a bell to call the spirits of the *enqaychu* and those of the Apus to assist in this ritual. Bride and groom, *padrinos* and *madrinas* observe every step with solemn serenity. The blackfaces make jokes and tease while they do this sacred work. Jokingly one of them uses his make-believe binoculars to make sure the work is done with precision.

Hatun madrina and *hatun padrino* place *coca k'intus* into the hole, followed by an offering wrapped in white paper with more *k'intus, untu, mukllu* (*coca* seeds), sweets, and all the other ingredients. The chief of the *yana uyakuna,* who has the primary responsibility for *surun pakay,* sprinkles alcohol into the hole and places the first *enqaychu* onto the *mesarumi* for the couple to view. "This is your house," he exclaims; everyone nods, the bell rings, and the *enqaychu* disappears in the hole. Next he says, "This is your car." Everyone laughs (except the couple) because there are no roads in Chillihuani. "This is your airplane." Again there is laughter. Most people have never seen an airplane. Then the stone money sinks into the earth. Effigies representing land, potatoes, *oqa, ulluku,* and *mashwa* are followed by those representing a llama, a sheep, a male and a female herder, a horse, and a glass of wine. Again alcohol is sprinkled into the hole and on its four corners. Everyone prays to the gods. Soil is dropped onto the *enqaychu,* and more prayers are said. Finally, when the treasures are almost covered, the chief of the *yana uyakuna* shouts enthusiastically, "This is your *chushllu.*" First water and then alcohol are sprinkled onto the large effigy of an alpaca before it is placed part way into the hole. The request for many healthy alpacas is most important for the couple, and this stone must stick out of the earth. More alcohol is sprinkled onto Pachamama as the *yana uyakuna* continue to pray, express hope, and joke.

The bell rings. The *yana uyakuna* kneel by the *mesarumi* facing the *surun pakay* and the musicians. Then they walk around the burial counterclockwise, exclaiming at the top of their voices, "*Allin ñan, allin ñan!*" (Have a good trip), referring to the trip to the spirit world and back. Together with the guests they laugh and dance and hope that the energy they create will bring joy and happiness to the couple and that the great Mother Earth will fulfill each wish that they have buried in her womb. The bride and groom look content, but they still do not speak, laugh, or display any outward signs of emotion.

The people of Chillihuani recognize the sites where *enqaychu* are buried. A year ago Luisa and Juan Mamani showed me with pride the *enqaychu* of an alpaca that stuck out of the earth close to their *mesarumi,* where it was buried at the occasion of their wedding. During fiestas such as Pukllay, San Juan, August 1, and Santiago, these stones receive libations of *chicha.*

The burial of the *enqaychu* is considered a success. Family and guests are in good spirits, and in appreciation of this festivity they reciprocate by putting donations on the table in the form of money and produce. This they call *aynikunchis qolqewan* (let us cooperate with money). *Hatun madrina* and *hatun padrino* collect the gifts and give them to the couple the following day. More visitors come from all corners of the village to congratulate the couple and to bring gifts and joy.

When the evening meal is ready to be served, a violent storm takes shape. Whirlwinds resembling small tornadoes lift clouds of dust into the air. "*Muyuq wayra*" (the whirlwind), the people whisper, but no one moves. In any event, there is not enough space for the wedding party and all the visitors in the two tiny houses. The cold wind forces the dust into the huts and through our clothing. It bends the *ramada* to the side. Luckily it does not break. This would be a bad omen.

Half an hour passes, then the wind subsides as quickly as it began. Food is served, perhaps with a little more dust than usual, but everyone thanks the hosts and the deities alike.

At night the bridal group disappears again into the storehouse to make offerings to the gods and to ask for good harvests, many animals, and general happiness. Close family members who could not participate the previous night are invited to join. After these guests leave in the middle of the night, *padrinos* and *madrinas* help bride and groom to change their clothes, a ritual act that shows that the couple has successfully performed another step in the transformation to a new married life. With their everyday clothes, they can now behave more naturally. They can again look at people, talk to them, and show their emotions. Yet, they must wait before they can participate in all activities without danger. The bride and groom remain in the *qolqa* with their guide and their *madrinas* and *padrinos.*

The guests and the blackfaces dance in the moonlit night to the enchanting melodies played by the band. They create joy that will last throughout the couple's life. After the forceful wind of the late afternoon, the night is unusually warm.

Dance is important in the Andes and almost everyone dances well. Yet, it seems the older people are the most accomplished dancers. Don Sebastián (Modesto's uncle), who is approximately eighty years old, dances without tiring, using intricate dance steps that are perfectly timed to the music. "This is the way we used to dance when I was young; we danced often, for days and nights on end," he says, smiling contentedly as he moves gracefully through the courtyard, recalling his long-gone youth.

On this night we sleep as little as on the previous one. Some visitors arrive, others leave, taking advantage of the moonlit night to reach the wedding party or to return to their distant homes. Every person who remains at the party finds a corner in which to sleep between alpaca hides. These are the simplest living conditions imaginable, yet life is marked by tenderness and generosity.

The Third Day—a Closer Look at the Blackfaces

With the rising sun, the laughter and joking of the blackfaces mixes with the thumping of dancing steps in the courtyard. The bride and groom have emerged from their cherished *qolqa* and have joined the *madrinas* and the *padrinos* in their dances on the earthen patio, happy and content. I have always known Justa as a lively person and, even more so, Salvador, who is talkative, outgoing, and very active. To remain silent for two days and nights and avoid eye contact shows that they take the marriage rites very seriously. They have passed this trial and can go on with some of their daily activities. Yet, they still cannot leave the compound and must remain in close proximity for six more days. They cannot work their fields or take their animals to pasture. Family, friends, and neighbors will do this for them. Neither can they attend fiestas or any other activity away from home. They must fulfill every task together; they walk together, sit together, prepare food together, and eat and drink together using the same plate, spoon, and cup. "They must show utmost discipline, this is most essential," the herders stressed several times throughout the festivities. Physical closeness symbolizes closeness in spirit. It is believed that if they stick it out for the required eight days, they will remain together for the rest of their lives.

In the morning the couple receives the *surun qolqe,* also referred to as *aynikunchis qolqewan,* which has been collected the previous day. This is a monetary gift to the bride and groom from family and guests to start their new married life together. The *ara padrino* hands it over to the couple. With this action, he no longer carries the tray with the twelve coins covered with a white cloth. The bridal group can now walk freely without proceeding in single file. But bride and groom still walk together—side by side. "Such are our customs," Ricardo explains. "We have always done it this way and so have our ancestors before us."

The music continues. Salvador asks me to dance. Then Justa asks Antolín, my *compadre* who has come from the valley, to dance in a group dance with two lines of dancers facing each other—the men on one side, the women on the other.[15]

One dance follows another. It is quite exhausting at this altitude after nights with virtually no sleep. But the herders do not mind. The blackfaces continue into the third day of vigorous activities without apparent signs of fatigue. Their repertoire of games and jokes is endless. They imitate married life, playing out scenes of jealousy and lovemaking while they dance. They do somersaults in the courtyard. Jokingly one of them throws himself onto the ground while another one whips him on his back; both laugh in their high falsetto voices.

As I observed the *yana uyakuna* for days and nights on end, my understanding deepened concerning the significant roles they play in the marriage process. Years ago in my first encounter with the blackfaces, I found it difficult to pass many hours in their company, listening to their shrill voices and seeing them engage in endless squabbles, fighting, joking, and screaming with glee. Now I recognize the symbolic significance of these characters. I appreciate their dedication to the couple as they struggle through days and nights with little or no rest to assure a safe and successful fiesta and a good life for the couple.

Although I am not aware that blackfaces participate in weddings elsewhere, I have seen similar characters during fiestas in Cusipata. There the blackface, called "*el negro*," and his "wife" play important roles during the festivities of the village saint, the virgin Asunta. *El negro,* with his face painted black, and his "wife"—a man in women's clothes with a red face—run in competition through the village. If the "wife" wins the race, the harvest will be good; if the husband wins, it will be bad. So all the villagers cheer for the "wife." Although dual forces—female and male—dominate this event, the male/female characters in Cusipata play only a small part of the roles the blackfaces take on during *casarakuy* in Chillihuani.

Yana Uyakuna and Ukukus—Andean Cosmology Comes to Life

During the wedding it became clear that the rituals the blackfaces perform and the powerful symbolism they carry are not restricted to *casarakuy,* but have significance within a much larger framework of Andean ideology. The longer I observed the *yana uyakuna,* the more I was struck by their similarities to the *ukukus,* which means "bears" in Quechua. These characters figure most prominently during the pilgrimage to Qoyllur Rit'i, to the glaciers of the Sinakara mountain range in the district of Ocongate in the province of Quispicanchis—a journey of twenty-seven hours on foot from Chillihuani. A comparison between the *ukukus* and the *yana uyakuna* can provide insight into the complex meaning and function of the latter, as well as yielding a deeper understanding of how the Andean people view their universe.

Scholarly writings shed some light on this aspect of Andean culture, as does information provided by Valerio Escobar, my former neighbor in Cusipata, who, until 1992 and for sixteen years of his life, was *capitán* of the *ukukus* of Quispicanchis. My own observations during the breathtaking pilgrimage to the glaciers of Qoyllur Rit'i in 1991 may further illuminate the meaning of the *ukukus* and thus the role of the blackfaces within the context of the duality of Andean thought (see Crumrine 1991:279 regarding processes of transformation and duality).

The pilgrimage to Qoyllur Rit'i (Star of Snow) or Qoyllurrit'i (Shining White Snow) starts one week before Corpus Christi, a holiday that can occur between May 20 and June 23 (Randall 1982:42). This holiday is based on the moon; thus there is moonlight every year for the fiesta (Randall 1982:46).

Qoyllur Rit'i, the largest pilgrimage center in southern Peru, is, as Randall (1982:38) pointed out, "probably the most impressive and dazzling spectacle in the Andes." The snow-covered mountain Qolqepunku, literally the "silver gate," rises from the steaming jungles of the Eastern Cordillera of the Andes to the icy heights of the Sinakara mountain range. Tens of thousands of people flock to Qoyllur Rit'i every year. Hundreds of villages send their dance groups in their special costumes. Most village groups carry the image of their village saint to this most important gathering (for an in-depth description, see Flores Ochoa 1990; Gow 1974; Ramírez 1969; Randall 1982; Sallnow 1991).

Qoyllur Rit'i is an ancient fiesta. Yet in 1780, the year of the uprising of Tupac Amaru II, the pilgrimage was given a Catholic interpretation by the church,[16] which invented a story that goes as follows: a miracle happened when the young pastoralist Mariano Mayta met an unknown young boy (Jesus Christ) high up on the pasture where he was herding his flocks. They became friends. Things started to go very well for the young herder and his family but ended in tragedy as Mariano died and his friend disappeared, leaving behind a cross imprinted in rock as evidence. A church was built to surround this miraculous rock at 4,900 meters above sea level and is now an object of annual pilgrimages.

Yet, the ancient Andean rituals that take place throughout the days and nights of the fiesta clearly overshadow the Christian element. In some ways the ancient beliefs and Christian elements mingle, but the Indians of the high Andes undertake the pilgrimage to Qoyllur Rit'i mainly for the same reasons their ancestors climbed to the glaciers long ago. They are attracted by the mountain and engage in this exhausting pilgrimage in honor of the mountains, who protect animals and provide the healing waters, snow, and ice that the pilgrims chop from the mountain and carry to their villages in the valley. The concept of health and fertility is strongly expressed in the fiesta of Qoyllur Rit'i, an event which may be related to the disappearance and reappearance of the Pleiades (Randall: 1982). Within Andean ideology, this is a time of chaos, uncertainty, and transformation, the end of sickness and the beginning of a new agricultural year.

As pilgrims enter the sanctuary, chaos is personified in sound and movement. Each group of dancers follows its own program without consideration for surrounding groups. Each band plays louder to overcome the sound of its neighbors, thus creating a cacophony of astounding proportions. Jumbled echoes return from the rocky mountains in the distance and add to the chaotic energy of the place.

Robert Randall (1982:68) captured the atmosphere well when he wrote:

> In contemporary Andean mythology, times of transition are also chaotic. Thus in daily life the transitions from light to dark (dawn to dusk) are particularly dangerous times when spirits of the past world have the most power. These spirits are also very much in evidence during Qoyllur Rit'i which ritualizes the transition from night to day (from one year to the next; from one world to the next). Perhaps one reason people stay up all night dancing and singing is to ward off these spirits; and it should be noted that the *ukukus* (who are protection against these forces) never sleep at night.

The similarity between the roles of the *ukukus* and the *yana uyakuna* is striking. The *ukukus* are central to the pilgrimage at Qoyllur Rit'i. Dressed in long robes made of shaggy alpaca wool, with their faces usually hidden by knit masks, the *ukukus* wander between this world and the supernatural. They have the strength to mediate between the two worlds. Some investigators consider them bear dancers; others believe they represent alpacas.

Like the *yana uyakuna,* the *ukukus* speak in high falsetto voices and joke with the people they meet. They dance in a rambunctious, disorderly fashion and engage in mock fights with other *ukukus.* Yet, in their dual capacity, they also keep order during Qoyllur Rit'i. Deborah Poole (1991:310) wrote: "The bear dancers or *ukukus* at Qoyllur Rit'i are solely responsible for maintaining order, preventing excessive drinking, and allaying theft at the sanctuary." Juan A. Ramírez (1969: 85) observed, "*Ukukus* are considered superior beings, they are potent and strong."

Like some *yana uyakuna, ukukus* carry a whip, a bottle, and a small doll[17] which is sometimes called a "*paulucha*" (Flores Ochoa 1990:83). Randall (1982:70) wrote that according to the chronicler Bernabé Cobo, "every Inca had an *idolo-guaoqui*, or brother idol, which received a house and food and was consulted during wars. There would seem to be some relation between the Inca's *idolo-guaoqui* and the *ukuku*'s *paulucha*." The practice of searching for stones that resemble desired items also exists at Qoyllur Rit'i, where thousands of people sit in the rubble along the hills making houses, fields, corrals, cars, and other things out of stones. They hope that God will help to make their wish built of stone come true.

We have seen the blackfaces acting out their utterly exhausting roles over the course of at least three days and nights during *casarakuy*. The *ukukus* offer their sacrifice in an equally daring fashion for three full days and nights. At 2:00 A.M. in bone-chilling cold, groups of *ukukus* start their ascent from the camp by the church to the glacier. First they climb across rubble and narrow ridges, and then they walk on the glacier, trying to avoid treacherous crevasses.

High up in the glacier, under the full moon, the ancient rites take place. New *ukukus* are initiated. They learn about their rights and duties and the roles they are to take on as protectors and keepers of order.[18]

As the sun rises, the young *ukukus* must undergo initiation that includes whipping. They leave a small amount of blood in the snow of the mountain. Established members of the *ukukus* confess on the glacier. Those who have sinned during the year also receive a whipping (Valerio Escobar, personal communication).[19] Sometimes an *ukuku* is swallowed at night by the icy crevasses of the glacier. This kind of death is tragic, but it is not mourned in the same way as other deaths; it is considered an offering to the mountain, a sacrifice to a cause that benefits everyone by bringing fertility to the land and health to people and animals. Before the *ukukus* return to their camp, they hack large chunks of ice from the mountain with which to heal people in the valley.

Although the festivities are different, the central roles the *ukukus* play at Qoyllur Rit'i mirror those of the blackfaces during the Chillihuani wedding. Both groups are essential to the festivity as they mediate between this world and the spirit world. They also exhibit the strength needed to confront the spirits of chaos that abound during times of great transition and transformation such as a wedding in Chillihuani or Qoyllur Rit'i, which marks the beginning of a new year when the Pleiades return in the sky.

The tremendous energy generated during these rituals in Chillihuani and Qoyllur Rit'i sustains the fiestas to their very end. The energy symbolically connects this world with the realm of the supernatural. It brings the past into the present and projects both into the future. Randall (1982:40) wrote: "Contemporary Andean mythology and 'pre-Hispanic cults' reveal an emphatic continuity in both thought patterns and contents. They demonstrate that 450 years of foreign rule have not changed the conceptual structure of the Andean mind."

In Chillihuani the wedding festivities continue as the third day gives way to the night. More visitors come; others must leave. On the morning of the fourth day the blackfaces leave as well. They have done their duty mediating between two spheres of existence, fending off evil forces, bringing joy to the occasion, and providing the *enqaychu* to fulfill all the couple's wishes for health, happiness, and prosperity. They have clearly represented the duality of forces in Andean thought.

Madrinas and *padrinos* also leave on the fourth day, as do the musicians. The length of time individuals remain with the couple varies from one wedding to another depending on the time available to them. The wedding party, the blackfaces, and the musicians, however, always remain for at least three days, after which the dangers of this transformation are thought to have lessened. On the fourth day the couple is again on its own but must obey certain rules until the full eight days are over. Therefore they cannot participate in the Fiesta de Santiago, held on July 25 and 26.

Eight-day periods are important in Andean ideology. Eight days after a person dies, his or her spirit is sent off in ritual form. Women stay in bed or around the house for eight days after giving birth. Pukllay lasts eight days. So does the wedding.

La Fiesta
de Santiago

"Huifa, huifa!" The exuberant yells of young riders mix with the thundering noise of their galloping horses as they race across the rugged terrain close to the perpetual snows of the high Andes. The landscape comes alive as more and more horsemen appear from all directions, their colorful ponchos fluttering in the wind like the wings of giant birds. Without saddles or stirrups, one with their horses, the riders swing their *warak'a* through the air with an expression of utter joy on their tanned faces. This is July 25, La Fiesta de Santiago, or, as the herders of Chillihuani call it, the Day of the Horse.

Already in February of 1988, when I first visited Chillihuani to celebrate Pukllay, the people urged me to stay until Santiago in July. "It is a great fiesta, you will like it," they said with radiant smiles. But I had to leave before July and could not return to Peru until the summer of 1990.

I arrived at a difficult time, a time of instability, inflation, and large-scale strikes. Peru was passing through its worst economic disaster in living memory. Getting a bus or car was no longer easy. At times there was not a single vehicle on the road. Stores and gas stations were closed all or much of the time. Eventually, with the help of many friends, we finally found someone who had saved some gasoline and who offered to take me to the countryside, though two days later than anticipated. But the *curandero* Juan Mamani, the community president with his shaggy little horse, and other *comu-*

neros from Chillihuani had waited for me in the valley.

Surprisingly, a small store in Cusipata was still open. Since there are no stores in Chillihuani, and few were open in Cuzco, I was happy to contribute to the upcoming fiesta with *coca* leaves, bread, sugar, and tea. My *comadre* Catalina gave me some carrots and onions, and another had made *chicha* for us to take along.

When times are difficult, my relationship with the parents of the children to whom I am a godmother is not only socially but also economically beneficial. We help one another as one would help one's own family. Early the next morning, off we went to the heights of Chillihuani, just in time for the *víspera,* the eve of Santiago.

An interesting and complex history surrounds the Fiesta de Santiago which sheds considerable light on the religious ideology of the Incas and also the Spanish. Santiago, the patron saint of Chillihuani, is a Spanish saint. In Spain he is represented as a mounted, sword-wielding warrior (Gade 1983:777), and effigies of Santiago on horseback date from the eleventh century (see Braunfels 1974, 7:34, in Gade 1983:777). In Spain, Santiago was believed responsible for thunder and lightning.

When the Spaniards invaded Peru, they soon discovered that in return for rain and protection against the devastating hail, the Incas held important rituals in July (midwinter in the southern hemisphere) which were of symbolic significance to the entire Inca religious and political structure. Sacrifices were made in honor of Illapa, the god of thunder and lightning (Gade 1983:775; Molina [1575] 1959:43–44). In an attempt to extirpate Andean religion, it was therefore convenient for the invaders to superimpose Santiago on the image of Illapa. Thus Santiago became the patron saint of Chillihuani and other high-altitude herding villages and has been worshiped widely throughout the Andes, where lightning is a constant danger to the people, their animals, and their homes (see Nash 1979:29 regarding Santiago in Bolivia). Federico Lunardi (1946:237) wrote: "Everything that had been attributed to the thunder was attributed to Santiago almost immediately after the arrival of the Spanish."

On our long hike to Chillihuani we talk about the forthcoming event. I ask my companions what Santiago means to them. "Santiago is a Spanish saint who always arrives with the lightning and knows how to make the *warak'a* roar like thunder," one of my traveling companions comments as he swings his arms into the air as though he were swinging the *warak'a*. This way of identifying the Inca deity with the Spanish saint was early recognized by Cieza de Leon, a soldier who came to Peru early in the conquest. He wrote ([1550] 1967:106) that the Andean people see the same characteristics in Santiago as in Illapa. Both bring deadly attacks—Santiago as a warrior, and Illapa as lightning.

Not everyone in Chillihuani views Santiago in the same way. One villager explained, "Santiago is a saint who believed much in Illapa. Perhaps he adored Illapa. This Santiago who believed in Illapa was certainly a man of the Andes who always rode a horse. For this reason he is always depicted on horseback. When Santiago died, the people believed that he could give orders to Illapa. And since the statue of the patron saint Santiago is in the church, people ask him to forego sending hail."

Another villager told me that "the man Santiago has died and his horse is also dead. What is left are the churches with his statue in many villages." For many people in the high villages, however, Santiago represents Illapa, and as such, the patron saint Santiago himself is believed to throw hail with a sling and make the lightning flash through the sky. Bernard Mishkin (1963:464) observed during his research in Kauri, Peru, that some people substitute Santiago for *qoa*—the mystical feline. *Qoa* is believed to incorporate Illapa's powers.

The Incas held a fiesta in honor of Illapa not only in July following the harvest and again before sowing a new crop, but also in December during the solstice of Qhapaq Raymi (Gade 1983:775–776) and again in February. The people of Chillihuani make offerings to Illapa or Qhaqya during the same times of the year as did their ancestors, the Inca, and on December 8.

In Chillihuani and other high-altitude communities Illapa is tied to the lives of the people in intricate and deep-seated ways. Ina Rösing (1990:69) found that among the lightning-related saints of the Callawaya of Bolivia, Santiago is the most powerful saint because he is in charge of lightning. To protect their beliefs, the Incas changed the ancient names of Andean deities to Spanish names. Abdon Yaranga Valderrama (1979:709), who did extensive research on Illapa in the high Andes, argued that the Andean people substituted the name Santiago for Illapa to escape the "extirpation of idolatry," a vast campaign in Peru that started at the time of the conquest and had as its goal the extermination of Andean religion. For the people in the heights of Chillihuani, the Fiesta de Santiago is also the Day of the Horse. The noise of horses' hooves beating the ground evokes the image of Illapa, powerful deity of the sky.

A statue of Santiago on horseback stands in the small church high in the wilderness of Chillihuani. The statue of Santiago carried through the streets of Cuzco during the Fiesta de Corpus Christi depicts a Spanish saint on a rearing horse, wielding his sword in the air. Below him, in fear, crouches a small, dark-skinned man in fear of being trampled. Shortly after the conquest, the Inca chronicler Guaman Poma de Ayala drew a picture of this scene (see figure 5).

The symbolic meaning inherent in the statue of Santiago is clear to everyone. In Chillihuani this meaning is seldom mentioned. During the many hours we walk uphill, my companions do not have much to say about the saint. Neither are they eager to talk much about Illapa or

Figure 5. "A Miracle Happened." The apostle Santiago descended to earth to defend the Christians in a battle with the Incas (from Felipe Guaman Poma de Ayala [1615] 1980: 376–377).

Qhaqya, their benefactor and destroyer. Perhaps they would call his attention by mentioning his name too often; perhaps they would anger him. I do not know, but I stop asking questions. Instead we talk about Kaballoq P'unchaynin, the great Day of the Horse, when the skilled horsemen of Chillihuani race across their high mountain world on their cherished horses, providing a superb spectacle for the people, the gods, and the spirits alike.

The sun has been burning mercilessly from the clear blue sky all day. Yet, our ascent is much easier during the dry Andean winter than it was during the rainy season, when the turbulent river ran across the trail, the earth was waterlogged, and we reached our destination only by means of considerable detours.

We arrive at the healer's home just as the sun disappears behind the snowy peaks in the distance. The barking dogs alert the Mamanis of our approach. Juan and his family pass through the tiny door to greet us. "It is good to see you after such a long time," Luisa says, smiling. She ushers us into her small adobe house, where a delicious hot soup with potatoes, *chuño,* and the high-altitude tubers *oqa, ulluku,* and *mashwa* awaits us. But Juan makes sure that I first enter the corral. He points to a young white alpaca with light eyes, a type which is rare and esteemed. With joy he asserts: "Never in my life did this happen to me." I think back to the Pukllay rituals I participated in two years ago, and I cannot help but wonder whether the gods of the Andes have smiled on me.

Back in the house it feels good to talk about all the things that have happened since my last visit and to discuss the upcoming Fiesta de Santiago, which in Chillihuani is second in importance only to Pukllay. We also discuss our plans for research and community work during the coming months. Eventually we fall asleep, rolled in the alpaca furs that stave off the intense cold of the Andean winter night.

In the morning, just as the rays of the sun begin to lick the frost from the stiff grass, we continue our ascent to *suyu* Llaqto, the highest sector of Chillihuani. The healer Modesto Quispe Choqque is this year's *carguyoq* (sponsor) for the Fiesta de Santiago. He has invited the *curandero* Juan Mamani and me to spend the fiesta with him and his family. We must arrive in time for the eve of Santiago.

The distance from the valley to the central area of Chillihuani, where the Mamani family lives, is 16 kilometers. From there to *suyu* Llaqto we have to cover another 15 kilometers to arrive at *condorwasi,* the house of the condor. Here Modesto Quispe lives with his family at an altitude of 4,600 meters above sea level, close to the perpetual snow of the Andes, one of the highest inhabited zones in the world.

The landscape becomes increasingly spectacular as we ascend. Rocky peaks of various shapes jut into the bright blue sky of the Andean winter. A small path leads higher and higher along precipitous mountain slopes. The ascent becomes more difficult as the air gets thinner. Alpacas and llamas balance on rocky inclines and cross the fast-flowing Rio Chillihuani to get to better pastures on the other side.

My bags sit firmly on the back of Juan's donkey while Juan and other Chillihuani friends offer to carry my cameras, tape recorder, and other breakable things. This allows me to keep up with the fast pace of these people, to whom altitude and distance mean nothing. They show no signs of fatigue. Many hours pass. Long stretches of rubble, precipitous mountainsides, clear rushing water. Two large hawks glide through the sky, graceful and majestic.

Finally *suyu* Llaqto comes in sight. A cluster of adobe houses resembling a small village surrounded by an adobe wall appears in the distance. On the far side this settlement is confined by a steep, high mountain range. Its slopes are deeply scarred by landslides, the dangerous *susuwas* where the spirits of the condemned languish. Whenever we come to a *susuwa,* people mention the dangers of these sites. Perhaps these stories serve to keep people from the scree, warning them of the actual danger of causing an avalanche of stone and rubble. The fear of the spirits of the condemned is, however, not excessive. A few days later during an excursion to the house of the village judge, we must cross this *susuwa* on a path that cuts horizontally across its extensive area. Here again the inventive mind of the Quechua people shows that potential spiritual danger need not always be avoided when, for practical reasons, the need is great and the daylight hours are short.

As we admire the landscape, so alive in the minds and spirits of the people and so much a part of life here, Alejandro Huaman, a young man with a radiant smile and an athlete's demeanor, comes running uphill. He left the valley at dawn and has already caught up with us, a true *chaski.* I always thought that people exaggerated the feats of the *chaskis,* runners during Inca times who carried messages throughout the Inca Empire and goods such as fresh fish from the coast to the highlands, but the people of Chillihuani have shown me that such feats can be accomplished.

Alejandro invites us to meet his family. The dogs bark as we approach the compound of adobe houses, and immediately this remote solitude comes alive as people in their colorful festive outfits emerge from their tiny houses to greet us. Touching shoulders in a loose embrace, they welcome us to their *suyu,* happy that we have arrived to celebrate the Day of the Horse among them at the very heights of their village.

The men of the house put blankets and ponchos on the ground for us and we sit down beside the *hatun rumi,* a large boulder deposited by a mountain glacier—or perhaps by the gods. This *hatun rumi,* a great and powerful rock, is at the center of sacred family rituals. Each family uses a large natural rock as an altar or a table from which to serve the gods. Rocks of intriguing shapes, either natural or carved, were sacred to the Incas and have not lost their power for the people of Chillihuani and other high-altitude communities.

Alejandro and his brother offer us *chicha* brewed by the women from maize bartered in the valley. They have also prepared a delicious meal using the tubers they have harvested and vegetables bartered in the valley. There is also alpaca *ch'arki,* a delicacy that must be present at every great fiesta.

Laughing, joking, and joyful exuberance fill the air. Yet, the people always maintain a degree of restraint, an elegance in their gestures, and respect in the way they address one another. With friendly smiles they offer us ever more food. Generosity is always present in Chillihuani, but is most visibly expressed during fiestas.

We thank our hosts for the generous meal and continue to the higher part of *suyu* Llaqto and the home of Modesto Quispe and his family. The landscape becomes more bizarre as we ascend. Its colors and forms project the image of another world, remote in time and space. Snow-covered peaks jut through crystal clear air into the cloudless blue sky, contrasting sharply with the earth-toned environment. This landscape above the tree line, barren and majestic, is alive, and is central to legends and myths that are rooted far back in the times of the great-grandfathers. Here and there springs emerge which keep the grass green. Their mineral content adds red and yellow-brownish colors to the smooth, undulating rocks. Some rocks look as though they have been carved by the hands of sculptors.

In the distance we can recognize *condorwasi,* the house of the condor, a two-story house built of stone. Two other houses and a large corral come into view. Every building and structure is made of stone, as is the bridge across a small creek and the fence that encloses the entire compound. Closer to the house we pass an altar made of stone. Earth is too scarce at this altitude to fashion adobe bricks, and Modesto and his family are experts in working stone.

We have been sighted. A band starts playing festive music (see photo 19). Young horsemen in their colorful ponchos come to meet us. Modesto Quispe, the healer of *suyu* Llaqto, greets us with a loose embrace. He and his family occupy this pleasant area, which sustains their alpacas and llamas.

I ask Modesto how long he has lived here. "All my life," he says. And where did his ancestors come from? "They have always lived here since the Incas and probably before," Modesto declares with a radiant smile.

We approach the house. The skeleton of a large condor hangs from its roof. A true *condorwasi*. Modesto honors and fears the spirit of the condor. Condors are the birds of the Apus, and to kill a condor may mean death for a person or a whole family. Yet, when a young herder who took Modesto's animals to pasture saw condors approaching a newborn alpaca, he used his sling to chase the voracious birds away. The stone he hurled hit one of the large birds and killed it. Modesto was shocked, knowing the revenge the Apus would take. He took the dead condor to his house and has been making offerings to the mountain gods ever since, asking for forgiveness.

The four musicians greet us with a loose embrace and continue to play enchanting tunes on their flutes and drums. Modesto introduces us to his wife Gregoria, her sister Jovita, his nineteen-year-old son Juan, and his young daughters Luswilma and Anali. In the name of all the people of Chillihuani I am given a gift, a weaving in which my name appears together with the name of the village. "This is for you," Modesto says with a smile, "so you always know where you belong."

Three-year-old Anali brings two cups from the kitchen. She fills them with water and gives one to me. "*Kuska ukyasun!*" (Let us drink together!), she says with a charming gesture. This perfect little hostess must have decided that I was *her* visitor, and she rarely left my side during my stay. Her four-year-old sister was a little shyer. Living so far from the mainstream of society, they had never seen a foreigner before, but they did not seem to mind that I looked somewhat different.

Modesto brings the *urpu,* a large vase-shaped earthen jar filled with *chicha.* With respectful elegance, he tosses the *ñawin aqha,* the first cup, to the east in honor of the gods. As a foreign guest I am served next,

Photo 19. Musicians play behind a *mesarumi* by the house of the *carguyoq*. The two men to the left play the *pitu* (flute); the musicians to the right play the *tinya* (small drum) and the *hatun tinya* (large drum). The author stands between the flute players.

then the elders, and then the other people present. Everyone sprinkles some *chicha* onto the ground in honor of Pachamama and some for the Apus, Qhaqya, and many other spirits. We talk about the Fiesta de Santiago—how it has been celebrated in years gone by and how it will be organized tomorrow. It is a joyous occasion. Everyone is content in the warm sun, so close to the eternal snow.

As soon as the last rays of the sun have disappeared behind the mountain peaks, an icy wind sweeps through the meadows. We hurry into the house to escape the wind's biting force, which penetrates to the very bones.

The house of Modesto's family is as tiny as the other houses of the village. It has an earthen floor, but the walls and the large stove are made of stone. Its facade reaches from the floor to the ceiling. Trapezoidal niches, as seen in Inca structures, are built into the walls to hold kitchen tools and anything else of value. An elevated platform at the far end of the room serves as bed and bench and is used as a base to reach the upper level of the house, which is reserved for the storage of alpaca furs and other necessities. There are two small glass windows in the house, a true luxury. On the wall above a small table hangs a first-aid case. Modesto uses some modern medicine in conjunction with mostly traditional medicine to cure his patients. Nothing else fits into this cozy home of stone.

Another feature that makes this house unique are two water taps, one inside the house and one outside; they bring spring water comfortably close.[1] No other house in Chillihuani is equipped with this modern convenience. There is no need for further luxury. Modesto and his family have more animals than other villagers and they live in a stone house. Yet their lives differ little from those of the other families in the village.

The women of the house resume their places by the stove to continue cooking today's meal and to prepare the meals for the coming days. As *carguyoq,* the sponsor of this year's fiesta, Modesto and his family must bear the costs for the band and for feeding the musicians and horsemen. He is also responsible for recruiting the horsemen for the central event, a horse race held on the high, windswept natural racetrack of Oqheq'asa Pata (*oqhe* = gray; *q'asa* = gorge; *pata* = high place—the high, gray gorge).

The meal is ready. The ladies of the house dish out the portions, while Modesto has the task of serving all his guests. Whether old or young, he serves each person with a deference fitting a solemn ritual. Nobody helps him. He himself offers the plates with both hands to every visitor. The guests accept the plates with both hands, thanking the host family for its great generosity.

Modesto does not eat. Alert and attentive, he offers second and third helpings as soon as a guest has finished the food. I am surprised to see Modesto express such deference during the entire fiesta. As time went on, it became increasingly clear to me that this fiesta, like Pukllay in February, centers on expressing respect for others. The hosts give respect to their guests. They, in turn, express respect toward their hosts, and in the course of a meal respect is always paid to the great Pachamama, the Earth Mother, who provides the life-sustaining food and drink, and to other deities—mainly Illapa, for sending rain and restraining the much-feared hail, the destroyer of all crops.

Although I have always been impressed by the elegant and respectful demeanor of the people of Chillihuani, whether during a celebration or in everyday life, it now is clear to me that the strong show of respect Modesto displays during this occasion, so characteristic of the people of the high Andes, has been mistaken for an attitude of submission by people in the valley towns who are not familiar with the practices of these high-altitude people.

Following the meal, the musicians continue to play music. We sing, dance, and joke until late at night. One person after another falls asleep wrapped in an alpaca fur.

The Day of the Horse—an Offering to the Thunder God

Only in the mornings, when thick frost covers the landscape, do I get the impression that my friends, too, feel the extreme cold, which can fall to -15° C. The water is frozen in the pipe. One's breath leaves white shadows in the air. Yet, despite the biting cold, everyone smiles, ready to joke, anxious to begin the day's events. The ladies of the house pull their *llikllas* tighter around their shoulders and start a fire in the open stove. Modesto brings the bucket of frozen water that he filled the night before. A hot, steaming breakfast soup is soon ready, eaten, and the dishes are washed before the sun finally penetrates the air, putting a halt to our shivering.

As the first warming rays of the sun appear between two steep mountain peaks to the east, we leave the icy house. Outside Modesto takes off his hat, and with his arms stretched upward he addresses the rising sun with the words "*Ay Taytay Inti, ñoqa valikuyki sumaq p'unchayta kawsanaykupaq pacha paqarimanta chisiyanankama*" (Oh my Father Sun, I implore you to make this a good day from dawn to dusk for everyone). The others whisper their supplications. (People may stand up or fall to their knees with their arms raised when they greet the sun.)

Orations to the sun were widespread throughout Inca times. Cristóbal de Molina ([1575] 1916:51) recorded these in the sixteenth century:

Uiracochaya punchao cachunto tacachum nispac nispacarischum yllarichum nispac nic punchao churi yquicta casillacta quispillacta purichic runa rurascay quictacanchay vncan campac viracochaya. Casilla quispilla punchao ynga runay anami chisay quicta quilla ricanchari ama honco-chispa amanana chispa casicta quispicha huacoy chaspa.

(Oh Creator! You who gave life to the Sun and then to night and day, dawn and light; move in peace, give protection and light to the people You created. Oh Creator! Oh Sun! Let there be peace and light for the people so they will not fall ill! Keep them healthy and safe!)

With sighs of relief everyone receives the rising sun. Almost instantaneously its rays warm our limbs as we sit down on the stone benches by the *mesarumi,* which Modesto covers with blankets and ponchos. A serene silence surrounds us, interrupted only by the occasional jubilant sound of a bird circling the snow-covered mountains, those sacred Apus, protectors of humans and animals alike. So close to us, the power of the mountains is omnipresent.

Modesto takes a seat by the *mesarumi.* He places the plumage of the condor which the young herder brought him long ago on the sacred stone table. The spirit of the condor is his soul mate, his ally. It gives him advice as he unfolds his *unkuña* and starts to read the *coca* leaves. Solemnly Modesto speaks: "*Apu Mallku, willaykuway sut'inta kuka qhawasqaykita*" (Spirit of the Condor, tell me the truth, what do you read in the *coca* leaves?).

I wonder about the significance of the condor's spirit on this Fiesta de Santiago. In the high Andes condors are believed to be the birds of the Apus and/or their spirits. As such, condors are related to the god of thunder and lightning, who also resides in the highest peaks.[2] Modesto smiles. "It will be a good day," he says with satisfaction. Yet, in respect and appreciation of the gods and to assure that everything goes well throughout the day, they must receive an offering.

Gregoria brings the *mama q'epe,* the bundle of sacred items, from its hiding spot. Modesto prepares the offering, asking Illapa, Pachamama, and the Apus to make the race a successful one, free of accidents. He opens the *unkuña.* A fine-grained stone in the shape of a horse appears, a most precious *enqaychu.* As is true for *enqaychu* of alpacas, llamas, or sheep, horse *enqaychu* can, with luck, be sought and found high up in the mountains on the winter solstice of San Juan, on June 24, or on August 1, when the earth is especially receptive to offerings. People search for the *enqaychu* of a horse on the racetrack of Oqheq'asa Pata.[3] Sometimes a fine-grained stone must be modified to better suggest the shape of a horse. As is true for the *enqaychu* of llamas and alpacas, a modified effigy has less *enqa* than does an unmodified stone. The horse *enqaychu* is placed on the *mesarumi* facing east during the entire ceremony (see photo 20).

The empty *unkuña* is then spread onto the *lliklla.* Modesto places a white sheet of paper on top of the *unkuña* and puts a handful of *coca* leaves on the table. All adults blow *k'intus* toward the east, requesting the gods to help make the race a spectacular one without accidents. Petals of white carnations for the god of thunder and red carnations for Pachamama and the Apus are also placed on the paper beside the increasing number of *coca k'intus* that are piled layer upon layer on the offering. Not one spirit may be forgotten. I frequently hear the name of the thunder god as *k'intus* are offered to this powerful deity, so highly venerated during Inca times and still so significant in the minds of the people today.

From time to time *chicha* and wine are sprinkled into the air and onto the four corners of the offering, in honor of the deities and the *enqaychu* and to quench their thirst. A toast of respect is given to the

Photo 20. The *curandero* Modesto Quispe prepares an offering for the deities, asking for a good day and a safe race. His son and grandchildren look on.

people present. Slowly Modesto walks to the *muyukancha,* where he burns this offering in the small cave-like *q'oyana.* As the smoke rises into the air, we avert our eyes to avoid offending the spirits who receive it and who are asked, in return, to protect the horses, the racetrack, and the riders; to restore life force to the *enqaychu;* and to maintain harmony among people, their animals, and all of nature.

Modesto now makes a separate offering. "It is for the *sirena,*" he whispers. The *sirena* (siren) is described as a beautiful woman with the tail of a fish who lives in the Rio Chillihuani, where waterfalls cause considerable turbulence. The idea of the *sirena* may have been introduced with the conquest. In earlier years when I worked in the Vilcanota Valley, people frequently mentioned the *sirena,* who, they said, "lives right here in the Vilcanota River." Half good, half bad, the *sirena* helps people and is especially concerned with horses. Yet she also entices people to her watery domain, from which some never escape.

Offerings to the *sirena* are much the same as those to major deities. The *coca* leaves and other goods are, however, placed on a yellow sheet of paper instead of a white one. I am curious to find out why the *sirena* is asked to help in the horse race. "Her character is capricious and thus in some ways similar to that of the horse," is the answer.

Everyone helps to prepare for this busy day. Being *carguyoq,* Modesto and his family must provide food, drink, and entertainment. Despite the multitude of tasks at hand, there is no sensation of rush. Everything is under control. At midmorning, the sound of galloping hooves announces the arrival of horsemen as they appear from all directions, swinging their *warak'a* high into the air. There are greetings and many good wishes. There is joy and laughter. Modesto opens another *urpu.* Libations are made to the gods. The four corners of the *mesarumi,* the four directions, and the four winds are recognized as the precious liquid sprays through the air.

The musicians pick up their musical instruments and play "Kaballopaq Taki" (or "Kaballo Taki"), the "Song of the Horse." Gregoria sings:

Ch'urumarka llaqtaymanta haykumurani
kaballuchaypi sillarusqa,
punchuchaywan punchurusqa
26 huliuchapi,
Haqhay chinpa orqomantan
iskay sultira qhawamuwan,
imaynatataq chinparusaq,

bandurriaytachus qichuruwanqa,
icha punchuchaytachus qichuruwanqa.

(I have come from my village Ch'urumarka
On my saddle-backed horse,
with my poncho on my body,
On this 26th of July.
From the mountain across
Two unmarried women look at me,
How will I pass to the other side?
Perhaps they will take away my mandolin,
Or perhaps they will take away my poncho.)

Exchanging personal items means that two people have fallen in love and become seriously involved with each other. The Fiesta de Santiago is, like all other fiestas, a time when young people meet and hope to find a partner for life.

More and more riders arrive for the fiesta. A steaming hot soup is served to everyone, followed by a second dish with potatoes, *chuño, moraya,* and meat. Then the new *carguyoq,* the sponsor for next year's Fiesta de Santiago, is elected. If no one volunteers to take over the *cargo* duties for a fiesta, a *carguyoq* is elected during the general assembly of villagers.

Usually two families sponsor the Fiesta de Santiago. One of the *carguyoq* must take care of church-related matters. He must ask the priest to come and read the mass. This is always done in conjunction with the weddings a few days before Santiago. He must also ask each family to contribute with money, potatoes, *chuño,* or other goods to pay the priest, and he must clean the church. The second sponsor is responsible for inviting the horsemen and musicians and for providing food and *chicha* for them.

Here and in other villages where I have worked, people usually agree that the *cargo* system, which was introduced by the Spanish conquerors, imposes significant hardship on the *carguyoq* and his family, who must provide both the money and the time for the required tasks. Yet, one of the horsemen who sits in Modesto's compound eating his meal volunteers to be *carguyoq* for next year's Fiesta de Santiago. The second sponsor will have to be found.

After the meal the horsemen leave to visit those people who sponsored the Fiesta de Santiago in past years. As they return, they assemble around the *mesarumi.* Each rider blows *coca k'intus* to the east, asking the deities for help. Each receives a last cup of *chicha* to offer to the gods and to quench his thirst. People are expected to drink in honor of the gods and in respect for people, but the riders may not behave in a drunken fashion. Drunkenness is not acceptable and I once witnessed how one of the young horsemen, who had peered too deeply into his glass and offered too little to the deities, was eliminated from the race.

We leave for the heights of Oqheq'asa Pata. The riders, sixty-four in all, fling themselves onto their horses, while the spectators—women, children, and those men who do not take part in the race—hurry after them, going still higher to where a natural racetrack has formed between two steep mountain ranges. On the far horizon one can see some peaks of the mountain range locally called the Cadena del Ausangate, or the Ausangate range, which includes the most sacred of all mountains, the mighty, snow-covered Apu Ausangate.

On a promontory, high up on Oqheq'asa Pata where the racetrack begins, the riders assemble around a *mesarumi*. Offerings are brought to the gods and specifically to Oqheq'asa Pata, the actual racetrack, considered one of the daughters of Pachamama. She receives offerings in her own right and is asked for a safe race. Many *k'intus* are blown into the wind as one rider after the other, while he says his prayers, places his hat on the *mesarumi* as a symbolic offering for the gods. The thunder god's name is whispered and carried into the wind.

The melodies of the musicians mingle with the whistling sound of the wind that blows through this high-altitude corridor. Spectators come from all corners of the village and assemble on the rolling hills close to the track, from where they will have a good view of the sacred spectacle.

The first group of four riders stands in position. People hush and there is complete silence as one of the three *qhawaqkuna,* the persons who watch and judge the race, calls out that the race is to begin. "*Hoq, iskay, kinsa*" (One, two, three), the voice of the *qhawaq* echoes through the mountains. The racers, none of whom have saddles or stirrups, take off. Colorful ponchos flutter through the air as the riders race toward the spectacular mountain range in the distance where snowy peaks glow in the evening sun. Benikunka, one of the mountain peaks at the horizon, is of reddish color. "*Apu Benikunka ñoqanchis hina churakun puka punchayta*" (The mountain peak Benikunka wears a red poncho as we do), people tell me proudly.

The racetrack is about 2 kilometers long. At the end of the track the riders tackle a steep mountainside and turn around. Swinging their *warak'a* over their heads, they yell, "*Huifa, Huifa, Kawsachun Pacha-mama, Apu Ausangate, Llaqto, Chullu, Qayara Chimpu, Chillihuani* [the four sectors of Chillihuani], *kawsachun Santiago, Santa Barbara, kawsachun iskay chunka pisqayoq julio killa p'unchay!*" (Long live the 25th of July). (Instead of *kawsachun*, sometimes the Spanish word *viva* is used, which also means "long live.") (The horse race takes place on the 25th or 26th of July.)

The *qhawaqkuna* who act as judges have no watch to keep time. They judge the general performance of each rider by the speed, the distance between the first rider to arrive and those who follow, and whether any contestant fell off during the race. Over the years I have seen several riders fall during the eight races I have witnessed in Chillihuani. Like acrobats they turn in the air before hitting the ground and usually land on their feet. Within an instant each rider is back on his horse. I have never witnessed an injury, though the terrain in some parts of Chillihuani where races take place is treacherous, especially when night falls.

At the promontory the jubilant riders are received with much applause from the spectators and their fellow horsemen. The winner of each heat rides again with other heat winners until a final winner is found. One group of riders after the other offers *k'intus* and drinks to the deities, waits for the signal, and dashes off toward the radiant mountains on the horizon, which gradually disappear in darkness as the race continues. Finally the horses and their riders are just shadows in the night. They become real only through the thundering sounds of their hooves as they gallop through the rough terrain, and by the jubilant exclamations of the riders and the joyful applause of the spectators. These horsemen are true "sons of the thunder," as they were called in the past (see photo 21).

Every contestant hopes to win. Yet, it is more important to participate, to celebrate this day, to remember the gods, to be together in joy and harmony. The competition is not a fierce one. The riders would make better time if they would lean forward on their horses instead of swinging their *warak'a* high in the air, calling the names of important sites and spirits.

The race is over. It was breathtaking. But I did not hear the name of a winner announced. I ask, but receive only smiles. Finally Juan points silently to Modesto. I congratulate him for having won this thrilling race. He smiles and shyly averts his eyes. Only later do I fully compre-

Photo 21. The race is on along Oqheq'asa Pata.

hend that winning is not the prime reason for staging the race, and I realize that it was not proper behavior to ask for the winner or to congratulate him openly. In an egalitarian society where respect for others is a primary concern, it is not considered polite to make much fuss about one person, stressing his individual achievement to the detriment of others.[4]

The race was a success. Everyone gave his best and it was a show of extraordinary vigor, endurance, dedication, and prime riding ability. The gods were pleased. There were no accidents. It was a great competition in which the riders competed *with* and not against one another. Everyone who witnessed or participated in this energetic ritual was equally important.

The winner receives a small prize. In 1990, for example, the prize was one million *intis,* at that time the equivalent of U.S. $1. No more mention is made of the fact that he won. The riders tell me that formerly, in some high-altitude villages, the winner had to capture his prize by passing, on the last race, through a scaffold while grabbing a live rooster with the prize attached to its legs. "We never liked the custom and we always do it our way," the horsemen assert.

Modesto is the winner of this spectacular race. At fifty years of age, he is older than most of the riders. Since he is *carguyoq* this year, he has been extremely busy preparing for the event and serving so many people food and drink. He had to descend several times to the valley at a distance of 31 kilometers from his house, and there was little time for sleep. He also had to offer much *chicha* to his guests, drinking with them to their health and in honor of the gods. Nevertheless, throughout the event he was completely alert and he was the fastest rider. I ask him about his secret. He smiles. Somewhat hesitantly he tells me that he knows well how to bring offerings to the gods, who help make it a good race and grant him a small advantage.

As the sun disappeared behind the snow-covered mountain peaks, and while the race was still in progress, *chiri wayra,* the icy wind, started to blow as it does every night in the middle of an Andean winter. It is especially cold and enervating along this natural corridor. Yet the drastic change in temperature disturbs neither the riders nor the spectators. Even after the race, people remain by the track, conversing, laughing, and celebrating. The women, whose festive outfits and sandals give little protection against wind and cold, seem undisturbed. Finally everyone hurries downhill to their homes.

Another steaming meal is ready to thaw our frozen bones. Again the host serves everyone. The women who cook get most of the praise, along with Pachamama, and are highly esteemed for providing the food. Although men are seen publicly as *carguyoq,* and women work more in the background, everyone knows that the success of a fiesta depends heavily on the cooperation of the women and their organizational skills.

After the meal Modesto goes out into the night. It is a meeting between him and the deities in which he thanks them for the excellent race and the harmonious fiesta. But it is not yet time to sleep. The dogs bark ferociously as music penetrates the stillness of the night. Groups of young women and men go from house to house to greet the hosts, their elders, and to dance and sing. They come to give respect to the elders, to bring and to find love. The young dancers hold their host and hostess in a loose embrace while they recite their good wishes:

Mamay Gregoria, kunan p'unchay, kusikaymi ñoqanchispaq, Taytanchis Santiago, munayniywan qhawaykuytan munani q'aya wata kunan p'unchayta hina, waynallata, allinllata, kusisqata. Kachuntaq allin qolqeyki, anchapawantaq kachun qoriyki, qolqeyki. Llipin munasqayki atisqa kachun ancha allinpaq.

(Mama Gregoria, this day is full of happiness for us; with the love of our patron Santiago I want to see you in the coming year as you are today, always young, always healthy, always happy and with good money and much gold and silver and may all your wishes be fulfilled!)

The same wishes are repeated for Don Modesto.

The musicians play throughout the night while people dance with spirited elegance. Juan, Modesto's son, dances with his young wife. Each holds two corners of the sacred *unkuña*. With the *unkuña* between them, they symbolically hold on to the four corners of Tawantinsuyu, the Inca Empire. "This is an ancient dance, from our great-grandmothers and even before," they tell me proudly (see photo 22).

The "Song of the Horse" and other love songs echo through the night. Some of the songs are old, and others are invented on the spot and make their way into the oral history of the village. Women take the lead in singing and inventing new songs, some of them sad, but most happy. The tremendous vitality and stamina that were felt during the race continue into the early morning hours.

Photo 22. The *curandero*'s son and his young wife dance in remembrance of Tawantinsuyu, as they hold on to the four corners of their *unkuña*.

The doors of the church have remained closed. The Santiago of the conquerors, as depicted by the Inca chronicler Guaman Poma de Ayala and carried through the streets of Cuzco during Corpus Christi, has no place on this day—or any other day when the people of Chillihuani celebrate their physical and spiritual freedom. As native sons of this, their mountain world, they do not view themselves as inferior beings, crouching beneath the patron saint Santiago, to be trod upon. Rather, they themselves ride their horses through their remote mountains, the realm of their ancestors. Theirs is a fair competition, a show of strength, endurance, and horsemanship. They are not out to conquer or dominate. Instead they give their best in respect for life in all its forms and in the hope that the great Illapa will respect their offering of a thundering race on the top of the world.

Qespisqa P'unchay— Independence Day in Tawantinsuyu

July is a great month for fiestas in Chillihuani. We have seen vibrant wedding celebrations, followed by the thundering race of Santiago which, in turn, gives way to the serene rituals of July 28, when Tawantinsuyu comes back to life again.

It is July 27, the eve of Peru's Independence Day. The sun has disappeared behind the rocky peaks to the west. Village children hurry to the plaza to deposit the roots of the *qayara* plant they have been collecting all day from different homes where they had been dried and stored. *Qayara* will provide the fuel for an enormous bonfire in the upper plaza where the people from the four corners of Chillihuani will congregate tonight.

While Luisa waits for her daughters to return home and to change into their best clothes for the children's parade around the lower and upper plazas, I leave with Juan to keep an invitation from the village council. As we approach the plaza, we see council members in their most beautiful ponchos and *ch'ullus* striding proudly toward the communal building.

The vice president (*vice presidente*), secretary (*secretario*), treasurer (*tesorero*), district attorney (*fiscal*), two members at large (*vocales*), and four young men who are called *cobradores* and *juntadores* in Spanish (or collectively called *chaskiqkuna* in Quechua), walk toward the office at the very left of the building, where they assemble in the president's hall. All of the above offices except for the *chaskiqkuna* have Spanish titles. The equivalents in Quechua for the Spanish expressions are rarely used.

The village president has the ultimate authority within the community. The vice president takes over when the president is absent. The secretary and the treasurer keep the books. The district attorney (*fiscal*) makes sure that there are no quarrels and that justice is done in the village council. Two members at large (*vocales*) inform villagers about important issues and replace committee members who are absent. The *cobradores* or *chaskiqkuna* are four young men who are elected for one year to perform rituals of respect in the public arena, where they simultaneously learn the tasks of the village authorities. They serve their elders food and drink and assist them in many other ways. They also collect dues and clean the offices.

The deputy governor (*teniente gobernador*), with his eight deputies (*agentes policiales,* sometimes referred to as *kamachiqkuna,* who also belong to the overall category of *chaskiqkuna*), and four musicians meet in the office next to the room where the village stores furniture and other goods throughout the year. The deputy governor represents the central government in Chillihuani and collaborates with the district governor of Cusipata. He resolves disputes within the community, calls people to *faenas,* and levies fines on those who do not participate in communal labors. During the festivities of Independence Day he is responsible for the organization of all political activities, which he carries out in coordination with all other village authorities.

The eight deputies (*agentes policiales*) are young men around eighteen years of age, sometimes older, who are, for one year, largely responsible for maintaining law and order in the community.

The municipal representative (*agente municipal*) who represents the mayor of the district of Cusipata meets with his treasurer (*síndico de rentas),* who is in charge of financial matters, and eight *arariwas* in the office beside the community hall. The municipal representative must take charge when, for example, one family's animals do damage to another family's property and the parties cannot resolve the conflict themselves. *Arariwas* are young men—two from each *suyu*—who are elected by the community for one year and are held responsible for the crops within village boundaries. They must assure that theft does not occur and must also bring offerings to the weather gods to assure plentiful harvests. At night they guard the fields against thieves and during the day they make sure that animals do not enter them. At night they often burn offerings for Pachamama, asking for plentiful harvests in the fields they guard. The Apus also receive burnt offerings with the request that the thunder god will not destroy the fields, but instead will bring the necessary rains. On Compadres Day the municipal representative walks with his *arariwas* through the potato fields of the village. They call the spirits of the potatoes and ask Pachamama and the Apus for a good harvest.

The village justice of the peace (*juez de paz*), who is elected for one year, enters his office with one of the eight young deputies (*agentes policiales*), who take turns assisting the justice of the peace and learning his tasks. The village justice of the peace presides over conflicts, robberies, and marital problems such as separation. In cases involving more serious legal trespass, a provincial judge must be procured. To elect the justice of the peace, villagers propose the names of two candidates to the community president, who sends the nomination to the provincial judge, who, in turn, determines which of the two people will serve as justice of the peace. Should the justice of the peace die, become incapacitated, or be away from the village, the second person will take over during his absence. Disputes over land, however, are handled by the community president. Occasionally the tasks of the justice of the peace can overlap with those of the deputy governor.

The next room is empty. It is the village jail, where the ill behaved are held. I have never seen it occupied.

The fifth political association in the village is made up of the parent representatives (*padres de familia*), a group of eight people (president, vice president, treasurer, secretary, and four members at large) with four assistants (*tenientes escolares*) who take care of the schoolhouse, learn the tasks of their elders, and respectfully serve them food and drink during festivities. They join in the lower plaza and then walk to their office, which is located in the old school building in the upper plaza.

All village authorities, except where stated otherwise, are elected in December for a period of two years and take over their duties in January.

The village fiesta organization in Chillihuani is in some ways based on the *cargo* system and is found in most Andean communities. But the Chillihuani herders are most concerned with ancient Andean ways that are still at the root of all activities. Young people give respect to their elders by serving them food and drink and, in return, learn from their elders by observing them perform specific tasks. At the age of approximately eighteen years, a young man starts an honorary and unpaid career leading toward village president. This begins with an apprenticeship that is performed in three stages. First he becomes a member of the group of eight *arariwas* who are elected between August and November during a community *faena* for a term of one year. After this rather demanding time, during which he and his age-mates must guard the crops in this widely dispersed village, the young man may be elected at the end of December to become a *cobrador,* a *cargo* he will also hold for one year. The following year or several years later at the end of December, the third stage of his apprenticeship starts as he is elected to become a deputy (*agente policial*) for one year. All elections take place in village meetings, where one adult of each household *must* be present.

The leader of each group of young men is called a *juntador.* He is the first to offer drinks to the authorities. His tasks also include cleaning the presidential office and unlocking the office door for every meeting. Each month a different *chaskiq* performs the task of *juntador* within the group to which he belongs.

After a young man has successfully carried out three years of apprenticeship, he can be elected secretary, treasurer, district attorney, or member at large. Later he can assume the post of deputy governor, municipal representative, and so on up the ladder toward village president.

Women also participate in this highly structured system by giving advice to their husbands and sons in all matters, by providing food and drink for the festivities, and by organizing other aspects of village fiestas. They also work through the Women's Committee, which is organized in a similar fashion, including a president, vice president, secretary, treasurer, and members at large. Their role is seen as parallel and complementary to that of men.

I enter the president's hall with the *curandero* and the vice president. The *chaskiqkuna,* consisting of one *juntador* and three *cobradores,* are already in the room preparing for the activities they are to perform tonight. They have brought drinking glasses, matches, pencils, paper, and some *trago* and arrange all items on the table. They will offer drinks to the authorities and address them with much respect.[1]

One village authority after another enters the president's room, greeting everyone in a loose embrace and wishing each one a happy life, health, youth, and prosperity. One hears people whisper, "*Q'aya wata kunan hina qhalillata qhawaykuyta munayman, waynallata allin qaqniyoqta, qoriyoq, qolqeyoqta*" (In the coming year I would like to see you just as you are today, healthy, young, well to do, with gold and silver). Some authorities deposit a bottle with *trago* or *coca* leaves on the table. Others leave some money to defray the evening's expenses.

We take a seat around a large rectangular table lighted by several candles. But the seat at the center of the table facing the *chaskiqkuna* remains empty. The village president, Salvador Illatinco Chino, will not be present at this meeting, during which decisions are usually made every year concerning the organization of the Independence Day celebrations and other urgent issues of the past and coming years. This is the eighth and final day of *casarakuy,* and Salvador is still walking with Justa as a unit—*warmi-qhari*—while coordinating their domestic activities close to each other and to their home near the dangerous *susuwa.* Regardless of what is demanded of a community president in his political career, his marriage is a commitment—not only to his wife, his family, his *padrinos,* his *madrinas,* and to society at large—but also to the spiritual forces, which must be properly acknowledged and respected.

In respect for the village president, no decisions are made on this night.[2] Everyone remains silent, hoping that the eighth and final day of the couple's transition to married life will pass without incident. No one speaks. Still, the rituals of respect, which are of the utmost significance to this meeting, take place in the same way as they do in any other year.

Juan Mamani places a handful of *coca* leaves on the table. Everyone fashions three perfect leaves into *k'intus,* blows on them while facing east, and asks Pachamama and the Apus for protection and to watch over this meeting so that harmony may prevail this evening, the next day, and always.

With an elegant gesture of deep respect, each member in the round offers his *k'intu* to one of the other council members, whispering, "*Hallpaykusunchis*" (Let us chew). *Coca k'intus* are offered, starting with the highest authority. The secretary, for example, offers a *k'intu* first to the president. In the absence of the president, as is the case tonight, the vice president receives the *k'intu* first, then the district attorney, the treasurer, and the members at large. Following this ritual, council members exchange *k'intus* without adhering to any precise order.

The young *chaskiq* Mariano opens a bottle of *trago.* He tosses the *ñawin aqha* toward the wall that faces east in honor of the deities. The person who serves is always the one to toss the *ñawin aqha* east. "*Sumaqllata ukyaykusun*" (Let us drink peacefully), everyone murmurs. Mariano serves drinks to the authorities. In the absence of the president, the vice president is the first to receive a glass of *trago.* He offers it to each person around the table in hierarchical order. Each accepts the glass, pretends to drink, and returns it. After everyone has received this gesture of respect, the vice president places some drops on the four corners of the table. (Sometimes it is sprinkled on the ground by the four legs of the table.) "This rite consecrates the sacred space occupied by the *mesa*, thus confirming its supernatural power" (see Sharon 1978: 41–42).

Using his thumb and index finger, the vice president sprinkles some alcohol toward the Apus. He asks all deities for their help, hoping that this evening and Independence Day will be harmonious. He then makes a movement with the right hand in the form of a cross on the rim of the glass to avoid any disharmony during this evening. He salutes the people sitting to the left and right, ingests the drink, and returns the glass to the *chaskiq* Mariano.

Mariano offers the next glass of *trago* to the other people around the table in hierarchical order. All engage in the same rituals of respect, offering first to the deities and then to everyone present, pretending to drink and returning the glass. Then Mariano is offered a drink by the vice president, who donated the bottle. Mariano takes off his *ch'ullu* and then continues with the same rituals of respect, asking permission of each authority before he empties the glass with one swallow.

The vice president receives a second glass of *trago* from Mariano. Holding it in his left hand, he traces four corners with the fingertips of his right hand above the glass as he softly disperses some of the liquid. Then with his right index finger and thumb forming a circle, and with his three remaining fingers stretched out horizontally, he traces three horizontal crosses in fast succession above the glass. These gestures occur in rapid sequence, with elegance and exquisite dexterity. Acknowledging his neighbors to the right and left, the vice president ingests the drink.

After each authority has had a second drink, Mariano takes off his *ch'ullu* again. He holds the bottle in his left hand and the empty glass in his right hand, crosses his arms, and gives glass and bottle to the vice president, who receives them halfway across the table. The vice president fills the glass and hands it back across the table to Mariano. Mariano sprinkles some *trago* on the four corners of the table, acknowledges all people present, ingests the drink, and returns the empty glass to the vice president. With his hands crossed, the vice president returns the glass (in his right hand) and the bottle (in his left hand, with his right arm over his left arm) to Mariano, who receives them halfway across the table. Concentration and pride are expressed on the young man's face.

When the bottle is almost empty, Mariano takes off his *ch'ullu* and with solemn concentration fills the glass. It is important that the glass be filled and that nothing remain in the bottle. He demarcates the four corners of the table with *trago,* salutes all people present, and swallows the drink. Then he wipes the bottle and, holding it with both hands, returns it to the vice president, who receives it with his right hand, demarcates a cross in the air, acknowledges the people present, and sets the bottle down in front of him.

The ritual passing of drinks that have been blessed by the deities symbolizes giving respect to the people present and asking their permission to drink, inviting everyone to participate peacefully, to cooperate, and find solutions together for the upcoming events.

Intrigued by these elegant and exquisite symbolic gestures, I later ask my companions for the meaning of these rituals, some of which are similar to those during *casarakuy* and other festivities. "They are done out of respect for the deities and all those present," is the answer I receive. "When we return glass and bottle, one participant must cross his hands, so that right hands meet across the table as do left hands. This must be done or else there would be no respect," the vice president asserts.

I am equally fascinated by the frequent use of the number four and the demarcation of horizontal crosses. The four corners of the table receive libations; the four directions are indicated as drops of *trago* spray into the air from between thumb and index finger. With thumb and index finger forming a circle and three fingers stretched out over the rim of the glass, four points are outlined and three crosses are drawn. The crossed hands add to this persistent pattern. These symbols continue to mark significant events throughout the next day.

The *chaskiq* Luis now takes his turn to serve *trago* from the second bottle. Like Mariano, he starts with the vice president, who receives the drink, toasts the people present, drinks, and returns the empty glass to Mariano. After the first bottle, *trago* is no longer tossed east or sprinkled onto the four corners of the table. Still, the rituals of respect continue as the bottle and glass pass from authorities to *chaskiq* and vice versa, with their hands crossed as they give and receive the bottle halfway across the table.

In the adjacent rooms, the authorities whom we followed earlier to their offices perform the same symbolic gestures as the people in the presidential hall. Only the number of people belonging to each group differs, as do their respective tasks. The rituals of respect are the same.

While the rituals continue, young men enter the president's room. They take off their *ch'ullus* and fall to their knees by the wall. With burning candles in their hands they whisper prayers beneath a picture of San Martín. In subdued voices they exclaim, "Long live San Martín, long live Chillihuani, long live the independence of Tawantinsuyu, and the 28th of July." As one group of young people leaves, another group enters.

José de San Martín, from Argentina, is the only one of the three freedom fighters who fought for Peru's independence in the 1820s to be honored during Independence Day in Chillihuani. Only San Martín gave any true recognition to the Indians. He acknowledged Quechua as an official language and confirmed the legal standing of the *ayllus*. Neither Simón de Bolívar nor Antonio José de Sucre is recognized in the prayers of the Chillihuani herders.

The sound of music penetrates the night. A band of four men enters the room. Two play the flute and two play the drum. The village authorities offer drinks and *coca* leaves to the musicians. The band then moves to the next room in the adobe building.

While the village authorities carry out rituals in the center of the village, their wives cooperate in their houses. They prepare meals for the coming event and organize the distribution of food and *chicha.* They are directly responsible for all sacred matters involving food and drink in both private and public spheres of life. The decisions the council members make during this meeting also include the ideas and suggestions of their wives and other family members. There has been considerable misunderstanding about gender roles in the Andes. Outsiders have frequently judged by the way in which major political decisions are voiced and have ascribed decision-making power to those who speak up in public, usually men. In Quechua society, however, women are strong decision makers, and men always consult with their wives and families before they voice their opinions on important issues in public. This becomes clear as one lives with the people of Chillihuani. (See Bourque and Warren 1979 for gender issues in other parts of the Andes.)

Back in the presidential room, Luis fills the last glass, making sure that nothing remains in the bottle. With his hands crossed, he returns the bottle to the treasurer who has donated it and who accepts it halfway across the table. Everyone thanks him for his generosity.

We leave the president's room to go out into the night. The candles in the lanterns of the school children who have assembled with their teachers in the lower plaza shine eerily through the pitch dark night. Each child carries the lantern she or he has made out of paper. To the music of the band, the children circle the lower plaza three times in counterclockwise direction and then walk to the upper plaza accompanied by all the villagers.

From far away we see flames flickering high into the night sky as they radiate from the center of the upper plaza. Everyone crowds around the bonfire, which provides heat on this cold winter night.

Village authorities and a teacher give short speeches inviting everyone to celebrate this important event. The paper lanterns are admired; the children respond with a mixture of pride and embarrassment. The teachers announce that I have been selected as the *madrina* (godmother) of the artistic competition. In this capacity I am given the difficult task of deciding which lanterns merit first, second, and third places from many beautiful models: animals, houses, airplanes, cars, and so on. The faces of the children reflect hope that their artistic talents and efforts will be recognized. Some children are close to tears; their crafts are devoured by flames as their candles touch the thin paper shells that swing in the wind. The talent expressed in all the lanterns makes it impossible to judge their merit in hierarchical order, and I decide to make a donation to the school to buy needed equipment for *all* the children. My decision is much appreciated by the villagers, but greatly disappoints most of the teachers who come from far in the valley. Two cultures clash in the heights of Chillihuani: a sense of competition and a traditional view of respect for everyone.

Celebrating Ancient Ways on July 28

The wives of the village authorities, of the parent representatives, and of the *chaskiqkuna* pass the morning of July 28 preparing food and drink. The teachers practice the dances and songs they are to perform with the children, and the village authorities meet in the community halls to further discuss the festivities of the day. In the distance we see village president Salvador Illatinco Chino, clad in his red poncho, hurrying toward the village center. With a radiant smile he greets everyone, ready to continue his duties as president after an absence of eight days. The authorities meet in the presidential room to discuss last-minute preparations.

The landscape looks bright and alive as villagers in their festive clothing appear from behind the hills and ravines of the four *suyus* to congregate in the lower plaza. With elegant gestures they greet one another. Together they move to the upper plaza, where the afternoon festivities take place.

Hundreds of people squeeze into the compound of the upper plaza, which is enclosed by an adobe wall and where the ashes from last night's bonfire mark the ground. The school principal sings the Peruvian national hymn; the villagers hum along. Then several speeches are made in succession. The principal explains Peru's major historic events. The community president, the deputy governor, the justice of the peace, the municipal representative, and the parent representative stress the importance of this special day, when *comuneros* meet with a strong sense of cooperation and solidarity. The school children from grade one to grade six get their turn to sing songs, deliver poems, and perform dances to much applause.

Then the teachers retire to their quarters as the people of Chillihuani organize themselves in the fashion in which they have celebrated Independence Day as far back as they can remember. Four groups of people form roughly parallel lines, one in each of the four corners of the compound.

Village authorities take seats on a bench behind a long table on the eastern side of the compound. Three past authorities are seated on the far right of the table, followed by the municipal representative, the deputy governor, the justice of the peace, the president, the vice president, the secretary, the treasurer, the district attorney, two members at large, and three other authorities who held office in previous years. On the opposite side of the table, young deputies (*agentes policiales*) are lined up facing their elders (see photo 23). They start by collecting the hats of the authorities. These are stored in a clean spot for the duration of the rituals.

On the western side, across the courtyard from the village authorities, their wives sit in a straight line on the ground facing east. The building behind them provides shade during the hot afternoon. They keep their *monteras* on their heads as they are attended to and given respect by the wives of the eight deputies (*agentes policiales*), who have taken off their *monteras* and form a line opposite their elders.

In the northern corner of the compound the male representatives of the parent association sit on a stone bench. They are attended by the

Photo 23. Male elders and young *chaskiqkuna* engage in rituals of respect during Independence Day festivities. An elder makes an offering to Pachamama before he drinks himself.

four male assistants (*tenientes escolares*), who line up facing their elders.

To the south, across the courtyard from the male parent representatives, their wives sit in a straight line. They are served by the wives of the assistants (*tenientes escolares*), who line up facing their elders. Here, too, the elder women sit in the shade with their *monteras* on their heads while the younger women take their hats off and stand in the blazing sun. The young women who serve their elders are referred to as *agenteq warminkuna* (wives of the deputies). Young male *chaskiqkuna* who are still single ask a female friend to take over the role of a wife serving the elder women (see photo 24).

On the far ends of the line formed by the wives of this year's village council sit the wives of past village authorities. One of them, Ignacia Choqque Quispe, has helped the community in many ways. Charming and outgoing, intelligent and extremely well organized, she not only raises four children and harvests excellent crops, but she also helps those who are most in need. She and her family own cows, a rarity in

Chillihuani, and she generously gives milk and a variety of food items to others. She has been elected president of the newly formed Mothers' Club, subsequently renamed as the Women's Committee. Like most other women in Chillihuani, Ignacia is illiterate and a monolingual Quechua speaker. This, however, does not keep her from doing everything in her power to improve the situation of the villagers. She wants to see a small-scale weaving industry develop in her village, and to achieve this goal, she has good ideas and a well-founded plan of activities that the women can engage in. When I agreed to cooperate with the Women's Committee several months ago, she looked at me with a radiant smile, and I could see many more plans springing into her mind. Ignacia is one of those Quechua women who has great capacities and who can put them to work. Throughout this day she participates in the rituals of respect with other female elders vis-à-vis the younger women.

Thus, within the festive compound, two groups of female elders and two groups of male elders sit comfortably on the sides of the compound, the male elders on benches in the sun, the female elders on the earth in the shade. Each line of elders faces young women or men, re-

Photo 24. Female elders and the wives or friends of the *chaskiqkuna* engage in rituals of respect parallel to those of the men.

spectively, who will stand for about six hours in the blazing hot sun serving their elders, showing respect and discipline, and proving their strength and endurance. Approximately every two hours, each group of elders and their younger attendants leave to obey nature's call. Leaving the group alone would be considered disrespectful, and the person would be expected to pay a fine.

The rest of the compound is filled with villagers. Previous authorities form a line sitting on a stone bench in the northeast. Young men who belong to the village soccer team sit together on a low stone wall on the southeastern side of the compound. Women with children occupy the southern to central part of the compound. The women prefer to sit on blankets on the ground, in close contact with Pachamama.

Two bands, each consisting of four musicians, assemble at the opposite ends of the courtyard, ready to play their instruments—two flutes (the *pitu* has six holes, while the *pinkuyllu,* which is used during Pukllay, has only four holes), one drum, and one bass drum in each band.

After a time of joyful greetings, shuffling, and last-minute preparations, there is complete silence in the upper plaza. Then the musicians play the festive tunes.

The first glass of *trago* is tossed east from each of the four corners of the compound, where the parallel lines of elders and younger people are located. As the sparkling offerings disperse against the dark blue sky and fall on the dry dusty courtyard, the divinities quench their thirst. The young people, starting with the person to the very right of the line, go on to offer *trago* in small glasses to their male and female elders, respectively. The elders often address the young people as *wawakuna,* young children, emphasizing the fact that they are just now beginning to learn the rituals of respect from their elders in the public arena. As was the case on the preceding night, amidst gestures of great elegance, the first glass offered to each elder makes its round within each group. The person who receives it offers it to his or her neighbor, who pretends to take a sip and returns the cup to its owner.

With the fingers of the right hand, the elders outline the four corners above the glass. With three fingers extended horizontally and making a circle with the index finger and the thumb, they trace three crosses over their glasses. Drops of *trago* are sprinkled on the four corners of the table. When offering to the deities, the elders take off their *ch'ullus.* These rituals of respect are identical in all four groups of people in the four corners of the compound. They last for several hours.

The sounds of people shuffling pots and plates comes from outside the adobe walls. Young men carry the *merienda,* the festive meal prepared by the women, into the courtyard. There it is first served to the elders by the young men and women who face their elders in the four corners of the compound. The meal consists of boiled potatoes, *chuño,* boiled grains of maize (*mote*), tortillas, rice, green beans, llama and alpaca *ch'arki,* carrots bartered from the lower villages, and *qochayuyu* (dark green algae from the high mountain lakes). *Qochayuyu,* also called *llulluch'a,* is a highly esteemed food item that is usually reserved for fiestas. Gade (1975:110) stated:

> *Nostoc* sp., *llullucha* or *kochayuyo* is a gelatinous, dark green alga that grows wild in lakes and ponds and is harvested during the dry season. Cobo ([1653] 1956, 1:179) mentioned it as a food in the early colonial period, and its use undoubtedly goes back to the Incas (Guaman Poma de Ayala 1966, 3:131). Today it remains an Indian item of consumption and is seen on sale in markets after it has been dried and pressed into rectangular blocks. *Llullucha* is usually eaten with capsicum pepper in a stew or soup during the food shortage season, and it provides much-needed vitamins to Indians living at high elevations. Possibly its main value is tied to the fact that it contains iodine, and therefore helps prevent goiter, a common deficiency disease in the valley.

Randall (1987:82) wrote that *llulluch'a* is dried and stored for times of hunger. Before *llulluch'a* is eaten, the dried plant is immersed in water, where it "comes back to life." In Inca times, women who were to be sacrificed to the gods were referred to as *llulluch'a* (sometimes *murqutu* and *siqlla*) since it was believed that they, too, would come back to life, communicate with the gods, and be transformed into oracles (see Hernández Príncipe [1622] 1923:61–62).

The people of Chillihuani use various terms for edible algae. *Mayuqochayuyu* (also referred to as *qochayuyu* or *qochayu*) is an algae that is found in rivers and lakes (*mayu* = river, *qocha* = lake), while *murmuntu* (small dark algae balls) is found in lakes and springs. *Layta* is another kind of algae, also dark colored, but flat and larger than *llulluch'a,* which likewise grows in lakes, swamps, and marshes. During the rainy season, both *llulluch'a* and *layta* can be found growing where spring waters flow.

The young people offer plates with food to their elders in a sequence that is determined by the elders' ages and their merits as *comuneros.* The *chaskiq* who stands at the rightmost side of the line starts serving.

Each elder offers his or her plate to the other elders, who pretend to take a small piece, or sometimes actually take one, and return the plate to the original owner, who with his right hand draws an imaginary cross over the plate. The people in each group start to eat only after each person has received a plate of food and has offered it to everyone in his or her group.

Subsequently the young people receive a meal from their elders. They engage in the same rituals, offering their plate to the people present at the table, asking their permission to eat as a gesture of respect.

Hundreds of people receive the delicious meal that is thus distributed, sponsored by the village authorities and other villagers whose crops have yielded some surplus. *Urpus* with *chicha* are opened and the *ñawin aqha* sprays through the compound, quenching the thirst of Pachamama and the Apus. Then the elders, the *chaskiqkuna,* and all villagers present are served *chicha.* The young people offer *chicha* to their elders, saying: *"Kuraqniy ukyay kay aqhata"* (My elder, please drink this *chicha*). The elders reply: *"Sulpay ukyasunchis"* (Thank you, let us drink).

After the meal is eaten, men assemble by the wall on the northern side of the plaza. On their knees they thank Pachamama for providing food and drink and well-being. Women do not publicly give thanks to the Earth Mother in the same way as the men. Women are considered as having a most intimate bond with Pachamama, with whom they cooperate and reciprocate directly. As the empty plates are collected by the young men, the musicians resume playing *waynus* (folkloric Inca music of dance and love songs) on their instruments.

The rituals of respect continue throughout the afternoon. The young people show no signs of fatigue. They perform the rites with great care, enduring stoically the intense rays of the sun burning down mercilessly from the cloudless sky. During Independence Day in 1994, unexpectedly and most unusual for the dry season, rain and hail poured onto the plaza in the late afternoon. Despite the discomfort this rapid change in weather caused, the people continued with their clothes drenched, with water dripping from their hair, until all rituals were carried out as usual with their customary elegance.

A sense of thoroughness and perfection, so characteristic of the people of Chillihuani, permeates the activities on this special day. On July 27 and 28, as during other festivities, the young people of Chillihuani learn not only to respect the deities, their elders, and one another through rituals in the public arena, but they also get an opportunity to demonstrate discipline and endurance, characteristics that are highly esteemed in this herding community. Simultaneously they acquaint themselves with the tasks of the various authorities, which, in due time, they will have to perform themselves.

At a young age men and women begin to work for the benefit of their society. When men reach the age of about eighteen years, they become responsible for maintaining order in the village. Like Inca *chaskis*, these young people run throughout the widely dispersed village to bring messages to every household whenever an emergency meeting is to be held in the plaza, somebody falls sick, or a theft has been reported. After a year, other young men volunteer or are elected to become the *chaskiqkuna* of the village. Apart from protecting the villagers, these young people also protect animals and crops. In the case of theft, they must find the thief. These tasks are challenging and demanding, and the young men are always praised for work well done. Needless to say, there have been few, if any, juvenile delinquents in Chillihuani.

As the evening approaches, the *chaskiqkuna* return the hats collected at the beginning of the afternoon to the authorities. The remaining food is distributed among the people present, mainly to those who are most needy.

During this festivity as well, considerable quantities of *chicha* and some *trago* are consumed by both elders and young men and women. Yet, although some people are tipsy, none of the authorities or *chaskiqkuna* behaves in a drunken manner or staggers while performing the rituals of respect. This is surprising since alcoholic beverages are virtually restricted to festivities and are seldom consumed during other times of the year.

As the sun sets behind the mountain peaks in the west, the people put the tables and benches into the adjacent adobe houses and start on their way home. For most of them, this means a long walk in the dark across difficult terrain. Groups of young people remain in the center of the village, from where they go in all directions throughout the night visiting families, playing, singing, and dancing for them in their small adobe huts and wishing them youth, health, happiness, and prosperity in the coming year.

For the people of Chillihuani, the "Day of Independence" is primarily a "Day of Respect." Respect for oneself, for others, and for the community is the paramount value that must be constantly reinforced in everyone's mind in both the private and the public arenas, and it must be practiced continually in order to be transmitted from one generation to the next.

A Timeless Balance—Gender Complementarity Now and in the Past

Rituals of respect are not the only aspects of pre-Columbian ideology revealed during this festivity. Since the first time I celebrated Independence Day with the people of Chillihuani, I have been amazed at the way in which men and women engage in parallel rituals. This agrees with Inca mythology, which states that authority should follow gender lines. The Incas explained the functioning of both the universe and society in terms of parallel hierarchies of gender (Silverblatt 1987:7). During Inca times there existed a strict hierarchy, with the sun at the apex of the male line and the moon at the apex of the female line. The Inca was considered the son of the sun; the Qoya (Inca queen) was the daughter of the moon, and as such presided over female priestesses and their worship of female deities. (Silverblatt 1987:7 refers to the tradition of parallel descent as pan-Andean.)

Early chroniclers (Cobo [1653] 1964, 2:141; Guaman Poma de Ayala [1615] 1956, 1:94; Murúa [1590] 1946:81, 85, 93, 181) observed that just as the Inca (the emperor) had authority over young men, so the Qoya (the empress) and women of the Inca aristocracy were surrounded by and had authority over young women of the Cuzco nobility and daughters of local leaders. "These young women were learning appropriate skills and tasks of government, following the same training process as their male counterparts" (Silverblatt 1987:63). It is a known fact that female hierarchies carried the same esteem and privileges as their male counterparts. Overall, women had great economic and political power (Horkheimer 1960:25).

Although male and female hierarchies were separate entities, this did not preclude their close cooperation and the exchange of tasks between males and females when the need arose. Martín de Murúa ([1590] 1946:97) noted that there was complete equality between king and queen among the Incas. He stated that the Qoya Anahuarque governed for a long time from Cuzco while her husband, the Inca Yupanqui, was absent. Not only did women participate in ruling Tawantinsuyu, but they also took part in conquering pre-Inca societies. John Murra (1986: 53), in his ethnohistorical research, found that "Andean armies included both women and men."

Parallel spheres of activities as they existed among the Inca nobility were also a strong principle underlying the social organization of the common people in pre-Columbian times. Zuidema (1977:254; see also Lounsbury 1964), in his ethnohistorical research on Andean societies, found that "here as elsewhere in South America, we see that men and women of a group were conceived as two different societies, each concerned with its own organization and its transmission through time." Zuidema further discovered that certain religious rights and duties were inherited from man to man and from woman to woman (see also Daisy Núñez del Prado Bejar 1975).

Women largely disappeared from the public scene after the Spanish conquest. In the seventeenth century the Inca chronicler Guaman Poma de Ayala ([1615] 1956 2:92) wrote that the *corregidores,* priests, and *encomenderos* ". . . take from women and their daughters, who should legitimately govern, the rights they have had since the time of the Incas, dispossessing them of their titles in order to favor rich Indian men. . . ."

Yet aspects of pre-Columbian ideology have endured and are found in present-day Quechua society. Catherine Allen (1988:73), in her study of the high-altitude community of Sonqo in the province of Urubamba, referred to the separateness of female and male spheres of activity and their potential for cooperation and integration. She found that the people of Sonqo "think about the world in a highly sexualized way— sexualized, not in an erotic sense, but in the sense that at any given moment, the object or activity at hand assumes a value associated with the sexes and with their interrelationship." Thus, the Andean people perceive some activities as "male" and others as "female." This, however, does not mean that only males or females can engage in the work symbolically assigned to their gender. In this context, Allen (1988:78) observed that "all handicrafts are *warmi ruway,* women's tasks, even those performed mainly by men" (see photo 25). Men's tasks are *qhari ruway,* but may be performed by women.

The people of Chillihuani remain faithful to the rules that governed their ancestors in a variety of ways. On July 28 the display of parallel male and female hierarchies becomes most obvious in a ritualized way. Yet, the complementary opposition of gender lines and their potential of integration and cooperation manifests itself at other occasions as well. During public meetings women always congregate in groups, sitting on the earth in close contact with Pachamama, with whom they in-

Photo 25. A young man performs *warmi ruway* (a woman's task).
Not only is he perfect at it, but he has also developed his own way
of holding the spindle.

timately identify, while men sit in a different area on chairs, benches, or
anything that is elevated. Thus, women occupy the horizontal plane
while men occupy the vertical plane.

Men speak up in public. Women seldom do. Yet, male and female
views are generally always integrated. Women who sit on the ground
with their children and apart from the men know that their opinions on
the issues to be discussed or voted on are well represented by the men
(Bolin 1990a:12). Similarly, everyone knows that women have powerful,

and often sole, decision-making power regarding household economics. Yet, their husbands are normally considered heads of households.

Regarding the separation of the public spheres of activities of men and women, it is interesting to note that not one of the women in Chillihuani wants to be part of the village council, which consists only of men. Women are eager, however, to participate in the work of the Women's Committee and to exert direct power through it. The young, unmarried women of Chillihuani as well as the married women without children wanted to be part of the club, and for the sake of correctness they insisted on renaming their club the Women's Committee, instead of "Mothers' Club," as such organizations are called elsewhere in Peru.

The Pre-Columbian Cross Comes Alive during Qespisqa P'unchay

Salvador Palomino Flores in his article "La Cruz en los Andes" (1968: 63–66) wrote that the cross is a historically and geographically universal symbol which existed hundreds of years before the spread of Christianity. Thus before these Americans came into contact with Europeans, the Incas, pre-Inca societies, and other aboriginal people knew the cross, but its meaning differed from the Christian one. Among the Diaguitas of Argentina, who lived in the past century, the cross was the symbol of the atmosphere and of rain. This belief may go back a thousand years.

Other scientists have also been concerned with the symbolic significance of the cross. Billie Jean Isbell (1985:138) believes that "the constellation of the southern cross symbolizes the synthetic union of male and female elements." The dichotomy of the horizontal as a symbol of femaleness and the vertical as a symbol of maleness has also been observed in other parts of the Andes (Bastien 1985:89), and is sometimes represented as a cross, denoting wholeness. Robert Randall (1987:89) discovered that "in Inca thought the number four signifies completeness. This is reflected in Tawantinsuyu, the Inca Empire." We know that the cross is, among other things, representative of the four *suyus* of Tawantinsuyu and the four crossroads leading through the Inca Empire. Douglas Sharon (1978:42) wrote: "Although to date we have no solid ethnohistorical evidence for the ritual orientation to the four cardinal directions in Peru, we do know that the practice was central to Indian cosmology and ritual throughout the New World."

During the night of July 27 and the day of July 28, it became clear that the cross and the signs designating the four corners are central to many rituals in Chillihuani. Sprinkling *trago* or *chicha* on the four corners of the table to demarcate sacred space, marking four points over a glass of alcohol with one's fingers wetted with the liquid, tracing three crosses over the drink in fast succession (or one cross over the plates with food), and reaching across the table handing glass and bottle from elder to *chaskiq* and vice versa with one's hands crossed are rituals that are as significant today as they must have been in pre-Columbian times.

It is certainly also significant that four hierarchies consisting of male versus female elders and their respective younger counterparts performed rituals in the middle of the four *suyus* of Chillihuani and at the four corners of the plaza. Guaman Poma de Ayala ([1615] 1987) described in detail the fiestas celebrated in ancient times in the central plaza of Cuzco in front of the church in the years 1608, 1609, 1614, 1615, and 1618. He mentioned that four richly decorated altars were erected in the four corners of the plaza where performances took place (see Zuidema 1991:816).

When we compare the way in which the four hierarchies of elders with young initiates are positioned on the upper plaza of Chillihuani on the 28th of July, we can see a mirror image of the four *suyus* of Tawantinsuyu, the former Inca Empire.

The "Day of Independence" in Chillihuani is not only a "Day of Respect" but also a day when Tawantinsuyu, the four quarters of the Inca Empire, return to life in symbolic form. Although an analysis of these symbols helps to illuminate the past, we depend on knowledgeable elders such as Roberto Yupanqui Qoa to lead us further into the ancestral realm to the roots of Andean culture and ideology.

Metaphors or Reality—
Visions from the Past

Each year and with every ascent to Chillihuani, new questions arise about intriguing and bewildering events and phenomena. Some mysteries are clarified as metaphors from ancient times are understood. Though certain of these metaphors are known to us from early Spanish documents, we cannot be sure that we understand them in the same way as did the Inca and pre-Inca peoples. Nor can we trust entirely in those early writings, which were often prepared by missionaries or soldiers, who had neither the eyes nor the mind set to understand or appreciate the Andean peoples.

However, an understanding of the past is indispensable to the comprehension of the ideology that underlies the rituals which the people of Chillihuani perform during ceremonies and in their everyday lives. We must interpret ancestral belief systems and worldviews to get a clearer picture of the forces that have shaped this society and to discern those ancient elements that have endured to the present time.

Elders in Chillihuani, as elsewhere, often cling to the past and are interested in discussing life as it was in former times. With radiant eyes they can talk of their youth, of the teachings they received from their respected elders, of the "good old days." With warmth, honesty, and a great sense of humor they recount both the good and bad things that have happened in their lives. Despite the daily hardships of high-altitude living, they are content in their mountain homes, so close to the Apus with their eternal snows and icy winds.

In the minds of the old people, ancient metaphors transmitted through oral history coexist with their more contemporary thoughts. It is therefore not always clear if, or to what extent, people separate metaphors and ancient belief systems from their personal views of the world, or how these two elements are related. I remember sitting with Roberto Yupanqui Qoa in the *curandero*'s house, contemplating what might happen after death. In a determined tone of voice Roberto assured me that it is of no use speculating about this matter since no one has ever returned to tell us. Yet, he is deeply devoted to the pantheon of Andean gods and often speaks of Pachamama, the Apus, and other deities, and of the worlds above and below, from which people arise and to which they return after death. He refers to these worlds as *hanan pacha,* the world above, *kay pacha,* this world, and *ukhu pacha,* the world below.

Whenever Roberto Yupanqui Qoa speaks of times long gone, he opens windows into the past and shares with us what he knows about a little-known ancient world. "We must speak about the times of our ancestors, they may not be forgotten," he says with an urgency in his voice as he invites me to his home high up under the sacred lagoon Waqraqocha.

I accept his invitation and the next day I follow Juan Mamani on a narrow path that winds up the steep mountainside to Roberto's house. On the way the *curandero* confides that Roberto is the one who knows best, that he is a great custodian of ancient customs. My previous encounters with Roberto testify to this, but I know that there is much more in his repertoire of knowledge about ancient times and I am grateful and very excited that he wants to share this with me.

The dogs bark ferociously as we approach Roberto's homestead, which is enclosed by a picturesque adobe wall. With a fast, energetic gait, and a smile on his wrinkled, weather-beaten face, Roberto comes to greet us. "I am honored that you visit me with my *compadre,* Doctora," he says, as he stretches his arms out to embrace us and proceeds to place a poncho on a stone bench by his adobe house. With an elegant gesture he asks us to take a seat. Two beautiful great-granddaughters in their teens and three small great-grandsons, all with charming smiles on their faces, come to greet us.

The young girls offer plates of steaming soup. Two villagers on their way to their own *suyus* stop by. They also receive a meal and decide to stay a bit longer. After the meal Roberto opens his *unkuña* and invites us to his *coca* leaves. We blow *k'intus* to the east, thanking the divinities for the food and asking them to be present at this encounter. We talk about the weather, the winds, the flocks, and the fields. Then I ask about life in the past in this village.

Roberto remains silent, his eyes focused on the adobe floor. Slowly a shimmer of enthusiasm flickers across his face. "There is so much to tell you, Señorita, so much," he says with some hesitation in his voice, "but I must try to get my thoughts together. It is not often that someone wants to talk of the past. My grandchildren and great-grandchildren do not want to listen. They say, "Grandpa, forget the old stories. Forget them.""

The great-grandchildren smile. They offer herbal tea to everyone. Roberto thanks the children. Then with a dignified voice he begins to speak. "When I was a child, I *had* to listen to the ancient teachings of our people. My grandparents told me about our ancestors every night. Often I was too tired to listen; I wanted to sleep. But my *qoyacha* (grandmother) and my *awkicha* (grandfather) insisted that I stay awake and listen, so I would know what has happened in the past, so I would know my ancestors. Sometimes my grandparents shook me hard if I fell asleep. 'Stay awake and listen,' they implored and commanded. 'You *must* know about our ancestors. You *must* tell your children and their children our story. It may never die.'" (See photo 26.)

His voice becomes hoarse as he continues. "Every night they told me about our ancestors. Sometimes we had secret meetings, many of us, in a cave under a rock. There I learned about the Yupanquis, about the Inca Yupanqui . . . about those Yupanquis. These were *our* Incas and they had *our* name." Roberto believes that he is a direct descendant of the Inca Pachakuteq Yupanqui. He takes a deep breath, sighs, and then there is silence. Pain is written on the face of the old man, the pain of his ancestors who lost their lives and an empire to a brutal conquest.

Some old people of Chillihuani and elders from other high-altitude villages confided that "in the past the *mistis* (mestizos, people of mixed background, living in the mainstream of Peruvian society) did not like it when they heard about our secret meetings. They did not like it when offerings were made to the Apus. They wanted us to do homage to God and the saints. So the priests came. We had to take over *cargos* for the saints with mass and priest."

About the Origins of Chillihuani

I ask Roberto whether his ancestors always lived in Chillihuani. He reflects. Then with an air of increased interest he explains how the grandparents of his grandparents (he uses this expression when he talks about times long past) came from Qolla, the area of Puno around Lake Titicaca. "The grandfather of my grandmother came to Llaqto Qocha. There he built a little house and then he went to Qayara Chimpu and also built a little house. Then he went to the heights above Tintinco, close to the high mountain lake of Chinchayqocha in the *puna*. He obtained land to cultivate potatoes, *ulluku, oqa,* and *mashwa,* and little by little he acquired a herd of llamas and alpacas. In those times there was enough land in the high-altitude zones to pasture herds of animals and to use large or medium parcels of land for cultivation. There were few people and there was enough land. There were only thirty-six families in Chillihuani who worked their land."

Juan Mamani nods. He declares that his ancestors also came from Lake Titicaca and that Mamani is a common name in the Lake Titicaca region. Other people in Chillihuani, however, among them Modesto

Photo 26. Roberto Yupanqui Qoa instructs my godson Rosas, who lives in the valley, to respect the teachings of their Inca ancestors.

Quispe Choqque, assert that their ancestors lived in the heights of Chilli-huani as long as anyone can remember.

None of the villagers, however, can remember the time when ances-tral migrations from Lake Titicaca to Chillihuani took place, or even put an approximate date to them. Perhaps these accounts are embedded in the myth of origin that states that the Incas came from Lake Titicaca and dispersed from there.

There are different versions of the myth of origin. The chronicler Molina ([1575] 1943:7) wrote that the Incas believed themselves to have arisen in Lake Titicaca. The creator god Wiraqocha told the first Inca, Manqo Qhapaq, as well as his brothers and sisters, to submerge them-selves below the earth and to move underground to the cave Paqariq-tanpu. From there they were to walk toward Cuzco in search of land on which to settle. Only where their golden staff would sink into the earth should they found their empire. (See also Aveni 1989:284 and Morote Best 1984 regarding the Inca creation myth.) Documents written by Rodrigo Hernández Príncipe ([1621–1622] 1923) also tell us about mi-grations from Lake Titicaca. Various scholars (MacCormack 1991; Sil-verblatt 1987; Zuidema 1973) analyzed these and other documents which reveal to us that people called *llacuas,* the legendary founders of descent groups, came from afar and conquered the *llactas,* also called *waris* (*huaris*), the original inhabitants of a region. In her ethnohistori-cal research, Irene Silverblatt (1987:68) wrote that the *llactas* adored di-vine relatives associated with the earth, symbolizing their local origin, while the *llacuases* often claimed Illapa, the god of thunder and light-ning, as kin. During his investigations in the late sixteenth and early seventeenth centuries, Padre Arriaga ([1621] 1968:117–118) discovered that *ayllus* were divided in this way throughout the Peruvian Sierra, but the people were not always called *llacuas* and *llactas*. It is possible that Chillihuani has been divided in this way and that part of the popula-tion who worshiped the god of thunder and lightning came from the Lake Titicaca region to conquer the Wari, the original inhabitants of this region. Remains of the Wari culture are found throughout the valley be-low Chillihuani.

People are known to have migrated from Bolivia on other occasions as well. In 1780 Bolivians joined Tupac Amaru II and his wife Micaela Bastides in their revolt against the mistreatment of the Indians.[1] Some of the people from Bolivia who participated in the uprising remained in the Vilcanota Valley region below Chillihuani.

Yet, long before these events took place, it was known that the Inca Pachakuteq Yupanqui brought stone masons from Lake Titicaca to Cuzco and other parts of the expanding Tawantinsuyu. On the ascent to Chillihuani one passes Pukara Punku, a large site with exquisite stone masonry, a possible site of migration for skilled stone masons.

When I mention Pukara Punku, Roberto sighs. "*Arí,* Pukara Punku, these stones, these big rosy stones! I must tell you about the beautiful stones of Pukara Punku." In an earnest tone of voice he explains: "Our Incas worked the stones and they moved them to their destinations with their *warak'a.* When our Incas used the whips, the stones moved by themselves."[2] The two visitors nod. They agree that the Incas lived at Pukara Punku and assert that in their youth many more rosy-red stones stood there. They also recount that one of the largest and most beautifully worked stones of Pukara Punku was taken to Cuzco.

Roberto imitates the action of whipping a sling, and with a victorious sparkle in his eyes tells the story of the rosy-red stone and the *ichu* grass. "The Spanish took many of our stones from Pukara Punku to Cuzco to build the cathedral; they left only a few for us. When they moved the precious stones, seeds of *ichu* grass were carried in the cracks of one of the stones. This stone was used to finish the cathedral and soon *ichu* grass grew right on top of the church. Yes, our *ichu* grass was stuck on top of the church!" he repeats, laughing with delight.[3]

But *ichu* seeds are not the only connection between the region of Chillihuani and the former Inca capital of Cuzco. Roberto tells us that long before the Spanish came, water from the heights of Apu Ausangate was led right to the Qorikancha, the Temple of the Sun in Cuzco, to a place immediately behind the present church. The other men agree with Roberto that the Incas built canals which brought water from Apu Ausangate to Cuzco via Yuraqwasi and Llaqtokancha. Juan further states that a straight wall of stone and mud (called *pirka*) still exists and that Inca canals also pass through Tintinco and above Pampaqolqa. This water was urgently needed when the city of Cuzco was reorganized and grew during the reign of the ninth Inca Pachakuteq Yupanqui, who ruled from 1438 to 1471. This Inca, sometimes referred to as Pachakuteq Inca Yupanqui (or Pachacuti Inca Yupanqui), was a most powerful ruler who is believed to have started the large-scale expansion of the Inca Empire (see Wolf 1982:62).

Hunger, Death, and Resurrection

"Water came from Apu Ausangate," Roberto repeats in a whisper. Then in an agitated voice he tells us that there was a time when the water was no longer sufficient. This was a "time of scarcity" (*muchuy*), which led to a "time of hunger" (*yarqay*). With sorrow written on his face Roberto explains: "There was no rain, no production, nothing grew. It did not rain for seven years. Every day people died during this time of hunger and sickness. Nobody could cure the people, not even *altomesayoq*, the most esteemed *curanderos.* This was the punishment of God. So many people died that they could not all be buried. People ate '*tuna de la altura*' (the fruit of the spiny *roq'a* plant that belongs to the genus *Opuntia*). They ate *qayara* (*Puya herrerae*); they even ate grass and stones. They ate the dry leather of the doors of their houses. They boiled it." With much concern he adds, "Yes, this was the 'time of the great hunger.'"

Seven years of hunger are recorded in ancient documents. Felipe Guaman Poma de Ayala ([1615] 1980:89) stated that during the reign of Pachakuteq Inca Yupanqui, many Indians died from hunger, thirst, plague, and the punishment of God; it did not rain for seven years—some say ten years. There were violent storms. People spent most of their time crying and burying the dead. Because of the lack of an objective time frame as we understand it, I cannot be certain whether Roberto refers to the "time of hunger" documented by this Inca chronicler, or to a different time of famine. (Regarding the consequences of severe droughts in recent decades, see Winterhalder 1994:26.)

This was not the only tragic time that remains vivid in Roberto's mind. There were other life-threatening disasters he learned about from his ancestors. His voice reflects deep sorrow as he continues: "Long ago big potatoes grew in Chillihuani. But then came the 'time of the endless rains,' which also caused hunger and death for many people. The father of my mother-in-law lived through these times of hunger when he was a child. It rained without stopping; rivers and lakes went over their borders and inundated the land. The rain caused rock slides that tore away the loose soil and destroyed crops in their path. Fields were buried beneath rain and rubble. Mountain peaks were covered with snow. This snow was like the snow of Ausangate, *wiñay rit'i* (eternal snow), snow that grows, or let's say, snow that never melts."

The old man sighs deeply, then continues: "Nothing was left to eat. There was nothing people could cook. Finally they had to eat ashes in order to have something in their stomachs to live. In other *ayllus* people also died in this time of hunger. It was a time of great sorrow. Then, little by little life returned to normal and finally happiness returned. Those who survived could work again and they produced again. The father of my mother-in-law died when he was very old."[4]

Llaqtayoq Mach'aqway—Village of the Great Snake

"There were other times when disasters happened in this *ayllu* and elsewhere," Roberto continues after offering *coca k'intus* to everyone. "There was the time when the big fire raged through the mountains." He seems agitated and somewhat disgusted as he relates: "It was long ago. There was fire everywhere. I don't know why they burned the *ayllus*. After the fire," he pauses, "I think there were two fires, the great snake was gone." I asked Roberto what kind of snake it was. "It was a big snake; it was dark gray. It lived in a cave high up on the slope above my house close to Waqraqocha. When it drizzled while the sun was shining, the snake emerged from its cave and rolled up on a flat stone (a *mesarumi*). This was Llaqtayoq Mach'aqway."[5]

The Chillihuani herders suggest that Llaqtayoq Mach'aqway means that the snake is the owner, master, or mistress of the village (*dueño del pueblo*). (See Arriaga [1621] 1968:117, n. 1: "*Llactayoc* is a shortened form of *llactacamayoc* or 'governor of the people.' *Llacta* means city."). Metaphorically, the "snake"—*mach'aqway,* also called *amaru*—governed the village.

Roberto's statement about Llaqtayoq Mach'aqway is significant as it reveals much about Chillihuani itself. It also sheds light on the use of metaphors in the organization of the Inca Empire and suggests ways in which the Incas viewed the universe and their empire within it.

Although Chillihuani is no longer officially a Llaqtayoq Mach'aqway—a Village of the Snake—Roberto believes, as do other villagers, that this snake still exists and manifests itself in different forms. On various occasions I was told that sometimes a snake moves in a ferocious whirlwind, called *ch'aki qhaqya wayra,* the dry thunder wind, above the high mountain lake Waqraqocha. People assert that the snake makes sounds—*chrchrchr*—similar to those of thunder but not as loud; one can still hear them at a distance. Lizards and green frogs also move around. "This is dangerous for people," Roberto and his visitors warn.

"When a person passes by and the wind takes a hold of him, it enters his stomach and the person dies of disease. It can even infect the clothes. The velocity of the wind is enormous. It can throw people against the rocky peaks surrounding the lake Waqraqocha." Roberto and all other villagers have, at one time or another, experienced these ferocious winds, usually in August.

I ask Roberto whether he has seen a big snake elsewhere. Slowly he stretches his arms toward the sky. "I have seen a snake in the sky, a snake with two heads. It moved through the air. Lightning came and burst into the snake along its whole body and blew it up. The snake disappeared."

Roberto's visitors nod. One of them notes, "My father has seen the snake several times. When it drizzled while the sun was shining a snake emerged from a spring and took to the air. Then lightning caught the snake, went into its body, and the snake disappeared."

I am excited about these accounts. I am aware of these metaphors from Inca legends I have read or heard, and from rock engravings I have seen. I have always wanted to know their meaning, but I never expected them to survive in the minds of living people. I would like to ask more questions, but I cannot come up with a formulation that would make sense to my friends. This is because I cannot fully comprehend what these symbols mean to the people of Chillihuani today or what they meant to the Incas. My friends do not seem to view myth and reality as separate entities, whereas I struggle to comprehend their ways of perceiving these phenomena.

It is late. I thank Roberto, his family, and friends for allowing me insight into the extremely complex and fascinating metaphorical world of their ancestors. Roberto laughs as I express my admiration for his *qoyacha* and *awkicha,* who kept him awake every night, and also for Roberto himself, who fought sleep throughout much of his youth to learn about his ancestors from his grandparents and great-grandparents. Roberto looks at me for a moment and then says in a determined tone of voice, "I will tell you more when you come again. You must know everything about our Incas. Our Incas may never die." He sighs, then repeats, "*Inkanchiskuna manan wañunankuchu*" (Our Incas may never die).

Because snake and lightning metaphors are so central to ancient Andean ideology and are still so deeply embedded in the lives of the high-altitude herders, they require closer attention.

The great snake, *mach'aqway* or *amaru*, is a powerful symbol in the Andes. It was, and still is, ideologically significant for the Andean people and plays an important role in myths and legends. The snake symbol appears in many different contexts. *Amaru* may have been the earthly symbol of Wiraqocha, the creator god (Urbano 1974:39). *Amaru,* the great snake, was intimately related to Inca Amaru and to the Inca Atahualpa (Pease 1972:60). *Amaru* is tied to fertility, agriculture, rebellion, and change in political power (see Seligmann & Bunker 1994:218–219). It is also a symbol of wisdom. In the form of a rainbow, *amaru,* the snake metaphor, ties the earth to the sky and to the underworld.

The snake symbol is deeply embedded in mythology. Douglas Sharon (1978:93) wrote:

> Valcarcel relates an ancient legend referring to two mythical serpents who operated on all three levels of the universe. They both began in the Underworld. When they reached this world, one of them, *Yacu Mama,* crawled and was converted into the Ucayali River, mother of the rivers. The second serpent, *Sacha Mama,* had two heads, walked upright, and was like an aged tree. Upon reaching the Upper World, the first serpent turned into lightning; he was now called *Illapa* and was god of the storm, thunder and rain. The two-headed serpent turned into the rainbow (*Coichi*), the deity that fertilizes and gives color to the earth and all living things. Thus the three worlds were united by these serpent gods of water and fertility.

In an even more metaphorical sense, *amaru* is perceived as a revolutionary force that dismantles a system which is out of equilibrium and then helps to bring back balance, harmony, and peace within a new system.

Within this multitude of meanings, what significance did the great snake have for Chillihuani? Most revealing in this context is the statement of the chronicler Sarmiento de Gamboa ([1572] 1960:225), paraphrased in Urbano (1974:38), who wrote, "The symbol *amaru* was very important. Whether we deal with a village, tribe or *ayllu,* the *amaru* are integrated in the life of Cusco since the beginning of the Inca domination of the valley. Sarmiento speaks of Amaru as though it was the town or the community of the *Ayamarcas.*" Roberto's referral to the snake as *Llaqtayoq Mach'aqway kaq,* which can be translated as "the snake is the village itself," echoes Sarmiento's characterization.

The observations of the chronicler Antonio de Calancha are equally enlightening as to the place Chillihuani may have occupied within the empire's organization. Zuidema (1967:50) stated that Calancha found that every one of the large villages conquered by the Incas was represented by a different kind of feline (or by a different subtype of *amaru*). *Amaru* was also considered the archetype of the felines (Guaman Poma de Ayala [1615] 1936). Subtypes of hawks (*huaman, halcon*) could also represent a village or a tribe (Zuidema 1967:50).

Given the above findings, it is probable that within the Inca Empire Chillihuani was one of those villages that was represented by the great snake. Yet Roberto tells us that the great snake (perhaps the snake metaphor) disappeared when the big fire came. Was the big fire again a metaphor? Or was it real? The sixteenth-century chronicler Pachacuti Yamqui (who wrote about the Inca Pachakuteq [also referred to as Pachacuti Inca Yupanqui] related:

> A new era began and a miracle happened in the air as an Amaru came from the mountain peak of Pachatusan. A wild beast, half a league long and bulky, two and a half arms wide and with ears, and fangs and a beard. It comes through Yuncaypampa and Sinca and from there it enters the lagoon Quibipay. Then from Asconcata emerge two comets of fire (*cometa de fuego*), one passes through Potina from Arequipa (the volcano) and another one comes from further down from Guamanca. There are three or four very high peaks covered with snow. They say those are animals with wings and ears and tails and four feet and on their backs they have many spines as do fish. And from far they say that it looked as though it was all fire. ([1613] 1927:184–185)

Pachacuti Yamqui's account relates most directly to Roberto's statement, especially where this chronicler wrote: "The powerful huge snake disappeared in the lagoon just before two comets of fire appeared and finally turned everything to fire." Did Roberto also talk about a *pachakuti* (turnaround of the world)—a change in government—when he referred to two fires that made the big snake disappear? Indeed, this may have been the case, given the chronicler's further account:

> And at this time the said *Pachacutiyngayupanqui* [Pachacuti Inca Yupanqui] leaves for his town of Kuzco where he finds his father *Viracochampayncanyupanqui* [Viracocha Inca Yupanqui] very old and sick. With great joy he gives a festivity honoring his arrival followed by the sacred celebration of *capacraymi* of *Pachayachachi*. And he presents his son, the grandson of the old man and prepares festivities honoring the child's birth, naming him *Amarottopaynqa* [Amaru Tupaq Inca].

Henrique Urbano (1974:41) characterized the comets the chronicler Pachacuti Yamqui talked about as symbolic replicas of the firebirds which represent the fire of Inti. He further argued that the arrival of Pachacuti after this "miracle" shows the primacy of fire over the *amaru*. The cycle of the *amaru* has been demolished and the dominion of Inti has imposed itself. Yet, the power of Inti is not absolute and cannot totally eliminate Viracocha, the distant god and his *amaru*. In other words, the era of *amaru* the snake (symbolizing water) gave way to the era of Inti, the sun (fire).

But, legend tells us, as does Roberto, that the snake and its symbol did not totally disappear as the "fire" raged through the countryside. Instead, the elders of Chillihuani recount that the snake retreated to the mountain lake Waqraqocha, where it occasionally appears in the whirlwind *muyuq wayra* or the even stronger *ch'aki qhaqya wayra,* the dry thunder wind.

The metaphorical merging of snake and lightning symbols (water and fire) is also central to the vision of the powerful ninth Inca Pachakuteq Inca Yupanqui. The chronicler Sarmiento de Gamboa ([1572] 1947:178) recorded this Inca's vision shortly after the conquest (see chapter 3 of this book). Sarmiento de Gamboa believed that Inti Illapa was considered the "brother" and "alter ego" of the great Inca Pachakuteq Yupanqui.[6]

Several days after our visit with Roberto, I climbed with three Chillihuani friends to a precipitous region across the Chillihuani River from Roberto's home. There on the steep rocky outcrop of Qaqa Letrayoq (the rock with the letters), we found engravings depicting five double-headed snakes in zigzag form. Below two of them were engraved round faces which my companions asserted symbolize the sun (*inti*), while the zigzag snakes represent lightning. I wonder whether perhaps in the past they represented Inti Illapa, the thunder of the sun, considered the alter ego of Inca Pachakuteq Yupanqui. Many more double-headed zigzag snakes were engraved in adjacent rocks.[7]

Is it possible that the emblem of the great Pachakuteq Inca Yupanqui is eternalized in stone on the steep rocks of Chillihuani? It is known that this Inca's wife, Mama Anahuarque, had lands in the *ayllus* of Sailla and Anahuarque, which are located in the district of Quiquijana in the valley just below Chillihuani.

The ancient rock drawings on Qaqa Letrayoq in Chillihuani, depicting both *amaru* and Illapa (i.e., water and fire), as well as an oral history which alludes to these metaphors and symbols, suggest that these phenomena must have been as important to Chillihuani's past as they were to the Inca Empire in general.[8] The insightful and fascinating accounts of the people of Chillihuani, especially those of Roberto Yupanqui Qoa, shed light on the intricate and highly metaphoric world of the Incas, which is still very much alive among the elders in the stormy heights of Chillihuani.

Waqraqocha

The last rays of the sun disappear behind the mountain range in the west, giving way to an icy wind. "*Chiri way-ra,*" Nicacia sighs, pulling her *lliklla* tighter around her shoulders. We have been sitting with the Yupanqui and Quispe families in the warm sun on Roberto Yupanqui Qoa's patio, feasting on *papa wathiya.*[1] Baked under-ground, these potatoes are a treat for everyone. With the sun gone, however, our fingers soon become too stiff to peel the potatoes. In June, the middle of the Andean winter, temperatures between day and night can drop abruptly. But the sudden gusts of wind that lift whole clouds of dust from Roberto's patio high into the air are unexpected at this time of year. The old man knows what causes these sudden violent disturbances, though. "Waqraqocha!"[2] he exclaims, looking with concern at the precipitous mountain peaks above us, which con-ceal the sacred lagoon. The others nod silently.

Almost a year has passed since my last visit to my friends who live below the lagoon Waqraqocha, the hub of ancient legends and present-day belief systems. They know the lagoon well; they feel her moods and seem to understand what motivates her. Strong winds, hail-storms, thunder, and lightning can be manifestations of her sudden outbursts of anger.

Throughout the Andes, high mountain lakes are re-spected and feared, venerated and worshiped. Myths, legends, and the Indians' accounts of their experiences with lagoons tell us of the role they play in the lives of the people and their animals. These high mountain lakes are associated with life, fertility, and procreation.[3]

Springs and lakes receive offerings and are considered the owners of the alpacas. This ancient association of the water with creation and fertility is common to both the Old World and pre-Columbian America (Eliade 1963:188–207).

For the Indians of the Andes, mountain lakes or lagoons (*qochas, lagunas*) are alive, powerful, and have personalities of their own. They aid the just and punish the offender who does not show respect for their sacred sites or for the animals, the plants, and inanimate objects in the vicinity.

"Waqraqocha is angry tonight," Roberto continues to express his concern. "She is as angry as I am for having lost my five llamas three days ago." He takes a deep breath. For Roberto and other herders, animals are not just an economic asset; they are also friends and companions. Roberto used to rent out his llamas to other villagers who have no animals or not enough animals to carry a heavy load. The person who borrows an animal for one day works for a day for the person who lent him the animal. "Your llamas," Juan adds with sorrow, "you will find them if you go to Waqraqocha and cry by the lagoon. This will make the thieves of your llamas fall to your tears." (To make thieves fall to your tears means to see what is happening, to recognize the thieves, to become clairvoyant.[4]) He pauses. "It helped me when my alpacas were stolen many years ago. While I was crying beside Waqraqocha I saw the thieves through my tears." Roberto nods. "Waqraqocha helped me often," he sighs. "Now my sadness is great, but I can no longer climb to the mountain peaks to meet her, I am too old now."

For the last two days Roberto has searched for his llamas in many parts of the village. But there was no trace of his animals. He fears that by now they are far beyond the mountain range in the distance. It was the first time in his life that any of his animals were stolen, and there was nothing else he could do. The village justice of the peace and his young deputies (*agentes policiales*) helped him in his search, but to no avail. Roberto laments that in former times an *altomesayoq*—one who can converse directly with the Apus—could have helped him find his animals. In those times, after conversing with the Apus, an *altomesayoq* had a vision in which he saw the thieves in the form of tiny men. He could then inform the rightful owner of the stolen animals about their condition, where they were, and who had stolen them.

Roberto names all the *altomesayoq* (shamans of the high table, who have the highest status) he has known in his life. He asserts that "they had great knowledge, they knew how to read *coca* leaves, they knew how to invoke the Apus." He laments that now only *pampamesayoc* (shamans of the low table) exist. "Some try hard, but they cannot speak directly with the Apus. Some cannot even read *coca* leaves." The *curandero* agrees: "*Yanqa kuka wayrachiq kanku*" (They are useless when it comes to reading *coca*). The others agree. Formerly some people who had great troubles went to church to ask the saints for help, but help never came. People usually believe that it does not help to complain to a judge in the valley, either, because he charges much money and at the end one knows no more than before. So there is only Waqraqocha.

"Waqraqocha, Waqraqocha!" Roberto laments, pointing to the sheer rocks that jut like dark omens into the night sky above us, concealing the lagoon. He turns toward me calmly, hiding the grief caused by the disappearance of his llamas, which he loved and needed so much. "Señorita, Doctora, you want to know? I will tell you about our lagoon. I will tell you what happened there long ago, when my grandmother was a child herding her flocks." We move through a tiny door into Roberto's small, cozy one-room house, from where the wind cannot carry the sounds high up to where Waqraqocha is listening. Teresa, Roberto's daughter-in-law, has kindled a fire and put a pot of soup on the earthen stove. We sit around the fire relishing its warmth.

Roberto takes *coca* leaves from his *unkuña.* Everyone selects three perfect leaves for a *k'intu,* blowing east in honor of Waqraqocha and the peaks surrounding her. Then there is silence. Roberto concentrates before he takes us back in time to his childhood, when his grandmother told him stories about her own childhood and her encounters with the lagoon.

He closes his eyes as he starts to speak of the powerful lagoon who teaches people respect, honesty, and discipline.

"When my grandmother was young, she often went to the shores of Waqraqocha. One day she arrived there at noon, a dangerous hour, a bad time. Close to the shore of the lagoon she saw a most beautiful flower. It was *werkantay*" (similar to the *phallcha* flower). The *curandero* nods and informs us that this flower can cure a cough and can also heal those young alpacas born with their heads tilted backward. Roberto continues to explain. "It was a big flower—red with yellow. My grandmother ran fast but could not catch the flower. As she approached the lagoon, step by step, the flower went further toward its center where it sank. If she had caught it, it would have pulled her down. So my grandmother warned me, never to go close to the shores of Waqraqocha and never to grasp anything that floats on it, not even the string of a hat, because it will pull a person down, never to appear again. She advised that one must sing a song or pretend to call somebody when one walks alone near the lagoon."

Roberto takes a deep breath. Everyone present agrees that the lagoon Waqraqocha is enchanted. She is the consort of the rocky peak Waqraqocha, who watches over her. "Señorita," Roberto resumes, "when a person goes there alone, beautiful flowers may appear, more beautiful than one finds in any other part." In a whisper he adds: "And golden bulls live in Waqraqocha." The others nod. I ask Roberto to explain.

"Sometimes bulls and cows rest with their young at the shores of the lagoon. When someone approaches, these animals get up, swing their tails, and go into the water where they become smaller and smaller as they approach the center of Waqraqocha. There they turn into *enqaychu* of pure gold and sink into the middle of the lagoon."

I recognize that this statement is profoundly symbolic. I have often heard people from high communities talk about the golden bulls and cows that hide in high lagoons, but they could not explain the meaning behind their appearance or the metaphorical significance of these golden bulls. The Andean scholar Abdon Yaranga Valderrama (1979: 714) suggested that certain symbols in the high Andes have changed and that the golden bulls are, in fact, *amaru,* the great snake.[5] When *amaru* is not satisfied—that is, if people do not cultivate their fields and breed animals—*amaru,* the shining snake of gold sent by Illapa, presents itself in the form of golden bulls. Since *amaru* is also considered a guardian of the earth and of agriculture, it can be assumed that this divinity watches over subsistence activities. The people of Chillihuani are not certain why or if this symbol changed when the Spanish arrived, but the realization that *amaru* is the symbol that hides behind the concept of the golden bull ties the ancient Andean context to a contemporary belief system.

Roberto tells us the sad story of a *misti* (mestizo) by the name of Espinoza. "This gentleman named Espinoza came from the heights of Pitumarca with his llamas carrying potatoes. At the shore of Waqraqocha he saw cows and thought they were real. He called out "*Qoy yaw!*" (Listen and surrender!). The cows startled, moved their tails, and hurried into the water. As he turned around to look at them and saw them getting smaller and disappearing in the middle of the lagoon, he lost his eyesight. If he had blown a *coca k'intu,* he could have avoided becoming blind, and perhaps he would have found an *enqaychu* for himself. But instead, blind and helpless, he crawled on all fours, his hands and feet full of the spines of the *roq'a* plant, until he found a cave to rest in. Many hours later, his relatives found him; he was in serious condition." (See Barthel 1986 and Paerregaard 1994:195 regarding the importance of showing respect to bodies of water.)

Roberto holds his hands with the palms facing in the direction of Waqraqocha as he continues: "My grandmother knew all about Waqraqocha; she learned it from her grandmother. She warned me never to go close to the lagoon, never to throw in rocks or disturb her in any other way, and never to startle animals in her surroundings. If she is disturbed, the lagoon becomes furious and punishes immediately, or sometimes later, by sending disease. But those who behave respectfully have nothing to fear, and the lagoon grants them their wishes." The others nod. "*Arí,* this is so."

Roberto mentions that above Waqraqocha there is another lake, equally sacred; this is Mama Waqraqocha. Both lakes are of emerald color surrounded by yellowish *ichu* grass that grows close to the eternal snow. Ignacia explains that the *qochas* are the eyes of the mountain and are guarded by the rocky peaks of Waqraqocha and Qellwaqocha (qellwa = gull).

Leandro looks at me intently. Then he quietly talks to Ignacia. I overhear him say, "*Q'omer ñawi*" (green eyes). Ignacia nods and looks back at me. "You must meet Waqraqocha," Leandro whispers, his eyes expressing a sense of urgency and insistence.

In the high Andes, people, animals, and all of nature are part of the same cycle of life and death. For Ignacia and her husband, who have never seen a person with coloring that so thoroughly resembles the mountain, there is only one explanation: I must be related to the mountain with its green lakes and yellow *ichu* grass.

This vision of the cosmos is alive in other parts of the Andes as well. Joseph Bastien (1985:56), in his study of the people of Mt. Kaata in Bolivia, noted, "Earth and humans no longer exist as dichotomies but rather as endless reflections of differently shaped mirrors. There is no need to look for the distinctions between earth and humans since they are essentially identical." He further stated (1985:190) that on Mt. Kaata, "*Apacheta* is the head, where the bunchgrass and wool symbolize the hair, and the lakes are the eyes." In this context David and Rosalind Gow (1975:141) observed that people in Pinchimuro, a village 15 kilometers from Ocongate, still live in very close contact with nature. Humans and their alpacas are believed to be part of the same empirical and spiritual world, to originate from the same source, and to be governed by the same supernatural powers.

Leandro repeats, "You *must* meet Waqraqocha." Through the tiny window I can see the dizzying heights where the Apus Waqraqocha and Qellwaqocha meet the night sky and where the sacred lagoon has her domain. "We can go tomorrow morning when the sun rises," Leandro insists. Ignacia agrees with a smile. The *curandero* hesitates and then nods with a questioning expression on his face. Roberto shakes his head. He warns that the lagoon can be dangerous and unpredictable. She does not permit anyone close to her shores. He stresses that "any kind of disturbance can cause her to get angry, to send horrible storms out of a blue sky and to obscure the sun with black clouds. *Chikchi parape*—a hailstorm—can arise, devastating the region with a shower of hailstones, killing anyone in its path." He pauses, shaking his head. "People become nauseated and dizzy with headaches that can break the skull." (He refers to *soroche* or *soroqch'i*—mountain sickness.) The others look at me in anticipation. I have climbed to many high places with the people of Chillihuani. Yet, to reach this lagoon, one must ascend for many hours along precipitous mountainsides, studded with rubble and *roq'a,* a cactus-like plant with needle-sharp spines. I also remember accounts of people who ventured alone to the lagoon. Waqraqocha did not welcome them, but afflicted them with dizziness, nausea, and even death.

Leandro recognizes my concern. "If you get tired, I will carry you," he says spontaneously. The thought of me being carried up these extremely steep mountainsides to meet the lagoon makes us laugh. Yet, I know that these people are amazing. I have seen them carry loads on their backs that I could not even lift from the ground. They run up the steepest hillsides without resting. Their stamina is beyond anything I have seen.[6]

I do not know for sure why Leandro and Ignacia are so eager to introduce me to their lagoon, but I can see that it is very important to them that I come. My own interest, of course, is also considerable since I have heard so much about this significant and powerful deity, central to many songs and legends. So I agree to meet Waqraqocha, but caution that I may have to rest at times during the steep ascent. My friends smile with understanding and relief.

"*Paqarinkama*" (Until tomorrow), everyone except Roberto exclaims with joy. We walk home in the moonshine under a sky full of the brightest stars. At altitudes over 4,000 meters, this is a paradise for anyone who loves the night sky.

At night I have difficulty falling asleep and sit upright, gasping for air. This is unusual as I have never had problems with high altitude. It is particularly disconcerting given the grueling ascent planned for the morning. At dawn a young man from *suyu* Qayara Chimpu brings the sad news to the *curandero* that his baby boy has died. Holding back his tears, he tells us that he died from the cold. A little later news comes that two other babies died that night from the same cause. Several animals in the vicinity are also dead, our neighbors inform us. This is the middle of June, the coldest time of the year, and in the night the temperature fell from very cold to extremely cold. In the absence of a heating system, one must cover up with many furs, but the air one breathes is still icy cold. I suspect that a change in pressure was also responsible for causing the unfortunate deaths and the problems I experienced. (The pressure at this altitude is only approximately half of what it is at sea level.)

Sleep or no sleep, I have made a promise and must stick to it. As the sun starts to lick the frost from the grass, we are off: Juan, my fourteen-year-old godson Rosas, and myself, to meet Ignacia and Leandro at Roberto's house. Leandro has already notified Modesto, the *curandero* from *suyu* Llaqto, and his son, who has also expressed interest in our excursion. They live at a distance of 15 kilometers. The system of communication in Chillihuani is amazing, as individuals or the whole village can quickly be notified about an important event by present-day *chaskis*.

To get to Ignacia and Leandro's house, we must walk uphill for forty minutes along the Rio Chillihuani and then cross the river at a very turbulent place on a wooden bridge attached to an enormous rock. Here we come to the foot of the steep Waqraqocha mountainside. On a narrow path we walk uphill past caves and rocks covered with *qayara* plants. Ignacia and Leandro's home is in a sheltered ravine close to a hardy native *kishwar* tree (*Buddleia incana*).[7] *Tayanka* and *ch'illka* shrubs grow in this region, both resinous species of the genus *Baccharis*. At high altitudes one can also sometimes see *keuña* trees (*Polylepis incana*), which reach up to the snow line.

Beside the house, Ignacia, Leandro, Modesto, and Modesto's son are already waiting for us. We greet one another excitedly in anticipation of our trip together. As we pass Roberto's house, he comes to wish us luck, but he looks worried. He is not convinced that we should go. Perhaps he knows something he did not dare to tell us on the previous night.

Ascent to the Eyes of the Mountain

To reach Waqraqocha, we must pass from the *puna* to the high *puna.* The area around Roberto's house and the region above are studded with rock outcrops, some of them uniquely shaped. One looks like a half-moon with a natural roof. Ochre-colored signs of various forms are painted onto the inner sides of the rocks. How old are they? Who were the artists? Nobody knows. "They have been here ever since people can remember," my companions tell me. In Inca times, and still today in Chillihuani and other parts of the Andes, rocks are sacred. Oddly shaped rocks and caves had special religious significance in the past. Given the multitude of forms, shapes, and types of rock, this whole area below the sacred lagoon must have been very important in ancient times.

We soon enter steeper terrain with loose rocks; some debris tumbles down the precipice at the slightest touch. The ground gives way to extended areas of the spiny *roq'a* plants which spread along the terrain, competing with the tough *ichu* grass wherever there is a speck of earth to cling to. Since it is very painful to step into these plants full of barbed spikes, we try to remain on the rubble, balancing our way up the steep inclines.

Here and there springs emerge, bringing water from the lagoon to the surface through underground rivulets. Subterranean waterways have always been of great significance in the Andes. The ancient Andean people had much practical knowledge of subterranean hydrology, and they developed advanced techniques for utilizing such waters. In her extensive research, Jeanette Sherbondy (1982:4, 24) found that an analysis of the mythology about lakes, subterranean canals, and passages offers empirical data about actual hydraulics. She also discovered that the ancient peoples of the Andes not only had practical knowledge of subterranean hydrology and developed techniques to utilize subterranean waters, but also elaborated a cosmology based on this knowledge which was useful in expressing concepts of ethnicity and political unity.

I see Ignacia blow a *coca k'intu* in recognition of this sacred landscape with its snow-covered peaks, rocks, creeks, rivulets, and springs. Since antiquity the native people of Peru have revered these phenomena of nature, which they consider places of origin or sacred sites (Carrion Cachot 1955:10).

One rock outcrop follows another. The midday sun burns mercilessly on our heads while the icy wind blows the sweat from our faces. The panorama becomes even more spectacular as we continue to ascend. In the distance Apu Ausangate, the highest and most sacred mountain of southern Peru, appears. Majestic, with a white cape of snow covering its 6,384-meter peak, it glows against the blue sky. A good omen. Myths and legends abound about Taytacha Awsanqati. This great mountain god is at the pinnacle of a hierarchy of Apus and receives daily offerings. It is honored and invoked during all ceremonies with *coca k'intus* and *ñawin aqha,* the first cup of *chicha,* taken from an earthen jar. During Ch'allaska the first handful of blood of a dying llama or alpaca is sprinkled east for Apu Ausangate, requesting that he replace the same animal and protect the herds.

Opinions differ about whether Apu Ausangate is a male or female deity. Although, as is true for most Apus, Ausangate is generally considered male, some people from Q'ero whom I met referred to this mountain as *madrina* or godmother. Jorge Flores Ochoa (1990:47), preeminent scholar of pastoral societies, studied ancient *qeros* which revealed that mountains are divided into male and female. He discovered that the highest snow-covered mountains can be female, though not all investigators agree.[8] We all blow *coca k'intus* in honor of the great mountain, asking for a safe trip.

The ascent continues, still steeper. I have to stop more often to catch my breath. I envy my companions, who climb easily and feel the effects of chewing *coca* leaves—alleviation of cold, hunger, thirst, and fatigue as well as the feared mountain sickness. Although I participate in the invocations and chew the leaves during sacred rituals, I have thus far not felt relief from the above symptoms.

More snow-covered peaks appear on the horizon. Occasionally a fluffy white cloud floats through the bright blue sky. The rocks and caves around us add to the awe we experience in these pristine surroundings. We pass a giant *mesarumi.* It is here where Llaqtayoq Mach'aqway, the great snake, owner and protector of Chillihuani, used to bathe in the sun. I feel an urge to explore these fascinating sites, but I must conserve my strength to ensure that I will be able to reach the lagoon, still higher up amid the rocky peaks.

Another hour, my companions tell me, and we will be there. But it takes almost two hours until we finally arrive at a promontory with level ground. At its far end, the peaks of the Apus Waqraqocha and Qellwaqocha hover over the still-concealed lagoon. We stop at a *mesarumi* in front of an oddly shaped rock, which resembles a person hunched over in meditation. "This is the guardian of the lagoon," Juan tells me. Modesto sits beside the *mesarumi* and places his *unkuña* onto the sacred stone. He lets a handful of *coca* leaves fall freely onto the *mesarumi,* reading the patterns displayed as they come to rest (see photo 27).

We wait silently in anticipation of his answer. Relieved, he whispers, "Waqraqocha waits." We all blow *k'intus* in honor of the lagoon, thanking her for permitting us to enter her sacred realm. Nobody speaks. My companions know, as do the people throughout the Andes, that approaching a high lagoon can be a dangerous undertaking (see also Sharon 1978:130–131).

Myths tell of people who have disappeared in the lagoon, who have become sick, or who were turned to stone. The theme of turning to stone is frequent in Inca mythology. When I studied the waterways in Yanahuara, in the district of Urubamba, in 1985, Solon Corazao, one of the village elders, told me a legend that describes how water was brought to Yanahuara from the high lagoon Yuraqqocha. In the course of this adventurous undertaking, two of the three daughters of Prince Irin Puqlla were turned into stone because they could not resist looking behind them as the thundering waters followed in their path. The third daughter withstood all hardships and triumphantly brought the desperately needed water to her village. Rocks representing the two petrified daughters mark the path from the lagoon to the village of Yanahuara.

Another myth describes the fates of four brothers as they emerged from the lagoon Yaurihuiri. The first turned into a lagoon, the second into *ichu* grass, and the third into stone, while the fourth became the founder of Andamarca (Cáceres 1986:115). Rebeca Carrion Cachot (1955:13–14) related myths about guardians of lagoons who were in charge of opening and closing gates to distribute water and to repair the system; eventually these guardians were turned to stone. Where we stand, at the entrance to Waqraqocha, the guardian in stone verifies the ancient myths and testifies to the great significance of this site.

The lagoon is near but not yet visible. Slowly we walk toward the rocky mountain peaks that surround it. We pass between two large boulders that form a gateway, and there it is, the mighty Waqraqocha, an emerald lake, its crystal clear waters reflecting the sacred Apus like a gigantic green mirror. We stand in awe, blowing *k'intus* in honor of these deities. There is total silence. Only the occasional cry of a bird can be heard and the whisper of the wind softly brushing the majestic landscape.

A feeling of eternal peace emanates from the deep green waters of the lagoon and from the guardian Apus, witnesses from time immemorial and beholders of ancestral spirits and malevolent winds. Small black-and-white ducks with big red feet, called *wallata* in Quechua (*Chleophaga melanoptera*), swim on the lake and immerse their beaks from time to time into its calm, cool water. In the rocks above we can see small caverns, the homes of condors.

Photo 27. Modesto Quispe Choqque reads *coca* leaves by Waqraqocha's stone guardian.

In Inca and pre-Inca cultures, high mountain lakes were considered the fountains of life and were associated with the origin of the world. According to legend, the first Inca, Manqo Qhapaq, and his wife Mama Oqllo, along with their brothers and sisters, originated in Lake Titicaca. Llamas and alpacas were also believed to have their origin in lakes. Pilgrimages were made to lagoons and springs to carry out ceremonies in request of water and good harvests (Carrion Cachot 1955:12). Water, in and of itself, has always had great religious significance in the Andes. Lakes and springs are considered daughters of the sea and have been worshiped since antiquity.

Perhaps the mythology that surrounds lagoons confers a special aura to this site. Perhaps it is the deep and serene religiousness of my companions or the enchanting remote environment. I cannot say for sure, but there is something gripping about this encounter, a feeling of a different reality, of a great mystery. Andean people do not view nature as existing apart from their own beings. Nature lives and every part of it has its own spirit, power, and personality. It must be approached with sensitivity, respect, and sometimes fear.

As I walk closer to the lagoon, I can see another *mesarumi* on its shore, half immersed in its waters. Juan tells me that on June 24 (the winter solstice and the Fiesta de San Juan celebration for the sheep) and on August 1, when the earth opens up, *paqos* (shamans) spend the night at the lagoon making offerings to Waqraqocha, the lagoon itself; to Mama Waqraqocha, the mother of Waqraqocha, a smaller lagoon found still higher in this rocky terrain; to the two Apus, Waqraqocha and Qellwaqocha; and always to the almighty Pachamama, the Earth Mother. The god of thunder receives special offerings as he is asked to bring rain and to refrain from striking people, their animals, their crops, and their houses.

The *paqos* also implore Waqraqocha to help them be successful diviners and healers throughout the year. At dawn, before the sun rises, they take a bath to purify themselves in the icy waters of this lagoon. On these occasions, *paqos* may approach and even enter the lagoon. This privilege is not granted to the uninitiated, who are believed to disappear in its depth or become ill.

My companions blow more *k'intus* honoring the lagoon and asking her, in return, to grant them a very special wish (see photo 28). Ignacia sits on an elevated rock overlooking the lagoon. There she twists her spindle, converting fleece into strong wool. Like the *paqos* who ask

Photo 28. Blowing *coca k'intus* in honor of Waqraqocha.

Waqraqocha to let them be successful shamans, Ignacia has her own request. As newly elected president of the Women's Committee, she hopes that she and all the women of the village will be successful in cooperatively raising alpacas, fabricating wool, and making weavings beyond their own needs to sell in the valley. The greatest wish of the mothers is to help their families even more in the endless struggle to survive, and Ignacia makes their wish known to the lagoon (see photo 29).

As she sits on the rock in an elegant pose so characteristic of the women of the high Andes, I remember the many occasions when she was the first to help others in spite of many obstacles. A mother of four, she has maintained her beauty despite excruciating work at home by the sooty stove, on the steep potato fields, and on the high pastures. Now she has even greater plans. Using her exceptional organizational skills, she wants to create work that can help everyone in the community. As always, she goes about it with determination, charm, and great joy. And she never forgets to ask the deities for their cooperation.

Photo 29. Ignacia requests Waqraqocha's blessings.

We retreat to a small area surrounded by rocks at a short distance from the lagoon. Leandro opens his *unkuña;* we blow *k'intus* in honor of the lagoon and the Apus, asking for permission to occupy these sacred grounds. Then everyone unpacks his or her contributions to a typical meal—alpaca *ch'arki,* potatoes, *chuño,* and *moraya.* I brought fruit from the valley and chocolates for desert. With great generosity, everyone offers food to the people present. Whether at the side of the sacred lagoon or in their own little adobe huts, daily activities, such as serving food or eating, are ritualized and seem more like sacred activities than everyday necessities.

Farther away from the shores of the lagoon we can talk, though quietly. Everyone is relieved that Waqraqocha has welcomed us with tranquillity. Although I know about the significance of the lagoon in the lives of the people, I do not fully comprehend the relationship between the people and their lagoon. But I will not ask more at this time. There are beliefs and sentiments between a person and the supernatural that must be kept private. Instead we talk about the animals and plants of this region. *Taruka* (deer of the high *puna*) and *wisk'acha* or *vizcacha* (*Lagidium peruvianum*), a rodent closely related to the chinchilla and about the size of a rabbit, are occasionally seen, as are foxes (*atoq*), and from time to time a puma. There are still vicuñas in the wilds of Waqraqocha. My companions tell me that until the 1930s they could be frequently seen, but their numbers have dwindled.[9]

We also see ducks (*wallata*). A bird with a bluish head flies over the rock beside us. "This is the *q'ello pesqo* or *para pesco* (*Sicalis uropygialis*), the rain bird," Modesto comments. He explains that wherever these birds congregate, it will soon rain or snow. None of the other animals that live in this remote region make themselves known. The mere presence of our group of eight people, although silent, keeps most wild animals out of sight. But then my godson points to the rocky cliffs and whispers with excitement, "Mallku!" (*mallku* usually refers to the chief or leader of the condors or to the deity within the condor). We look toward the steep cliffs where Apu Waqraqocha meets the sky. Two condors perform an elegant dance. Their powerful wings almost touch as they circle around each other. Then they take off together, tracing loops against the blue sky before they disappear behind the cliffs.

"These are the birds of the Apus," Modesto whispers. "The Apus are the owners and protectors of wild animals. People who disturb or destroy wild animals bring the anger of the mountain spirits upon themselves. An Apu, when angered, can send malevolent winds (*uraña wayra*)." Yet, many animals are hunted. Their hunters are normally not the Indians themselves, but mestizos and people coming from as far as Bolivia; they have brought animals close to extinction.[10] Everyone agrees that these hunters respect neither the Apus nor the powerful spirits of the animals themselves.

Juan leaves to collect the thin branches of the *maych'a* bush, to use as firewood on June 24, when he will make an offering to Pachamama and the Apus, asking these deities to watch over the health of his sheep. This firewood will be a powerful asset to the ritual. With a *k'intu* he asks Pachamama for permission to reap some of her riches.

While we wait for Juan to return, the slight wind that started to blow increases in strength. Waqraqocha, whose surface was as smooth as a mirror, now sends waves to her shores; their gurgling noises echo against the towering rocks. Then the wind starts to roar ferociously as it hits the rocky peaks above, sending gusts of tremendous intensity our way. The force of the icy wind makes it difficult to open our eyes. "Please hurry!" Modesto exclaims as we pick up our belongings from the ground and run out toward the promontory, past the petrified guardian and its *mesarumi*. "Juan has not returned," I call out into the storm. "He will catch up with us," I faintly hear one of my companions respond. Steep inclines appear. The ground is loose and slippery. I slip, but catch myself before hitting the ground. Ignacia and Modesto come running toward me. Holding hands, we virtually fly down the mountainside. Occasionally I slip, but Modesto and Ignacia, strong and extremely alert, tighten their grip in the brink of time as we continue our race downhill on the flowing rubble, trying to evade the thorny *roq'a* plants. Juan comes in sight, still high up, half buried under a big bushel of *maych'a*.

The downhill race continues. To evade loose and spiny ground, we take constant turns, somewhat like skiing around moguls. Modesto slips close to the edge of a precipice. Like an acrobat he catches himself in midair before ending upright on what could have been a most uncomfortable landing spot. Despite the danger, Modesto and the others laugh, amused by this awkward incident. It is amazing how my companions in their open rubber sandals manage to run sure-footedly through this treacherous terrain. They obviously don't need good hiking boots to master their mountains.

As we reach lower altitudes, the wind subsides and finally dies. Everyone is relieved. I ask how much actual danger this violent storm represented apart from the tremendous cold it brought. "*Ch'aki qhaqya wayra,* the dry thunder storm, is very dangerous," Leandro explains. "It lifts people and animals from the ground and can throw them against the rocks." Everyone nods in agreement. This wind and *muyuq wayra,* the whirlwind, are the kinds of storms believed to carry *mach'aqway,* the great snake, as well as lizards and frogs, in their turbulent funnels. I am glad we escaped its ferocious power, about which I have heard people talk so often.[11]

With the danger gone, we take our time to collect the goods the mountain has to offer. Ignacia discovers seaweed brought from the lagoon through a subterranean rivulet that ends in a small spring. Seaweed, called *qochayuyu* or *llulluch'a,* is a delicacy which we ate during various festivities such as the wedding and Independence Day. We also collect *taqya,* the dried dung of llamas, alpacas, and sheep. It will be used to make a fire in the earthen stoves. Without smell or other unpleasant side effects, this dung is extremely important to the livelihood of people living at high altitudes, where trees are scarce or nonexistent. Dried *qayara* roots that Modesto's son found are equally important.

The sun disappears behind the mountains as we resume our rapid pace; we must arrive at Roberto's house before nightfall. We thank one another for the companionship in this journey to the lagoon, an adventure that has brought us closer together. We were in great danger but Waqraqocha spared us. "We must return some day," Modesto suggests with a smile. "You must also meet Mama Waqraqocha!" Juan nods in agreement. He knows that he came too close to the sacred lagoon when he collected firewood. But nobody mentions it and he will make offerings to the great Waqraqocha, asking for forgiveness.

Roberto awaits us in front of his house. The old man knows about the storm. Perhaps the dark shadows that moved across the rocky peaks told him that Waqraqocha was aroused.

Tragedy and Triumph—
Chillihuani Will Call
Forever

Icy nights, dusty whirlwinds, torrential rains, hail and thunder, deadly bolts of lightning—these are the realities of Chillihuani. Still, they are soon forgotten as I yearn to go back. Images flash through my mind of the hot days in July when the mountainsides have turned velvety brown with patches of yellowish *ichu* grass that sways softly in the wind. Where springs emerge and rivulets crisscross the landscape, the grass takes on different shades of green which stand out against the brown and reddish hues of the soil. Gray rocks in suggestive shapes stud the captivating landscape with its majestic Apus in their white ponchos that glow against the horizon. I think of the mornings when the first rays of the sun fall onto millions of tiny frost crystals, converting the landscape into a silvery sparkling paradise that slowly gives way to the velvety brown of a dry, sunny day.

With the early rains of spring, the fields and pastures take on a light-green hue that intensifies during the rainy season. Fog conceals the mountains much of the time. Yet, when the wind blows away the fog's thick cover, permitting the sun's rays to penetrate, the landscape assumes a luminosity of an almost surrealistic nature, reflected in the billions of raindrops that cling to the damp vegetation. Only the wind, the occasional cry of a bird, and the shuffling feet of grazing alpacas interrupt the silence. And sometimes, when the fiestas and *faenas* are in progress, the silence is broken by the laughter of a wedding party, the hooves of galloping horses, or the busy shuffling of communal work parties clearing the village paths. During fiestas the large *niwa* hats of the herders' festive attire join the *ichu* grass swaying in the wind, while the colorful symbols woven into their clothes contrast with the soft umber hues of the landscape.

As I think of Chillihuani I remember the spiritual serenity and wisdom of the herders' lives today; the insight they provide into a once-glorious past and a most unpredictable future. I treasure the *chansana-kuy*—the joking and laughing—and the dancing throughout the night to the haunting melodies of the flute and drum that make one forget the problems of everyday life.

Just as the beauty of the landscape can, in an instant, turn into a playground for deadly forces bringing devastating winds, hail, and lightning, so the lives of the people can take swift, unexpected, and tragic turns. In August the winds *muyuq wayra, ch'aki qhaqya wayra,* and sometimes *tutuka wayra* are devastating as they attack houses, animals, and even the strongest of people who cross their paths. In September I received an envelope with my address written in a handwriting that I did not recognize. It contained a letter folded in the same complex way in which offerings are wrapped during rituals. I froze as I read the words: "Our beloved mother has died suddenly as she returned from her potato field at night. We found her on the trail leading to our house. We are so very, very sad. Please return soon." It was signed by Ignacia's fifteen-year-old daughter in the name of her family. This was at the end of August, when the *uraña wayra,* the devastating winds, are most ferocious.

Ignacia exemplified the indomitable spirit of the high-altitude herders. Joyful and exuberant, she went about her work for family and community alike. She wanted to see progress, to improve her people's living conditions without changing their Indian identity. She insisted on maintaining the Quechua language, traditional clothing, indigenous religion, and worldview, and she felt it was right to remain *punaruna,* a Quechua person of the high *puna.* Her limitless initiative, insight, and energy made up for her lack of formal education. She always went forward, even in the face of almost insurmountable obstacles. From the first time I met Ignacia, I knew she would be capable of helping her society rise above its marginal economic existence with just a little support. But she died young.

When I returned to Chillihuani a year later, I was still full of sadness about the loss of this special friend. Three of Ignacia's children came to meet me at the *curandero's* house. I asked for their younger brother, an intelligent eight-year-old boy. "He died when we prepared *chuño,*" the children lamented. Thus he had died shortly before his mother. We cried together. For some time I was worried about this family. How would they make out in view of these tragedies? But in the course of the dry season, it became quite clear that the children followed in their mother's footsteps. Telesfora, the sixteen-year-old daughter, almost seamlessly took over the role of her mother. She holds the family together and performs the manifold tasks of a woman in the high Andes. Little six-year-old Cerila clings to her sister and respects her decisions in the absence of her beloved mother. She has begun to learn from her sister to weave the intricate ancient patterns into her clothes. Esteban, their eighteen-year-old brother, a handsome young man who has learned the responsibilities of a son and who is being initiated into those of a community member, does much-appreciated work with his father in the private and public spheres of life.

The death of Ignacia caused much sadness, but her spirit continues to dwell in the village and her ideals become realities through her children and other outstanding villagers. Again, the resilience of the highland people comes to the surface.

The famous Peruvian author and anthropologist José María Arguedas grew up with the Indians of the Andes and became a most outspoken defender of Quechua Indian rights. But he lost hope that the situation of the Indians would ever improve. At a meeting with friends who were saddened by his depressed outlook, one of them asked: "José María, what can we do so you will regain hope and a will to live?" The answer of this preeminent Peruvian was, "Prevent the arrival of the conquerors." In 1969 José María Arguedas committed suicide.

For eight years I have had the good fortune and honor to participate in the serene and captivating life of Chillihuani. I have learned much, but I know there is still much more to discover. The understanding I have thus far gained leads me to believe that the people of this village, and the essence of their culture and their worldview, will survive for a long time to come. As I watch them weave intricate Inca symbols into their clothes, honor their ancestors, till the soil of their beloved Pachamama with pride and dedication, sing and dance through the night to ancient tunes and ride their horses across the precipitous barrenness of the high *puna,* or walk for miles through thundering storms to help others in distress, I know they have the strength to survive in their beloved mountains, one of the most marginal regions on earth. At any time, but especially when life becomes too difficult—almost unbearable—they perform their rituals of respect. With these gestures they place their grief in perspective and absorb new strength from the cosmos of which they are a part and with which they share *enqa,* the force that transcends all life.

NOTES

Chapter 1 · Ascent to the Realm of the Apus

1. *Compadres* are neither consanguine nor affine parents, but rather spiritual parents. They are usually selected for the baptism of a child, a first hair cutting, or a wedding. *Compadre* is a reciprocal term of address between parent and godfather of a child; *comadre* is the godmother of the child. Godparent and godchild assume reciprocal rights and responsibilities.

2. To make *chicha,* maize (corn) must be soaked in water for several days. It is then placed into a pot covered with vegetable matter such as *ichu* grass. After one or two weeks the maize sprouts, at which time the substance is referred to as *jora* or *wiñapu. Jora* contains the enzymes necessary to change starch into sugar. In order to prevent further germination, the *jora* must be dried in the sun. It is then ground on a millstone and is mixed with water to form a dough. Little by little the dough is mixed with boiling water, is kept boiling for several hours, and is then kept in the pot overnight. The next morning it is boiled again, strained through a piece of cloth, and put into an *urpu,* a large jar, where it ferments for three days.

3. Catherine Allen (1988:23) showed remarkable perception in her exploration of the deep significance of *coca* in the lives of the highland Indians.

4. Daniel Gade (1975:155–156) explained: "Quinoa stalks are macerated, dried and burned; the ashes are then collected and formed into a ball the size of a golf ball, a bit of which is chewed with *coca* leaves to extract the alkaloid in the leaf."

5. Peruvian obstetrician Sara Teresa Rivero Luque (1995:240–241) has listed the elements in 100 grams of *coca* leaves (306 calories) as follows: proteins 18.9 g; carbohydrates 46.2 g; fat 3.3 g; fiber 14.2 g; water 7.2 g; vitamin A 14,000 iu; alpha carotene 2.65 mg; vitamin B1 0.68 mg; vitamin B2 1.73 mg; vitamin B6 0.58 mg; beta carotene 20 mg; vitamin C 53 mg; vitamin E 44.10 mg; vitamin G; nicotinic acid 5 mg; vitamin H 0.54 mg; organic acids 3.2 mg; natural alkaloids 75 mg. Minerals: Al 49 mg, C 1.1 mg; P 911.8 mg; Ba 17 mg; Cr 0.23 mg; Mg 0.37 mg; Bo 24 mg; Sr 204 mg; Mn 0.5 mg; Ca 1,540 mg; Fe 45.8 mg; K 1.9 mg.

6. Daniel Gade (1975:104–106) divided the vertical zones of the Vilcanota Valley into six major ecological regions based on Inca tradition: Puna, Suni, Quechua or Keshwa (I use Keshwa, as pronounced by the Indian people), Chaupiyunga, Yunga, and Rupa Rupa. The first three, which are the higher zones, exist in the area we must traverse.

7. During the 1980s International Development efforts between Peru and Germany (GTZ) helped to provide enough irrigation water to allow peasant farmers to plant a second crop, mainly vegetables (see Bolin 1987, 1990b, 1994).

8. Antolín explains that this malevolent wind causes an illness called *soq'a wayra*. People may be affected by becoming thin and weak; often they cannot speak; they sweat and freeze intermittently and froth at the mouth. A person may die within a few hours. Only *curanderos* can cure this sickness.

9. I was told this same story and sometimes parts of it several times later in Chillihuani, mostly by older people. Upon those occasions I asked when the time of the god Churi will come to an end. I received different answers. An old lady asserted that six harvests (years) will go by. The centenarian Roberto predicted that when the snow on Apu Ausangate has melted, this world will come to an end. He believes this will take between 100 and 150 years.

10. Trepanation was practiced during Inca times when square, rectangular, or round holes were cut into skulls. We do not know the degree to which the Incas knew about the brain or the purpose these procedures had apart from releasing pressure.

11. Sabine MacCormack (1991:425) described burial practices in *mach'ayas* (mountain caves) in the Sierra. In her comparison of funerary ceremonials, p. 427, she pointed to significant continuities in belief and ritual.

Chapter 2 · Suyay Ch'isin—a Night of Secret Rituals

1. See also Bastien (1985), Flores Ochoa (1977), Oscar Núñez del Prado (1984a). Thomas and Helga Müller (1984:168) observed during their fieldwork in Q'ero that "most of the fiestas which are said to be Christian (because of their denomination and the date at which they occur) or Western are, in fact, explicitly Andean."

2. Ina Rösing (1990:40) observed among the Kallawaya in Bolivia that *illa* water is collected from various springs. It contains the souls of white, brown, and black alpacas and llamas.

3. David and Rosalinda Gow (1975:149) stated: "This is the most secret of rituals and it is almost impossible that outsiders can observe it." At a later date when we had become close friends, the Mamani family and other families gave me permission to describe the rituals in detail for this book and to publish pictures.

4. Anthropologist Douglas Sharon (1978:42) wrote that performing a *mocha* (blowing a kiss) is a pre-Columbian gesture of reverence for sacred places

and objects that has maintained its importance to the present day among highland Indians.

5. Although the Apus are much honored during this night, the people of Chillihuani assert that the most important of all deities is Pachamama, the Earth Mother, of which the Apus are a part.

6. David and Rosalinda Gow (1975:150) found that in spite of considerable regional variations, the words *enka, enkaychu, inkaychu, hispa,* and *illa* are synonymous. The rituals in Chillihuani clearly show, however, that *enqa* is the life force contained within the *enqaychu.* John Rowe (1963:297) found that *illas* were used in pre-Columbian Peru as amulets; see also Flores Ochoa (1977:211–237).

7. Arriaga ([1621] 1968:11) observed that Indians recognize deity in small things. Gow and Gow (1975:147, 150) remarked that *enqaychu* in the form of alpacas possess the spirit and life force of the livestock.

8. Some people in Chillihuani maintain that *ch'allay* and *ch'uyay* have the same meaning. Others say that *ch'allay* is to sprinkle *chicha* into the air or onto the animals proper while *ch'uyay* means to pour *chicha,* wine, or alcohol onto the *enqaychu* or onto the four corners of an *unkuña* or a *mesarumi.*

9. The herders of Chillihuani refer to an offering as *haywa, ofrenda* (S), *despacho* (S), and *pago* (S). *T'inka* is a ritual toast which is made by flicking drops of a beverage into the air using thumb and forefinger. *Phukuy* is a ritual offering in which one blows over *coca* to share it with the deities. See also Glynn Custred (1979:380–381) regarding the terminology used to designate an offering.

10. Tom Zuidema (1982:430) stated that the reason why in the preparation of sacrifices during Inca times "all *huacas,* places of worship, trees, wells, mountains and lakes would obtain part of the sacrifice, was that they held it as an omen that no one would be missed, in order that the one that was missed in the sacrifice would not be angry and out of angriness would punish the Inca."

11. The chronicler Martín de Murúa ([1590] 1946:294) wrote that the old people who lived in Inca times recounted that when they made a sacrifice they offered, among other things, seashells, which they called *mollo,* to the fountains and springs, saying that the seashells were daughters of the sea, mother of all waters.

12. The people of Chillihuani and Cusipata explain that incense (*q'apachi, incienso* [S]) is obtained by burning the hardened resin of the incense tree. Bastien (1985:137) stated that this incense is the resin of a tree slashed so that it cries and its tears harden to be collected by another harvester in the year following, who then slashes another tree to reciprocate.

13. Terry West (1988:196) stated that among the Aymara of Bolivia the *illas* are sprinkled with the blood of a sacrificed animal. This is not a custom in Chillihuani.

14. See also Rösing (1990). Jorge Lira (1953:128) commented on the danger of watching an offering burn. Ellen White, in a personal communication, stated that among the Coast Salish tribes of British Columbia, Canada, the burning of ritual items is too sacred to be observed.

15. Irene Silverblatt (1987:185) stated, "The indigenous metaphor for giving offerings and showing devotion to divinities was 'feeding them.' And ever since the Spanish conquest, when Christian gods began to compete with native deities, the *huacas* were hungry: the normative prescription that guided the relationship between Andean people and their deities had been undermined."

Chapter 3 · Thunder God and Sacrifice

1. Father Pablo Joseph de Arriaga (1968:23) wrote the following in 1621 in his book, *The Extirpation of Idolatry in Peru:* "They [the Indians] also worship Libiac, or lightning, which is very common in the mountains, and many of them take the name and surname Libiac or Hillapa, which means the same thing." During the seventeenth century, as part of a campaign against animistic beliefs, names such as Liviac, Llibia, or Santiago, given to a baby born when lightning brightened the sky, were forbidden. Gade (1983:779) referenced Arriaga ([1621] 1968) and Villagomes ([1649] 1919:267). Yet, occasionally one can find these names in the heights of the Andes.

2. Gade (1983:770, 772) stated that Illapa tends to have a figurative meaning today, while Qhaqya, onomatopoeic in derivation and Aymara in origin, has a more concrete usage than Illapa and may also imply the evil spirit in lightning. He further remarked that Qhaqya is in some regions of the Andes referred to as *kaxya, ccacya,* or *caccha.* These are Aymara words which are also used by Quechua speakers in southern Peru. The people of Chillihuani explain that the expression Qhaqya is sometimes replaced by the Spanish term *rayo,* which literally means "thunderbolt" in Spanish but may also include lightning and the sound of thunder. When lightning flashes intermittently through the sky, the Chillihuani herders refer to this phenomenon as Qhaqya *lliphipipimusian.* Some herders assert that lightning is female while thunder is male.

3. The divine tripartite deity Illapa, the Inca god of thunder, is in different parts of the Andes known under a variety of other names such as Lipiaq, Libiac, and Chuki Illa. See Yaranga Valderrama (1979:697).

4. María Rostworowski (1983:21) stated that in the chronicles we find that each divinity has its double, called "brother" by the indigenous people. They believed that each god had a replica in the same way as each Inca had his *huauque* or "brother."

5. For more information on Illapa see also Acosta ([1589] 1962), Cobo ([1653] 1956), Gade (1983), Rösing (1990), Rowe (1963), Yaranga Valderrama (1979), and Rodrigo Hernández Príncipe ([1622] 1923), a priest whose aim it

was to get to the roots of idolatry in the northern highlands of Peru.

6. Antimony (Sb) is a silvery white, brittle, metallic chemical element of crystalline structure which is found only in combination.

7. Angélica Aranguren Paz (1975:127–128) observed among the herders of Puno that animals that have died by a stroke of lightning receive the same burial rituals as do humans. After eight days the departure of their spirit is acknowledged through rituals. This is not practiced in Chillihuani. She further observed that during the celebrations of *compadres* and *comadres,* offerings are made to the thunder god by those who have been punished by this deity.

8. Mary Ann Cooper (1980:134) in her article "Lightning Injuries: Prognostic Signs for Death" stated that "many civilizations have revered ground frequently struck by lightning as sacred."

9. Rostworowski (1983:22–23) stated that the indigenous people saw the world in double perspective in such a way that opposite forces were at the same time complementary.

10. These happenings are considered miraculous events; the medical literature, however, discusses in great detail how lightning can paralyze the nervous system, momentarily stop the heart, and lead to spontaneous recovery. See Cooper (1980), Gade (1983:775), and Taussig (1968).

11. Gade (1983:782) wrote, "Eye witnesses to a lightning strike are considered to be future victims, because Santiago does not like to be surprised in the act. For that reason, an unscathed cohort looks away from his stricken companion rather than rush to his aid."

12. In the course of his research in the Vilcanota Valley, Gade (1983:781) found that a black metallic stone of this type (*bala*) is believed to have been brought to earth by lightning.

13. Other investigators have observed that Qoa (Ccoa) is central to a myriad of metaphors widely perceived in the Andean world. Bernard Mishkin (1963: 463–464), in his study of Kauri near Cuzco, learned that Ccoa, sometimes called Cacya, is the most active of the spirits, the most feared, and intimately involved in the daily lives of the people. It destroys crops and kills with lightning. Douglas Sharon (1978:98) wrote that "today it is believed that during the rainy season the *ccoa* cat emerges from highland springs (*puqyos*) in the form of clouds." He further stated that it is believed that this supernatural being strikes the novice with lightning (p. 99).

14. Flannery, Marcus, and Reynolds (1989:83–84) described a sacrifice in the Ayacucho region of Peru which differs in several aspects from that in Chillihuani. Flannery et al. explained that the animal's feet are tied together; it is rolled over on its side. The person in charge cuts through the back of the neck into the juncture between the atlas vertebra and the occipital condyles of the skull. He then cuts the spinal cord. The pain is brief. The llama's feet must be untied quickly in order to enable it to kick, which indicates that the llama's spirit is running back to the corral.

Terry West's (1988:196) observations of the sacrifice of llamas and sheep in Pampa Aullagas in Bolivia are different as well. There the animal is cut in the throat and the blood is sprinkled over the *illas.*

15. Pre-conquest Andeans saw parallels in the creation of both humans and camelids. Wiraqocha, the creator god, is considered to be a divinity that incorporates both male and female elements. David and Rosalinda Gow (1975:150) were told by their informants that "*la pancha*" was an alpaca born with male and female sexual organs and that it was regarded with great respect. If anyone were to kill a *pancha,* this would put the whole herd in danger. Informants furthermore asserted that the first alpacas were female and black and that their ancestors (*machula*) had had black alpacas for a long time.

16. Sabine MacCormack (1991:171) in her ethnohistorical studies discovered that "llamas were represented as interacting with humans on an equal footing, and indeed as adopting human roles—this being what they still do in the puna around Cuzco."

Chapter 4 · Fertility Rites in the Muyukancha

1. *Curanderos* say that *maych'a,* a bush with small yellow flowers, is also used as medicine in case of a sprain, break, or blow. It is rubbed into the skin or plastered onto it. *Maych'a* is also a derogatory term for a healer.

2. Sabine MacCormack (1991:167) quoted Cristóbal de Molina, who witnessed sacrifices during Inti Raymi, the Festival of the Sun, shortly after the conquest. As the sun rose, a prayer was said: "Maker, Sun and Thunder, may you always be young, may the peoples multiply, and may they live in peace."

3. For example, to make *kispiño, chuño, moraya,* flour, and wheat are mixed with blood. *Lonqa* (tripe), is also cut up and mixed with blood. *Chalchi* is prepared with blood, onion, potatoes, *chuño,* and so on. It looks like a cake and is delicious when cooked.

Chapter 5 · Pukllay Martes—the Incas Invite

1. Gade (1975:203) stated that the Andes have given the potato to the world. It was probably first domesticated in the altiplano of southern Peru and northern Bolivia. "In this region one finds the greatest amount of speciation and clonal elaboration as well as the highest degree of integration of this crop in the culture." Gade also found that the potato grows from 1,850 to 4,340 meters above sea level.

2. In making *chuño,* the potatoes are sorted according to size and put on dry *ichu* grass spread out on the ground. Depending on the size of the potatoes and the degree of frost at night, they are left out for about ten days, exposed to the extreme cold at night and the drying sun during the day. Each morning some family members—sometimes the whole family—walk on the potatoes with their bare feet to squeeze out the moisture. The dehydrated potatoes be-

come hard and turn a grayish-black color. They are then placed into a *taqe,* a cylindrical basket-like container made of straw, where they can be kept for up to ten years.

3. The processing of *moraya* is more complicated than that of *chuño.* Usually, high-quality *mallqu* potatoes are placed onto *ichu* grass and covered with *ichu* for about six days and nights. Then, with their bare feet, people squeeze the moisture out of the potatoes which, in the process, become flat, and lose their skins and their acidity. In this state they are placed into a pond or rivulet where they remain for about ten days before they are again put onto the ground on top of *ichu* grass for another week. During all this time they are covered and thereby retain their whitish color. Finally they are squeezed again in the usual way, dried, and stored in a *taqe,* where they can be kept for up to three years.

Timing is important in the preparation of *chuño* and *moraya* and differs in relation to environmental factors as well as the kind of potato used. Both *chuño* and *moraya* lose most of their weight during the freeze-drying process. During Inca times many storehouses were kept full of freeze-dried potatoes in anticipation of drought, flood, or other agricultural catastrophes.

4. Poole (1991:337) stated that "circular dances called *qashwas* are frequently performed during carnival and harvest festivals from May to June. These circular dances . . . are specifically associated with fertility rituals and the ritual battles that are believed to lead to increased fertility for both competing sides." See also Alencastre and Dumezil (1953).

5. *Taki* means song; *tusuy* means dance. Yet *taki* can stand for both song and dance. John Rowe (1963:290) stated that among the Incas, "the usual name for a ritual dance was *taki,* which also means singing." As is the case in Chillihuani today, the dance steps were very simple in ancient times.

6. Deborah Poole (1991:337) stated that in pre-Spanish dance traditions, circular forms were specifically associated with war dances—see Cobo ([1653] 1956:271)—or with the recitation of imperial historical narrative. See also Betanzos ([1551] 1924:158) and Murúa ([1590] 1922:130–131).

7. Whipping during a dance has been noticed by other investigators. Carter (1977:208) described an Andean dance in which whipping plays a central role. "The band began to play, and they danced first a *waynu,* the Aymara love dance, punctuated by threatening gestures of their whips. The music then abruptly changed to the tune of the *achuqalla,* and each dancer began to whip the other violently on the calves of his legs. After some five minutes, the music reverted to the original *waynu* tune, the whipping and threats ceased and a symbolic reconciliation occurred as the partners changed steps, alternatively locked arms and hands, and pursued the classic dance of endearment and social acceptance." Allen (1988:184) found that when women participate, they whip even stronger. Men were expected to seek out partners from other communities. See also Remy (1991) for an analysis of ritual battles.

Chapter 6 · Survival Today and a Look into the Past

1. In different regions the ritual festivity of *señalupampay* may be called one of the following: *señaluqepi, señalay, ninriseñala, ninrikuchuy, ninripampana,* or *ninripampay.*

2. In recent years I have helped to introduce solar cookers funded by the Landkreis Böblingen in Germany, which are much appreciated during the dry season but cannot be used throughout much of the lengthy rainy season; see Bolin (1992).

3. I asked other people whether in the past the predominant color for hats and outfits was white and black. No one was certain or even knew about it. Perhaps Roberto talks about times long past. The chronicler and priest Bernabé Cobo ([1653] 1956:208) stated that the Incas wore black-and-white costumes during certain fiestas at the time of the conquest. Tom Zuidema's (1990b:161) ethnohistorical research revealed that "on the night of the full moon after the December solstice noblemen and women, dressed in black and crowned with white feathers, danced through all the streets of the town. . . ."

4. Roberto and his age-mates used to wear braids. He told us that men wore one braid down the back of the head and that women have always worn two braids.

5. Gary Urton (1993:132) wrote: "Unripened peaches and *tunas* (cactus fruit) were the missiles of choice in Pacariqtambo in the ritual battles of the 1980s and in the playful taunting between youths in the 1940s, as described by Muelle."

6. Modesto explained that a *pillu* is like a hat that protects the back of the head and neck. It is made of llama and alpaca fur of various colors. The *pillu* is no longer used.

7. José María Arguedas wrote in his famous book *Los ríos profundos* (*Deep Rivers;* 1991:14): "The Indians call these turbid rivers "*Yawar mayu*" . . . and they also call the violent time of war dances, "*yawar mayu*" (river of blood)."

8. See also Alencastre and Dumezil (1953) and Gilt Contreras (1966). Robert Randall (1987:87) wrote that a ritual battle symbolizes the victory of abundance and fertility over hunger and drought in the past and today. Michael Sallnow (1991:299) reported that in Qamawara, in the Department of Cuzco, forty years ago "the *tinkuy* was explicitly portrayed as a sacrifice, or at least a bloodletting, to the local *Apus* in return for the fertility of the soil and the welfare of people and animals."

9. The *yawar mayu* is part of a whole choreography of dances called *maqt'acha tusuy.*

10. In North America, Europe, and various other parts of the world, crowds cheer during Spanish bullfights, boxing matches, football, hockey, auto racing, and other potentially injurious events. In Germany in the past, and still today, students belonging to certain fraternities engage in a type of fencing

which leads to injuries, primarily in the face, which draw blood and lead to scars which some young men carry with pride. In Spain people continue to mutilate themselves as they walk on their bare knees with chains around their ankles along asphalt or cobblestone streets during Holy Week. In Hindu societies, while in a state of trance, people push hooks through their skin and thin iron rods through their tongues and cheeks during Thaipusam. Terrible physical pain is endured in the Philippines by young men who have themselves nailed to a cross at Easter.

Chapter 7 • Munanakuy—Falling in Love

1. Several investigators have observed this type of opposition between the *puna* and the *llaqta* (town) in different parts of the Andes. Sallnow (1991:301) stated that "the descent from the high *punas* to the intermontane valley is a movement from the unbounded field of wild, uncontrolled fertility to the bounded domain of society and controlled reproduction." In the same context, Deborah Poole (1991:330) observed that "a typical Andean settlement pattern, for example, opposes a central village to the fields which lie around it, while these lands are subsequently opposed to the less populated, uncultivated, and hence symbolically 'wild' *punas*." Billie Jean Isbell (1985:89–97) discussed opposing forces—the "savage *puna*" versus the "civilized village" —in Chuschino social and economic organization.

2. In Chillihuani the high *puna* is referred to as *hatun puna*. Some investigators refer to the high *puna* as *sallqa*. The herders of Chillihuani assert that *sallqa* means an inaccessible region.

3. Carter (1977:185) stated that in the high Andes a certain degree of hostility on the part of the young woman's family seems to be both expected and ritualized. William Stein (1961:138–139) observed during his studies in the Peruvian village of Hualcan that "the traditional occasion for courtship is when the girl is pasturing on the hills. The boy passes by while the girl is watching her herd. He throws a stone or a clump of dirt at her, and if she returns in kind, the occasion is ripe for his approach." Stein further stated that the lovers meet often in the *cuklla* (called *ch'uklla* in Chillihuani), a brush hut, which remains a sentimental object even after marriage for the people from Hualcan. Old couples sometimes make arrangements with each other to meet on the hill, where courtship can be a never-ending process.

4. Carter (1977:181–183) described a similar organization, called Q'achwa, in the Bolivian Aymara community of Irpa Chico, which was created as a meeting place where young people can dance and get to know one another.

5. The healer tells me that formerly the fighting at borderlines was more forceful in the last attempt of a young man to prevent the woman he loves from dancing into another man's *suyu*. He asserts that nowadays only "clean fighting" is allowed—that is, only bare hands can be used.

6. *Suwanakuy,* the stealing game, has never included force. The young

people of Chillihuani often plead with a big smile on their faces: "Steal me, please steal me and take me to your country." Carter (1977:183) observed that in the highlands of Bolivia, "Most liaisons begin with what is commonly referred to as bride theft. Since such theft is always with the full consent of the girl and, in fact, often is something she imposes on her lover, the act can hardly be called theft."

7. Dances performed by high-altitude dance groups often portray this much-cherished custom of stealing a bride or a groom. In the dance the young man carries the young woman over his back, or the woman carries the man, which causes laughter among all.

Chapter 8 • Rimanakuy—a Wedding Andean Style

1. *Rimanakuy* means literally "conversation among various people." The term *rimanakuy* is used when a young man asks the parents of a young girl their permission to marry. In some regions a wedding is referred to as *warmichakuy* (Oscar Núñez del Prado 1984b:124), *tincunacuy* (Carter 1977:178), or *serviciado* and *huatanacuy* (Carter 1977:214).

2. I did not participate in this night of rituals. I obtained the information from the people involved and from many discussions on the subject area with other villagers.

3. The first hair cutting, called *chukcha rutukuy* in Quechua, is believed to be a pre-Columbian custom. It takes place when a child is between the age of one and six years. In 1994 I was asked by the parents of Anali, a five-year-old who lives in the heights of Chillihuani, to be *madrina* of her first hair cutting. On the day of the ritual, together with family and friends, we took a seat on a stone bench by the *mesarumi*. An empty plate and a pair of scissors with a white ribbon attached were placed on the *mesarumi*. As *madrina* I started to cut the first lock off her hair and put it into the plate together with a gift in the form of money. Then I gave the scissors to Anali's father, mother, aunts, uncles, and visitors. Each person cut off a lock and placed it into the plate together with a gift. Antolín was elected to be secretary, and he noted the gifts given and/or promised on a sheet of paper. Among other things, Anali was promised clothes, an alpaca, and a sheep. After the second round of hair cutting, Anali's cut hair was put into a little bunch and tied together with a red string. When all promises are fulfilled—that is, when Anali has received all her gifts—her hair will be buried at a sacred place in the womb of Pachamama. The kind and amount of gifts a child receives depends on the property a family owns and the behavior of the young people. Love for a child and responsibility shown on the part of an offspring also figure prominently in what a child receives.

4. *Cargo* is Spanish for "burden". All men of an Indian community are expected to take part in the *cargo* system, in which young men start with such tasks as cleaning the church or the office of the village council and may end

up as village judge and/or village president. These *cargos*, combined with the sponsoring of fiestas, lead to much prestige, but they are financially draining.

5. Zuidema (1973:19) further explained that in Inca times "all the descendants of a great grandfather could be called metaphorically 'brother' and 'sister' as they included all the nonmarriageable kin."

6. For the interpretation of some symbols, see Desrosiers (1992), Franquemont, Franquemont, and Isbell (1992), Phipps (1992), Ann Rowe (1987), Silverman-Proust (1991), Ulloa Torres and Gavilan (1992), and Zorn (1987).

7. The first son or daughter is called in Quechua *piwi* or *kuraq*, the second one is *chawpi*, the third *sullk'a*. Further children are referred to as *chanakuman qatiq* (not all people agreed with this). The last is always *chanaku*.

8. *Varayoq* derives from the Spanish term *vara* (staff) and the Quechua term *yoq* (with); thus "the one with the staff." A *varayoq* is an individual who has a *cargo*, which is a political or religious office in the political-religious hierarchy, the *varayoq* system of a community. All men of an Indian community are expected to take part in the *varayoq* system. In the beginning young people must assume simple *cargos* (burdens) such as carrying messages or cleaning offices and the church. Later they must take over major *cargos* such as sponsoring a fiesta. As a villager moves up through this hierarchy of obligations, he is rewarded with increasing prestige.

In Chillihuani the *cargo* system is still maintained but the authorities no longer carry a staff.

Chapter 9 • Casarakuy

1. In some regions of the Andes, *casarakuy* is referred to as *runachakuy* or *warmichakuy* and by the Spanish terms *matrimonio religioso* (religious wedding) and *matrimonio católico* (Catholic wedding).

2. Processes of transformation as they occur during weddings and other rites of passage are of deep concern to the Andean people. Morinis and Crumrine (1991:11) look at pilgrimage as a way to achieve transformation: "While pilgrimages are not rites of passage in the strict sense of birth, initiation, marriage, or death, all share important features. Like the latter, pilgrimages are meant to be transformative processes, from which the individual emerges altered from his or her previous situation. While in rites of passage this change is focused on alterations in social status, in pilgrimage the transformation is more commonly concerned with changing personal matters such as health, mental state, and spiritual life."

3. The transitory aspect of male and female elements becomes further evident in that in Andean society there are "male" tasks and "female" tasks. This does not mean, however, that males always engage in male tasks and females always do female tasks. Some female tasks, such as weaving and knitting are, in fact, often carried out by men.

4. Irene Silverblatt (1987:90) quoted early investigators who observed that

the Incas celebrated yearly mass marriages in the villages they conquered. Tom Zuidema (1992:271) noted that in Inca times, "Marriages were concluded in the dry season," as is the case in Chillihuani as well.

5. Gerardo Reichel-Dolmatoff (1978:18–19), in his studies in Colombia, observed the counterclockwise circuit in certain rituals of the Kogi Indians. He has maintained that this ritual is based upon the fact that "the sun delimits sacred space by tracing a line from left to right (west to east) and then continues northward." He noted that "the concept of inversion, which is so important in the Kogi worldview, is obviously related to the ray of light falling through a focal point, which is the articulation of two cones joined by their tips, as exemplified by the chain of inverted temples."

6. One also hears the melody at dawn, at about 5:00 A.M., to get up; next to take breakfast, between 7 A.M. and 8 A.M.; for lunch, between 12 P.M. and 1 P.M.; and for supper, between 4 P.M. and 5 P.M. (as well as after meals and on selected other occasions).

7. This prayer goes as follows: "Bendito y alabado sea el santísimo sacramento del altar y la virgen concebida sin mancha y sin pecado original desde el primer instante de su ser natural. Amen."

8. This plant, which grows in rocky fields, has delicate dark spines, yellow flowers, and dark red seeds which are used to make a refreshing drink. It also has medical properties and is used against fever.

9. The disrupting element represented by the *yana uyakuna* is also found in dance groups elsewhere. Poole (1991:322–323) stated: "The alzados (Spanish: 'rebel; mutineer; insolent; or fraudulent person'), are one of a number of dance groups in Cuzco which represent clowns, ruffians, or 'wildmen.' Like other dancing trickster figures, the alzados have a highly improvisatory choreographic style, based for the most part on mocking and satirizing through chaotic or obscene gestures the formations of the other, more serious dances theirs is intended to deride. Alzados not only chide the sobriety of other dancers, but also flaunt in the most extravagant and lewd manner possible the established order of the entire fiesta. As such, they represent a chaotic element of disorder constantly present at the fringes of the pilgrimage and procession they attend."

10. Processes of transformation or transition relate to a multitude of phenomena. Randall (1982:44) wrote: "Evil spirits called *soq'a* are also said to cause diseases and death and have their greatest powers at dawn, dusk and the full moon (all periods of transition)."

11. In the highlands of Peru, winter is the dry season, which lasts from May to October and is characterized by hot sunny days and very cold nights.

12. I observed the same sequence of events with straight and circular movements during a wedding in 1992.

13. Several researchers have studied the meaning of linear and circular movements. Zuidema (1982:444) stated: "Descriptions of modern rituals of

people addressing themselves (i.e. traveling) to a shrine, make clear that traveling to the shrine is done in as direct a way as possible; returning from the shrine however is done in a non-ritual way—by following the normal road (e.g., Bastien 1985, chapter 9)." Deborah Poole (1991:326) suggested that the ordering of dance sequences "resembles the sequential structure of pilgrimage itself: linear hierarchical movement into a sacred center; movement around the sacred precinct; and the renewal or regeneration of individuals as a result of this combined linear and circular movement."

14. Isbell (1985:138) wrote that the cross is a dominant Andean symbol that has multiple referents. Among other things it symbolizes fertility and abundance.

15. Poole (1991:326–327) has argued that dance formations are initially structured around two parallel columns of dancers. "Parallel hierarchies of dancers evoke the dual organization of moiety-divided communities, in which each moiety maintains its own hierarchy of political-religious authorities (Palomino 1984; Urton 1984). A similar dual structure provided the foundation for the elaborate Inca imperial system of parallel dynasties and 'brother' kings (Zuidema 1964, 1982) and also appears in models of Inca and Quechua kinship systems (Isbell 1985; Zuidema 1973)."

16. In 1780 Tupac Amaru II and his wife, Micaela Bastides, began a rebellion against the injustices done to the native people. This rebellion also gave rise to a revival of Inca customs and religion. Qoyllur Rit'i, located within the general territory of Tupac Amaru II, was a meeting place for tens of thousands of indigenous people from many different regions and a center for a revival of the traditional Andean religion. Randall (1982:41) related that in 1780 the Archbishop Moscoso "seized the opportunity to try to replace a pre-Conquest rite with a Catholic one." See also Gow (1974:55) and Randall (1982:40) for details regarding this apparent miracle.

17. Among the blackfaces it is not a common practice to carry a doll. Yet during Salvador and Justa's wedding one of the blackfaces' "wives" wore a small doll.

18. In all the festive and sacred occasions in the high Andes in which I have participated, it has been consistently believed that what happens during a particular festivity will become the rule throughout the coming year. Thus the strong element of order represented by the *ukukus* within the chaos of sound and movement at Qoyllur Rit'i reflects the cosmological order of the coming year. The chaos in which the world finds itself after the disappearance of the Pleiades will return to order with the reappearance of this important constellation.

19. Deborah Poole (1991:320) suggested that "whipping has long been an important part of initiation ceremonies in the Andes where it symbolizes regeneration and renewal." See also Cobo ([1653] 1956:210–211) and Molina ([1575] 1943:100–101).

Chapter 10 · La Fiesta de Santiago

1. In 1992, with funding from the Red Cross of Stuttgart, Germany, I assisted in the installation of a drinking water system for the central part of Chillihuani serving the health clinic, the school, the house of the Women's Committee, and the facilities of the village council.

2. Langer (1990) observed that the Aymara of Bolivia believed Condor Nasa, one of the highest peaks of a region, to possess extraordinary powers and to be traditionally associated with lightning, the ancient Aymara god of war.

3. Horses are treasured by the herders of Chillihuani, although only one in four families can afford one. These shaggy mountain horses live about twenty years and reproduce only one to four times in their lives. They graze on the meadows, but do not eat the hard *ichu* grass preferred by llamas and alpacas. They die a natural death and their meat is not consumed.

4. Erick Langer (1990:242) quoted Tristan Platt (1986), who observed in the Andes that in *tinkuys,* for example, "outright winners are never declared." Michael Sallnow (1991:299) stated that in *tinkuys* which are staged on politico-territorial boundaries in the high mountains, no permanent winners and losers are disclosed and that coalitions may be in a constant state of flux.

Chapter 11 · Qespisqa P'unchay—Independence Day in Tawantinsuyu

1. Joseph Bastien (1985:143) stated that the custom of young people serving their elders is also an important social principle in Mount Kaata in Bolivia.

2. Normally on this evening the authorities review issues pertaining to Independence Day and sometimes a council member may be elected to replace someone who has died or become incapable of continuing with council tasks. In the absence of this kind of emergency election, new authorities take office (*cargo*) on the first day of January. In the past, people voted by lifting the right hand. Now the secret vote is used and each adult community member receives paper of different colors which designate different candidates, one of which is placed in the voting box.

Chapter 12 · Metaphors or Reality—Visions from the Past

1. Lillian Estelle Fisher (1966:ix) wrote that this uprising "stretched from Tucumán to Colombia and Venezuela through Peru, Bolivia, northwestern Argentina, and part of Ecuador, covering a larger territory than that of the war for independence on the North American continent, our Civil War, or most of the European conflicts preceding the world wars. It was the greatest Indian revolt in the Americas and fully taxed the resources of Spain and the genius of military officials to put it down."

2. People from the high-altitude communities of Chupani and K'unkani,

high above the Sacred Valley of the Incas, also assert that the Incas made stones walk with their *warak'a.*

3. This idea of victory of the indigenous people over the invaders is expressed in other contexts as well. In the pilgrimage to Qoyllur Rit'i, the Ch'unchu Indians of the jungle regions decorate some of the crosses that are carried up into the glaciers with orange feathers, thus putting an indigenous mark on this ritual occasion.

4. Roberto's conceptualization of time agrees with Catherine Allen's (1988: 64) observation in the high-altitude community of Sonqo. "*Runakuna* conceptualize time as discontinuous, as a series of stages punctuated by apocalyptic interruptions. But when a given world 'turns around' and is finished, it does not cease to exist. Previous *timpus* (eras) continue to exist in a different but less immediate state than the present, and they can affect this world indirectly." See also Altamirano and Hirabayashi (1997:11) and Golte (1981: 123) for Andean conceptualizations of time and space.

5. At a later date Roberto said that some big snakes are brown with black. They emerge when it drizzles while the sun shines, a meteorological phenomenon called *chirapa* (or *garua,* which is considered dangerous).

6. Sabine MacCormack (1991:271) wrote that "at the holy place Chuquipalta near Cuzco, the Maker Pachayachachic Intiillapa, the 'Thunder of the Sun' who was also the 'brother' of Pachacuti Inca, and Punchao were represented together as three upright stones and received joint sacrifices."

7. There are a variety of other sites from different time periods where symbols of snakes, lightning, and related metaphors exist. Metaphors of snakes with one or two heads in the form of zigzag configurations must have carried considerable significance even in pre-Inca times. They are found engraved, for example, in rock outcrops of La Caldera in the province of Arequipa in Peru. See Eloy Linares Malaga (1978). Daniel Gade (1983:782) wrote that early in this century in the Lake Titicaca region "Bandelier—1910:107—noted roof crosses overlain by a pair of snakes. In native Andean symbolism, the serpent has represented a lightning flash." On a variety of structures in Cuzco and surroundings, we find engravings of snakes and zigzag lines. Douglas Sharon (1978:93) has used legend to explain Andean ideology. He found that a one-headed snake turns into lightning while a double-headed snake turns into a rainbow.

8. *Amaru,* although representative of the snake, is considered the archetype of the felines, which are related to the sun. Illapa, the fiery lightning god, in turn, is related to water, as it brings rain. This intricate interconnection of elements and phenomena is reminiscent of the yin/yang principle.

Chapter 13 · Waqraqocha

1. *Papa wathiya* are prepared in the following way: Clods or lumps of dried earth are shaped into a small mound-like kiln or oven, about half a

meter in height. Inside the kiln a fire is lighted using thin firewood and dry animal dung. The potatoes are placed into the ashes. As the kiln collapses, the hot clods of earth roast the potatoes. They are delicious.

2. *Waqraqocha* literally means "horn lake" (*waqra* = horn; *qocha* = lake or lagoon). The two mountain peaks rising from the sides of the lagoon look like horns.

3. Gow and Gow (1975:149) also observed that around Apu Ausangate there are several lakes which are associated with the fertility of the livestock.

4. Tears are seen on most important personages in Inca and pre-Inca iconography. They may be related to water, rain, fertility, or to procreation. The creator god of Tiahuanaco on the Gateway of the Sun, for example, is depicted with something like tears running from his eyes. But there may be more to this metaphor related to tears. It is possible that the gift of knowing, the gift of a shaman, the gift to see past, present, and future may be related to the representation of tears. I have often wondered about the meaning and only now, as I witness the two men discussing this matter, which is clearly so important to them, is more light shed on this question.

5. Yaranga Valderrama (1979:713–714) wrote, "*Illapa* sends the luminous golden Amaru—Qori Amaru Kachamuq—the snake of shining gold. In today's belief system Amaru, also known as Wata Puñuy (preserver of the year), is the divinity from the water with a human face, the body of a snake and four extremities. In many places the symbol of Amaru has changed. It is represented as a bull, a pig or a golden bull."

6. Peter Hochachka et al. (1991:1720, and personal communication), in their research on metabolic and work efficiencies during exercise in Andean natives, found that "from numerous previous studies it is evident that indigenous Quechuas of the high Andes in South America display a number of functional and structural adaptations allowing them to at least partially circumvent the main metabolic problem they face: maintaining an acceptably high scope for sustained aerobic metabolism despite reduced availability of O^2 in the inspired air." See also Hochachka (1992) and Monge (1953:4–21) on high-altitude stress.

7. *Kishwar* is a full-branched, medium-sized tree on average 7–17 meters high. It is shorter in the few places it is found in Chillihuani. It has simple, opposed, dark green leathery leaves which are whitish on the underside, and red-orange flowers. It is especially predominant in the landscape above 3,400 meters. *Kishwar* is highly valued for its wood in this wood-poor region. It supplies the basic material for agricultural tools.

8. In the Quechua language eternal snow is called *mamarit'i*, which literally means "mother of the snow" and conceptually means "eternal snow." The denomination *mama* refers to the eternal, the immense, the original. Thus Pachamama is Mother Earth or universe and Mamaqocha is the ocean.

9. Luis Millones (1975:50) wrote that at the beginning of the nineteenth

century, *vicuña* hunting became a widespread activity. Traps were used, which drastically reduced the species.

10. In 1965 Peru, with the help of the German Agency for Technical Cooperation (GTZ), started to cooperate in creating the National Vicuña Reserve of Pampa Galeras in the Department of Ayacucho at an altitude of 4,000 meters above sea level (see GTZ 1978).

11. Johan Reinhard (1992:107) noted that during his high-mountain expeditions he experienced violent storms which came out of a clear blue sky with lightning and static electricity. He wrote that this type of storm can build to a dangerous intensity, capable of knocking people unconscious; his cameras no longer functioned.

GLOSSARY

Words of Spanish origin are designated by (S). All other words are Quechua. Alternate frequently used spellings of Quechua words are in parentheses following the spelling I have used.

ahijada (S), *ahijado* (S): goddaughter, godson.

alawaru: a musical phrase used to indicate stages of a ritual sequence (derived from *alabado* [S], prayer).

alcalde (S): mayor.

allin ñan: have a good trip!

altomesayoq (*altomesayuq* or *altomisayoq*): diviner of the highest level.

amaru: large snake, serpent, deity. Also perceived as a symbol standing for a variety of concepts such as water, wisdom, revolution, and revolt.

antara (*zampoña* [S]): indigenous Andean musical instrument; panpipes.

Antisuyu: eastern quadrant of the Inca Empire.

apacheta (S) (*apachita*): sacred cairn consisting of stones that were deposited by worshipers for the spirit guardians of a particular place.

Apu: powerful mountain deity or other powerful sacred place; lord.

aqha (*aha*): fermented beverage; see *chicha* (S).

ara madrina and *ara padrino:* horizontal sponsors at a wedding (*ara* means altar or flat surface).

araphoqtoy: twelve silver coins carried on a silver platter by the *ara padrino.* A symbolic gift for the bride.

arariwa: guardian of agricultural fields.

arpa (*arpay*): offering; sacrifice of a llama or alpaca.

awki: protective ancestral spirit and mythical personage living in the highest mountain peaks.

awkicha: grandfather (*hatun awkicha* means great-grandfather).

ayllu: kin group, lineage, or indigenous community with a territorial base and members who share a common focus.

ayni: balanced reciprocity, aid to be reciprocated in kind.

ayranpu (*ayrampo*): (*Opuntia soehrensii*) a cactus-like plant used for medicinal purposes. The dark red seeds are used as a dye.

barquilla montera (S): hat with wide brim and small conical center, similar to the *montera* but without fringes, worn by Andean men and women on special occasions.

cargo (S): literally, "burden"; a duty Indian community members take on within the political-religious hierarchy to serve their community.

carguyoq: a person who holds a *cargo* (S); e.g., sponsor of a fiesta.

casarakuy: church wedding. In some places wedding is referred to as *runachakuy* or *warmichakuy*.

ch'aki qhaqya wayra: dry thunder wind.

chakitaklla: foot plow from Inca times.

chakra (*chacra*): agricultural field.

Ch'allaska (Ch'uyaska, Ch'uyasqa): the ritual of spraying liquid (e.g., *chicha*) in a gesture of symbolic purification.

chanaku: the last child to be born to a family.

chansanakuy: having a good time while joking together.

ch'arki: dried llama or alpaca meat. The English word *jerky* is derived from *ch'arki*.

chaski (*chasqui*): runner who carried messages and goods in Inca times.

chaskiqkuna: young men who perform rituals of respect and learn the tasks of village authorities.

chicha (S): fermented beverage made out of corn or *quinoa; aqha* in Quechua.

chikchi wasi (*casa de la granizada* [S]): house of the hail.

Chinchaysuyu: northern quadrant of the Inca Empire.

chirapa (*garúa* [S]): a condition of drizzle during sunshine.

ch'ullu: knit hat with colorful symbols worn by men.

chullumpi: honorable address for llamas during rituals.

ch'unchu: dancer at Qoyllur Rit'i representing indigenous people from the jungle regions.

chuño (S) (*ch'uñu*): freeze-dried potatoes.

ch'uru: seashell; see also *mullu*.

chushllu: honorable address for alpacas during rituals.

ch'uspa: small woven bag men use to carry *coca* leaves and money.

coca (kuka): leaves of the *coca* plant chewed with the ash of certain plants act as a mild stimulant and alleviate fatigue, hunger, and thirst. A dietary supplement as well as a central ingredient in all ritual offerings to the deities and central to social interactions.

coca k'intu: see *k'intu.*

coca mukllu (kuka mukllu): coca seed.

Collasuyu: see Qollasuyu.

comadre (S): co-mother, godmother.

compadrazgo (S): ritual-fictive kinship.

compadre (S): co-father, godfather.

condenado (S) *(kukuchi):* soul of the condemned that must do penance.

Coricancha: see Qorikancha.

corregidor (S): Spanish administrator during the late colonial period.

curandero, curandera (S): male healer, female healer.

cuy (S) *(qowe* or *qowi):* guinea pig.

despacho (S): offering to the gods.

encomendero (S): Spanish administrator who was replaced by the *corregidor* (S) during the later colonial period.

enqa: life force contained in the *enqaychu.*

enqaychu: a small, natural or slightly worked stone usually resembling an animal, sometimes a human or an object, believed to contain life force and the power to promote fertility, happiness, and luck.

faena (S): communal obligatory work party.

garbanzo (S): chickpea; nutritious and thus considered one of the best foods in an offering to the deities.

hach'u (kuka hach'u or *khullu):* wad of chewed *coca* leaves.

hach'u p'anpay: ritual burial of chewed *coca* leaves.

hacienda (S): landed property or estate.

hallpay: to chew *coca* leaves.

Hanan Cuzco (Hanan Qosqo): upper part of Cuzco.

hanan pacha: upper world where the spirits reside.

hanku haywa (ofrenda cruda [S]): raw offering.

hatun madrina and *hatun padrino:* vertical sponsors at a marriage (*hatun* means principal, big, or erect).

Hawkaypata (Haucaypata) (Plaza de Armas [S]): the principal plaza in Cuzco.

haywa: ritual offering; see also *pago* (S), *despacho* (S), *ofrenda* (S).

Hurin Cuzco (Urin Qosqo): lower part of Cuzco.

ichu (*ichhu, stipa ichhu*): favored high-altitude grass for llamas and alpacas; can be used for a variety of purposes.

illa: see *enqaychu.*

Illapa: god of thunder and lightning; see also Qhaqya.

Inti: sun, sun god.

iphiña: usual enclosure for camelids and sheep.

irpay (*irpa*): ceremony of marking alpacas, llamas, or sheep. In Chillihuani, also considered a ritual wedding of young animals.

iskay kapun, iskay kapunku: now there are two in one; commonly expressed by spectators after two people get married.

kantunka: belt with woolen tassels attached to it which is worn by men during Pukllay.

kawsachun (*¡viva!* [S]: long live! (kawsachun Chillihuani = long live Chillihuani!)

kay pacha: this world, the world where we live.

keuña (*qewña, kehuiña*): native Andean tree which grows between approximately 3,000 and 4,800 meters above sea level (*Polylepis incana*).

killa (*quilla*): moon, moon goddess.

k'intu: offering of usually three perfect *coca* leaves placed green side up in a bouquet.

kishwar (*kiswar*): indigenous Andean tree (*Buddleia incana*).

Kuntisuyu (Cuntisuyu): western quadrant of the Inca Empire.

kuraq: elder.

k'uychi: rainbow.

llant'a: firewood.

llaqta: town, village, community.

Llaqtayoq Mach'aqway: snake, master, or mistress of the village; village of the snake.

llayta: flat, dark-colored algae.

lliklla: woven shawl with symbols used by Andean women from Inca times to the present.

llipht'a: compressed ash of certain plants, chewed with *coca* leaves to release alkaloids.

llonqhetaku: paint obtained from red earth which is used on the fur of animals in a marking ceremony (*llonqhe* is paint; *taku* is red earth).

llulluch'a: algae from mountain lakes which makes up an important part of the highland Indians' diet.

mach'aqway: serpent, snake.

mach'ay: burial cave.

machu: old one, ancient one. May refer to an ancient spirit which may be either benevolent or malevolent.

mallku: spirit of the condor; leader of a group of condors.

mama q'epe (*mama q'epi*): bundle consisting of various ritual paraphernalia wrapped into a colorful *lliklla*.

Manqo Qhapaq (Manco Capac): first mythical Inca.

markachana: small cave in the ceremonial corral used to burn an offering; see also *q'oyana*.

mashwa (*maswa;* also called *añu* or *isañu*): an important food staple in the Sierra (*Tropaeolum tuberosum*).

maych'a: medicinal high-altitude plant which is also used to start fires for offerings. Also used as a pejorative reference to a healer of dubious skill.

mayu: river, also Milky Way.

mayuqochayuyu: type of edible algae found in rivers.

mesarumi: literally *mesa* (S) for table; *rumi* for stone. A table of stone. This is an altar where sacred rituals take place.

misti (*mestizo* [S]): person of mixed Indian and Spanish descent.

montaña [S]: literally, "mountain," but the term also designates the eastern slopes of the Andes mountains.

montera (S): flat hat with fringes.

moraya: dehydrated potatoes. Similar to *chuño*.

mullu: large seashell used in rituals; sometimes referred to as *ch'uru* or *qocha*.

murmuntu: dark edible algae found in lakes and springs.

muyukancha: corral used during sacred rituals.

muyuq wayra: whirlwind.

ñawin: eye.

ñawin aqha: eye of the *chicha* (S), i.e., the first cup of *chicha* from a vessel which is offered to the deities.

niwa: long-stemmed grass (*Cortaderia quila*) used to make the festive hats worn by men during Pukllay and some other festivities.

ñusta: Inca princess.

ofrenda (S): sacred offering; also referred to as *despacho* (S), *pago* (S), or *haywa.*

oqa (*oca*): tuber that serves as one of the food staples in the *puna* region of the Andes (*Oxalis tuberosa*).

pacha: time, earth, space, universe.

Pachakuteq Inca Yupanqui (Pachakuteq Inka Yupanki, Pachacuti Inca Yupanqui): the ninth Inca emperor, who made many changes within the empire which earned him the name "transformer of the world."

pachakuti (*pachacuti*): reversal of the world.

Pachamama: Mother Earth, the Great Mother.

pampamesayoq: diviner of ordinary status; of the low table.

paqo: diviner, ritual specialist; see also *altomesayoq, pampamesayoq.*

phukuy: the action of blowing across *coca* leaves in a ritual offering to the deities.

pinkuyllu: musical instrument similar to a flute which is used to play traditional music, especially during Pukllay.

pitu: musical instrument similar to the flute. Used during weddings and at the Fiesta de Santiago.

pollera (S): woman's skirt.

Pukllay (Puqllay): literally, "play" or "game." A major festivity in the Andes, also referred to as Carnavales (S), Carnival Week.

pukuchu: bag made of the fur of an alpaca that is aborted as a fetus, is born dead, or dies immediately after birth.

puna: high-altitude region with tundra-like grasslands.

puru (*poro*): drinking vessel used during rituals made of gourds from tropical regions.

puruña: an earthen jar used in rituals to hold water.

qañiwa: nutritious indigenous Andean plant with tiny seeds; similar to quinoa (*Chenopodium pallidicaule*).

qantu: a red flower, sacred to the Incas and national flower of Peru (*Cantua buxifolia*).

q'apachi (*incienso* [S]): incense.

qayara (*Puya herrerae*): a bromeliad which reaches about 1.5 meters in height and is used as fodder for some animals. Its roots are used as fuel.

qellwa: an Andean gull.

Qellwaqocha: a mountain peak and high mountain lake in Chillihuani.

q'eperina, q'epirina, q'epina: woven carrying cloth for women and men.

qero (*kero*): vase-shaped container used for drinking and for ceremonial purposes. A *k'ullu qero* is made of wood; a *qespe qero* is made of glass.

Qhaqya: Andean god of thunder and lightning; see Illapa and *rayo* (S).

qhashwa (*qhaswa*): circular dance of Inca origin. Also the name of an organization in Chillihuani in which young people have a chance to meet one another.

qhawaq: the one who watches and observes.

qocha (*cocha, laguna* [S]): a tarn; a high mountain lake or lagoon.

qochayuyu (*cochayuyu*): algae; a part of the highland Indian's diet; see also *llulluch'a*.

Qollasuyu (Collasuyu): southern region of the Inca Empire.

qolqa (*collca*): storage area for food; storehouse.

qolqelazo: threads of silver-colored yarn used in ritual offerings.

qolqelibro: thin slices of silver-colored paper used in ritual offerings.

Qorikancha (Coricancha): the Temple of the Sun in Cuzco.

qorilazo: threads of gold-colored yarn used in ritual offerings.

qorilibro: thin slices of gold-colored paper used in ritual offerings.

qoya (*coya*): queen, sister/wife of the Inca.

qoyacha: grandmother (*hatun qoyacha* means great-grandmother).

q'oyana: see *markachana*.

qoyllur: star.

Qoyllur Rit'i: object of a pilgrimage to the high, snow-covered mountains of the Sinakara range.

Quechua: native language of the Incas and still the predominant indigenous language of the Andes.

quinoa (*kiwina*): a nutritious, high-protein grain with small white seeds grown at high altitudes in the Andean highlands (*Chenopodium quinoa*).

ramada (S) (*toldo* [S], *apaki*): hut constructed of branches or reeds.

rayo (S): thunderbolt, lightning flash, Andean god of thunder and lightning; see Illapa and Qhaqya.

rimanakuy: marriage in the traditional Andean way.

rit'i: snow.

roq'a: plant of the cactus family (*Colletia spinosa*). Used in folk medicine.

runa: human being; refers to an indigenous Andean person; plural is *runa-kuna.*

runa pusaq: guide.

runasimi: the language of the people, i.e., Quechua.

ruphasqa haywa (*ofrenda quemada* [S]): burnt offering.

rutuchikuy: ritual first hair-cutting ceremony. The practice is of pre-Spanish origin.

sank'ayllo: chicha boiled with *coca* leaves, alcohol, and sugar.

sierra (S): highlands.

sirk'a: vein.

soltera (S): unmarried woman.

soq'ana: sling made of wool; used to throw stones and also used as a whip in dances during Pukllay; see *warak'a.*

soroqch'i (*soroche* [S]): mountain sickness.

susuwa: steep field of rubble or scree slope where the *condenados* (S) or *ku-kuchi*—dead people who have sinned during their lives—must struggle their way uphill every night until only the bones of their bodies are left.

suyu: region, division, territory.

taqe: bin made of reeds where freeze-dried potatoes are stored.

taqya: dried dung of alpacas, llamas, and sheep.

Tawantinsuyu (Tahuantinsuyu): land of the four quarters; the Inca Empire.

t'inka: a libation or toast for the deities made by flicking drops of a beverage into the air using thumb and forefinger.

tinku (*tinkuy*): encounter, e.g., during ritual battles. Confluence of streams.

tinya (*caja* [S]): small drum; *hatun tinya* (*bombo* [S]): bass drum.

trago (S): sugarcane alcohol.

Tusuna Q'asa Pata: the site above the ravine between the high mountain peaks where the dances take place during Pukllay. There are several of these sites in Chillihuani.

uchu: chili.

ukhu pacha: world below, underworld.

ukuku: bear dancer seen mostly during Qoyllur Rit'i. Some investigators believe that *ukukus* represent alpacas.

ulluku:. high-altitude tuberous food plant (*Ullucus tuberosus*).

unkuña (unkhuña): small woven cloth used to hold *coca* leaves and in rituals and dances.

untu: pure fat from the chests of alpacas and llamas.

uraña wayra: a terrible wind that is believed to cause severe stomach pains, vomiting, and *susto* (S), a state of extreme fear.

urpu: earthen container for *chicha* (S).

uywa: animal.

vara (S): staff.

varayoq: literally "with staff"; the one who possesses the staff of office. A member of the indigenous civil-religious hierarchy of an Andean community.

víspera (S): eve.

waka (huaca): sacred place or divinity.

Waqraqocha: literally, "horn lake." Sacred high-altitude lake in Chillihuani.

warak'a: see *soq'ana;* woolen whip used to throw stones. Also used in some dances. A weapon in Inca times.

warak'anakuy (juego de la Honda [S]): an ancient game with connotations of fertility where participants use the whip.

Wari (Huari): a pre-Inca culture characterized by urban settlements, such as Pikillacta near Cuzco, with large buildings for administration, storage, military, and other purposes.

warmi-qhari: literally, "woman-man"; couple.

wathiya: potato baked in a makeshift earthen stove.

waynu (huayno): folkloric Inca music and dance.

wayra: wind.

wayruru (huayruru): brilliantly colored beans used in rituals and as a love charm.

willka (*villca*): sacred.

wira: animal fat.

yacana: dark stars in the Milky Way believed to represent a llama.

yanantin: pair; bride and groom.

yana uyakuna: blackfaces (*yana* = black; *uya* = face; *kuna* denotes plural).

yawar mayu: river of blood; part of a whole choreography of dances known as Maqt'acha Tusuy, a dance during Pukllay.

BIBLIOGRAPHY

Academia Mayor de la Lengua Quechua
1995 *Diccionario Quechua-Español-Quechua.* Qosqo, Peru: Municipalidad del Qosqo.

Acosta, José de
[1589] 1962 *Historia natural y moral de las Indias.* Mexico City.

Albó, Xavier
1972 Esposos, suegros y padrinos entre los Aymaras. Paper presented at the Symposium on Andean Kinship and Marriage. Seventy-first Annual Meeting of the American Anthropological Association, Toronto.

Alencastre, G. Andrés, and Georges Dumezil
1953 Fêtes et usages des Indiens de Langui. *Journal de la Société des Américanistes,* n.s. 42:1–118.

Alford Andrews, Michael
1982 *The Flight of the Condor: A Wildlife Exploration of the Andes.* Boston: Little, Brown.

Allen, Catherine
1988 *The Hold Life Has: Coca and Cultural Identity in an Andean Community.* Washington, D.C.: Smithsonian Institution Press.

Altamirano, Teófilo, and Lane Ryo Hirabayashi
1997 The Construction of Regional Identities in Urban Latin America. In *Migrants, Regional Identities and Latin American Cities,* ed. Teófilo Altamirano and Lane Ryo Hirabayashi, pp. 7–23. Society for Latin American Anthropology Publication Series, vol. 13. Jeffrey David Ehrenreich, General Editor.

Antuñez de Mayolo, R. Santiago
1981 *La nutrición en el antiguo Perú.* Lima: Banco Central de Reserva del Perú, Oficina Numismática.

Aranguren Paz, Angélica
1975 Las creencias y ritos mágicos religiosos de los pastores puneños. *Allpanchis* 8:103–132.

Arguedas, José María

1991 *Los ríos profundos*. Lima: Editorial Horizonte.

Arguedas, José María, and Ruth Stephan

1957 *The Singing Mountaineers: Songs and Tales of the Quechua People*. Austin: University of Texas Press.

Arriaga, Pablo Joseph de

[1621] 1968 *The Extirpation of Idolatry in Peru*. Trans. and ed. L. Clark Keating. Lexington: University of Kentucky Press.

Ascher, Marcia, and Robert Ascher

1981 *Code of the Quipu: A Study in Media, Mathematics, and Culture*. Ann Arbor: University of Michigan Press.

Aveni, Anthony F.

1989 *Empires of Time: Calendars, Clocks, and Cultures*. New York: Basic Books.

Bandelier, Adolph F. A.

1910 *The Islands of Titicaca and Koati*. New York: Hispanic Society of America.

Barthel, Thomas S.

1986 El agua y el festival de primavera entre los Atacameños. *Allpanchis* 28: 147–184.

Bastien, Joseph W.

1985 *Mountain of the Condor: Metaphor and Ritual in an Andean Ayllu*. Prospect Heights, Ill.: Waveland Press.

Bauer, Brian

1995 *Astronomy and Empire in the Ancient Andes: The Cultural Origins of Inca Sky Watching*. Austin: University of Texas Press.

Betanzos, Juan de

[1551] 1924 *Suma y narración de los Incas*. Ed. H. H. Urteaga. Colección de Libros y Documentos Referentes a la Historia del Perú, ser. 2, vol. 8. Lima.

[1551] 1987 *Suma y narración de los Incas*. Madrid: Atlas.

Bolin, Inge

1987 The Organization of Irrigation in the Vilcanota Valley of Peru: Local Autonomy, Development and Corporate Group Dynamics. Ph.D. diss., University of Alberta, Canada.

1990a The Hidden Power of Women: Highland Peru and West Sumatra Compared. *Development and Cooperation* 1:12–13.

1990b Upsetting the Power Balance: Cooperation, Competition, and Conflict along an Andean Irrigation System. *Human Organization* 49(2):140–148.

1992 Achieving Reciprocity: Anthropological Research and Development Assistance. *Practicing Anthropology* 14(4):12–15.

1994 Levels of Autonomy in the Organization of Irrigation in the Highlands of Peru. In *Irrigation at High Altitudes: The Social Organization of Water Control Systems in the Andes,* ed. William P. Mitchell and David Guillet, pp. 141–166. Society for Latin American Anthropology Publication Series, vol. 12. Jeffrey David Ehrenreich, General Editor.

Bolton, Ralph

1973 Tawanku: Intercouple Bonds in a Qolla Village (Peru). *Anthropos* 68: 145–155.

1977 The Qolla Marriage Process. In *Andean Kinship and Marriage,* ed. Ralph Bolton and Enrique Mayer, pp. 217–239. A Special Publication of the American Anthropological Association no. 7. Washington, D.C.

Bourque, Susan C., and Kay Barbara Warren

1979 *Women of the Andes: Patriarchy and Social Change in Two Peruvian Towns.* Ann Arbor: University of Michigan Press.

Bowman, Isaiah

1938 *Los Andes del Sur del Perú.* Arequipa, Peru: La Colmena.

Braunfels, Wolf, ed.

1974 *Lexikon der Christlichen Ikonographie.* 8 vols. Freiburg.

Brush, Stephen

1977 *Mountain, Field and Family: The Economy and Human Ecology of an Andean Valley.* Philadelphia: University of Pennsylvania Press.

Burchard, Roderick E.

1992 Coca Chewing and Diet. *Current Anthropology* 33(1):1–24.

Cáceres Ch., Efraín

1986 El agua como fuente de vida: Traslación y escape en los mitos andinos. *Allpanchis* 28:99–122.

Cadorette, Raimundo

1986 Perspectivas mitológicas del mundo aymara. *Allpanchis* 10:115–136.

Cahlander, Adele

1980 *Sling Braiding of the Andes.* Weaver's Journal Monograph IV. Boulder: Colorado Fiber Center.

Calancha, Antonio de la

[1638–1639] 1974–1981 *Corónica moralizada del Orden de San Augustín en el Perú.* Ed. I. Prado Pastor. Lima.

Carrion Cachot, Rebeca

1955 El culto al agua en el antiguo Perú. *Revista del Museo Nacional de Antropología y Arqueología* 2.

Carter, W. E.

1977 Trial Marriage in the Andes. In *Andean Kinship and Marriage,* ed. Ralph Bolton and Enrique Mayer, pp. 177–216. Special Publication of the American Anthropological Association no. 7. Washington, D.C.

Chávez, Sergio Jorge

1981 Note on: Further Inquiries into the Case of the Arapa-Thunderbolt Stela. *Ñawpa Pacha* 19:189–191.

Cieza de León, Pedro

[1551] 1967 *Del señorío de los Incas.* Lima.

Cobo, Bernabé

[1653] 1956 *Historia del Nuevo Mundo.* Vol. 92, *Obras del P. Bernabé Cobo de la compañía de Jesús,* ed. P. Francisco Mateos. Biblioteca de Autores Españoles. Madrid: Ediciones Atlas.

[1653] 1964 *Historia del Nuevo Mundo.* 2 vols. Madrid: Biblioteca de Autores Españoles.

Cooper, Mary Ann

1980 Lightning Injuries: Prognostic Signs for Death. *Annals of Emergency Medicine* 9:134–138.

Crumrine, N. Ross

1991 A Pilgrimage Fiesta: Easter Week Ritual at Catacaos, Piura, Peru. In *Pilgrimage in Latin America,* ed. N. Ross Crumrine and Alan Morinis, pp. 269–279. New York: Greenwood Press.

Cusihuaman G., Antonio

1976 *Diccionario Quechua Cuzco Collao.* Lima: Ministerio de Educación, Instituto de Estudios Peruanos.

Custred, Glynn

1979 Symbols and Control in a High Altitude Community. *Anthropos* 74: 379–392.

Davis, Wade

1996 *One River—Explorations and Discoveries in the Amazon Rain Forest.* New York: Simon and Schuster.

Desrosiers, Sophie

1992 Las técnicas del tejido ¿tienen un sentido? Una propuesta de lectura de los tejidos andinos. *Revista Andina* 10(1):7–46.

Duviols, Pierre

1971 *La Lutte contre les religions autochtones dans le Pérou colonial: L'Extirpation de l'idolatrie entre 1532 et 1600,* Documentary Appendix. Lima and Paris: Institut Français d'Etudes Andines.

1974 Duality in the Andes. Paper presented at the Andean Symposium II, November 20, American Anthropological Association Meeting, Mexico City.

Earls, John, and Irene Silverblatt

1978. La realidad física y social en la cosmología andina. *Actes du XLIIᵉ Congrès International des Américanistes, Paris* 4:299–325.

Eliade, Mircea

1963 *Patterns in Comparative Religion.* Trans. Rosemary Sheed. New York: Meridian Books, New American Library.

1965 *The Two and the One.* London: Harvill Press.

Ereira, Alan

1991 *From the Heart of the World.* A film produced by the BBC, directed by Alan Ereira, distributed by Mystic Fire Video, 524 Broadway, Suite 604, New York, N.Y. 10012.

Escalante Gutiérrez, Carmen, and Ricardo Valderrama Fernández

1992 *Nosotros los humanos—Ñuqanchik runakuna. Testimonio de los Quechuas del siglo XX.* Cuzco: Centro de Estudios Regionales Andinos "Bartolomé de las Casas."

Fisher, Lillian Estelle

1966 *The Last Inca Revolt, 1780–1783.* Norman: University of Oklahoma Press.

Flannery, Kent V., Joyce Marcus, and Robert G. Reynolds

1989 *The Flocks of the Wamani: A Study of Llama Herders on the Punas of Ayacucho, Peru.* San Diego: Academic Press.

Flores Ochoa, Jorge A.

1977 Enqa, Enqaychu, Illa y Khuya Rumi. In *Pastores de puna: Uywamichiq punarunakuna,* comp. Jorge A. Flores Ochoa, pp. 211–237. Lima: Instituto de Estudios Peruanos.

1979 *Pastoralists of the Andes: The Alpaca Herders of Paratía.* Trans. Ralph Bolton. Philadelphia: Institute for the Study of Human Issues.

1988a Clasificación y nominación de camelidos sudamericanos. In *Llamichos y paqocheros, pastores de llamas y alpacas,* ed. Jorge A. Flores Ochoa, pp. 121–137. Cuzco: Centro de Estudios Andinos.

1988b Mitos y canciones ceremoniales en comunidades de puna. In *Llamichos y paqocheros, pastores de llamas y alpacas,* ed. Jorge A. Flores Ochoa, pp. 237–251. Cuzco: Centro de Estudios Andinos.

1990 *El Cuzco: Resistencia y continuidad.* Cuzco: Centro de Estudios Andinos.

Flores Ochoa, Jorge A., and Ana María Fries

1989 *Puna, Qheswa, Yunga: El hombre y su medio en Q'ero.* Lima: Banco Central de Reserva del Peru, Fondo Editorial.

Frankfort, H.

1965 *Kingship and the Gods.* Chicago: University of Chicago Press.

Franquemont, Christine, Edward Franquemont, Wade Davis, Timothy Plowman, Steven R. King, Calvin R. Sperling, and Christine Niezgoda

1990 *The Ethnobotany of Chinchero, an Andean Community in Southern Peru.* Fieldiana: Botany, New Series, No. 24. Chicago: Field Museum of Natural History.

Franquemont, Edward M., Christine Franquemont, and Billie Jean Isbell

1992 Awaq Nawin: El ojo del tejedor—La práctica de la cultura en el tejido. *Revista Andina* 10(1):47–80.

Gade, Daniel

1975 *Plants, Man and the Land in the Vilcanota Valley of Peru.* The Hague: W. Junk.

1983 Lightning in the Folklife and Religion of the Central Andes. *Anthropos* 78:770–788.

Garcilaso de la Vega

[1609] 1966 *Royal Commentaries of the Incas and General History of Peru, Part One.* Trans. Harold V. Livermore. Austin: University of Texas Press.

Gavilan Vega, Vivian, and Liliana Ulloa Torres

1992 Proposiciones metodológicas para el estudio de los tejidos andinos. *Revista Andina* 10(1):107–134.

Gelles, Paul

1985 Coca and Andean Culture: The New Dangers of an Old Debate. *Cultural Survival Quarterly* 9(4):20–23.

German Agency for Technical Cooperation

1978 *Utilization of Vicugnas in Peru.* Eschborn: GTZ.

Getzels, Peter

1984 Los ciegos: Visión de la identidad del runa en la ideología de Inkarrí-Qollarí. In *Q'ero, el último ayllu inka,* ed. Jorge Flores Ochoa and Juan Núñez del Prado B., pp. 170–201. Cuzco: Centro de Estudios Andinos.

Gilt Contreras, Mario Alberto

1966 *Las guerrillas indígenas de Chiyaraqe y Toqto.* Cuzco. Mimeographed.

Golte, Jürgen

1981 Cultura y naturaleza andinas. *Allpanchis* 17–18:119–132.

Gow, David D.

1974 Taytacha Qoyllur Rit'i. *Allpanchis* 7:49–100.

Gow, David, and Rosalinda Gow

1975 La alpaca en el mito y el ritual. *Allpanchis* 8:141–174.

Guaman Poma de Ayala, Felipe

[1615] 1936 *La nueva crónica y buen gobierno.* Paris: Institut d'Etnologie.

[1615] 1956–1966 *La nueva crónica y buen gobierno.* Ed. L. Bustios Galvez. 3 vols. Lima: Ministerio de Educación.

[1615] 1956–1966 *La nueva crónica y buen gobierno.* Translated into modern Spanish by Luis Bustíos Gálvez. 3 vols. Lima: Editorial Cultura.

[1615] 1980 *El primer nueva crónica y buen gobierno.* Ed. John V. Murra and Rolena Adorno. Translated from the Quechua by Jorge L. Urioste. 3 vols. Mexico, Madrid, and Bogota: Siglo Veintiuno Editores.

[1615] 1987 *La nueva crónica y buen gobierno.* Ed. John V. Murra, R. Adorno, and J. Urioste. Madrid: Historia 16.

Guillet, David
1994 Canal Irrigation and the State: The 1969 Water Law and Irrigation Systems of the Colca Valley of Southwestern Peru. In *Irrigation at High Altitudes: The Social Organization of Water Control Systems in the Andes,* ed. William P. Mitchell and David Guillet, pp. 167–187. Society for Latin American Anthropology Publication Series, vol. 12. Jeffrey David Ehrenreich, General Editor.

Harris, Olivia
1978 Complementarity and Conflict: An Andean View of Women and Men: In *Sex and Age as Principles of Differentiation,* ed. Jean Sybil La Fontaine, pp. 21–40. London: Academic Press.

Harrison, Regina
1989 *Signs, Songs, and Memory in the Andes.* Austin: University of Texas Press.

Hemming, John
1970 *The Conquest of the Incas.* New York: Harcourt, Brace, Jovanovich.

Hernández Príncipe, Rodrigo
[1621–1622] 1923 Mitología andina. *Revista INCA* (Lima) 1:25–70.

Hochachka, Peter W.
1992 Principles of Physiological and Biochemical Adaptation. High-Altitude Man as a Case Study. In *Physiological Adaptations in Vertebrates—Respiration, Circulation, and Metabolism,* ed. Stephen C. Wood, Roy E. Weber, Alan R. Hargens, and Ronald W. Millard. New York: Marcel Dekker.

Hochachka, Peter W., C. Stanley, G. O. Matheson, D. C. McKenzie, P. S. Allen, and W. S. Parkhouse
1991 *Metabolic and Work Efficiencies during Exercise in Andean Natives.* The American Physiological Society.

Hopkins, Diane
1982 Juego de enemigos. *Allpanchis* 20:167–187.

Horkheimer, Hans
1960 *Nahrung und Nahrungsgewinnung im vorspanischen Peru.* Berlin: Colloquium Verlag.

Hrdlicka, Ales
1978 La trepanación en los pueblos prehistóricos de América. In *Tecnología andina,* ed. Roger Ravines, pp. 687–695. Lima: Instituto de Estudios Peruanos.

Huanca Mamani, Teodosio
1990 *Manual del alpaquero.* 2d ed. Puno, Peru: Proyecto Alpacas INIAA-CORPUNO-COTESU/IC.

Hugues, A. Juan
1974 La fiesta en los Andes. *Allpanchis* 7:3–5.

Isbell, Billie Jean
1977 Those Who Love Me: An Analysis of Andean Kinship and Reciprocity within a Ritual Context. In *Andean Kinship and Marriage,* ed. Ralph Bolton and Enrique Mayer, pp. 81–105. Special Publication of the American Anthropological Association, no. 7. Washington, D.C.
1985 *To Defend Ourselves: Ecology and Ritual in an Andean Village.* 3d ed. Prospect Heights, Ill.: Waveland Press.

Kent, Jonathan
1988 El sur más antiguo: Revisión de la domesticación de camelidos andinos. In *Llamichos y paqocheros: Pastores de llamas y alpacas,* ed. Jorge Flores Ochoa, pp. 23–35. Cuzco: Centro de Estudios Andinos.

Langer, Erick D.
1990 Andean Rituals of Revolt: The Chayanta Rebellion of 1929. *Ethnohistory* 37(3):227–253.

Lehmann-Nitsche, Robert
1928 Coricancha: El Templo del Sol en el Cuzco y las imágenes de su altar mayor. *Revista del Museo de la Plata* 31:1–256.

Liebscher, Verena
1986 *La iconografía de los keros.* Lima: Herrera Editores.

Linares Malaga, Eloy
1978 Prehistory and Petroglyphs in Southern Peru. In *Advances in Andean Archaeology,* ed. David L. Browman, pp. 371–391. The Hague and Paris: Mouton.

Lira, Jorge A.
1953 Puhllay, fiesta india. *Perú Indígena* 4(9):125–134.
1968 *Diccionario Kkechuwa-Español.* Cuzco: Edición Popular.

Lounsbury, Floyd G.
1964 Some Aspects of the Inca Kinship System. Paper presented at the Thirty-sixth International Congress of Americanists, Barcelona.

Lunardi, Federico
1946 El rayo y su culto en los Andes. *Revista de Historia* 2:215–243.

MacCormack, Sabine
1991 *Religion in the Andes: Vision and Imagination in Early Colonial Peru.* Princeton: Princeton University Press.

Maclean y Esteños, Roberto
1952 "Sirvinacuy" o "Tincunacuspa." *Perú Indígena* 2(4):4–12.

Malengreau, Jacques.
1972 Les Limites de la communauté à Cusipata, un village des Andes péruviennes. Ph.D. diss., Université Libre de Bruxelles.

Mayer, Enrique
1985 Production Zones. In *Andean Ecology and Civilization: An Interdisciplinary Perspective on Andean Ecological Complementarity,* ed. Shozo Masuda, Izumi Shimada, and Craig Morris, pp. 45–84. Tokyo: University of Tokyo Press.

McCorkle, Constance
1988 *Manejo de la sanidad de rumiantes menores en una comunidad indígena andina.* Lima: Comisión de Coordinación de Tecnología Andina CCTA.

Meneses, Georgina
1992 *Tradición oral en el imperio de los Incas—Historia, religion, teatro.* San José, Costa Rica: Editorial del Departamento Ecuménico de Investigaciones.

Metraux, A.
1934 Contribution au folklore andin. *Journal de la Société des Américanistes de Paris* 26: 67–102.

Miles, Ann, and Hans Buechler
1997 Introduction: Andean Perspectives on Women and Economic Change. In *Women and Economic Change: Andean Perspectives* 14:1–12. Society for Latin American Anthropology Publication Series. Jeffrey David Ehrenreich, General Editor.

Millones, Luis
1975 Economía y ritual en los Condesuyos de Arequipa: Pastores y tejedores del siglo XIX. *Allpanchis* 8:45–66.

1993 Representando el pasado: Desfiles y disfraces en los Andes. In *El mundo ceremonial andino,* ed. Luis Millones and Yoshio Onuki, pp. 275–288. SENRI Ethnological Studies no. 37. Osaka: Museo Nacional de Etnología.

Mishkin, Bernard
1963 The Contemporary Quechua. In *Handbook of South American Indians,* ed. Julian H. Steward, 2(143):411–470. New York: Cooper Square Publishers.

Mitchell, William P.
1991 *Peasants on the Edge: Crop, Cult, and Crisis in the Andes.* Austin: University of Texas Press.

Molina, Cristóbal de
[1575] 1916 *Relación de las fabulas y ritos de los incas.* Lima: Imprenta y Librería Sanmartí y Ca.

[1575] 1943 *Fabulas y ritos de los incas.* Buenos Aires: Editorial Futuro.

[1575] 1959 *Fabulas y ritos de los incas.* Buenos Aires: Editorial Futuro.

Molinié-Fioravanti, Antoinette
1986 The Andean Community Today. In *Anthropological History of Andean*

Politics, ed. John V. Murra, Nathan Wachtel, and Jacques Revel, pp. 342–358. Cambridge: Cambridge University Press.

Monge, Carlos M.

1953 Biología general y humana: Características de los seres aclimatados en el altiplano: Revista de conjunto sobre la función respiratoria del andino. *Perú Indígena* 4(9):4–21.

Morinis, Alan, and N. Ross Crumrine

1991 La Peregrinación: The Latin American Pilgrimage. In *Pilgrimage in Latin America,* ed. N. Ross Crumrine and Alan Morinis, pp. 1–17. New York: Greenwood Press.

Morote Best, Efrain

1984 Un nuevo mito de fundación del imperio. In *Q'ero, el último ayllu inka,* ed. Jorge A. Flores Ochoa and Juan V. Núñez del Prado, pp. 158–169. Cuzco: Centro de Estudios Andinos.

Muelle, Jorge C.

1950 Pacarectambo: Apuntes de viaje. *Revista del Museo Nacional* 14:153–159.

Müller, Thomas, and Helga Müller.

1984 Cosmovisión y celebraciones del mundo andino. *Allpanchis* 23:161–176.

Murra, John V.

1956 The Economic Organization of the Inca State. Ph.D. diss., University of Chicago.

1965 Herds and Herders in the Inca State. In *Man, Culture and Animals,* ed. A. Leeda and A. P. Vayda, pp. 185–215. American Association for the Advancement of Science Publications 78. Washington, D.C.

1985a "El archipiélago vertical" revisited. In *Andean Ecology and Civilization,* ed. Shozo Masuda, Izumi Shimada, and Craig Morris, pp. 3–13. Tokyo: University of Tokyo Press.

1985b The Limits and Limitations of the "Vertical Archipelago" in the Andes. In *Andean Ecology and Civilization,* ed. Shozo Masuda, Izumi Shimada, and Craig Morris, pp. 15–20. Tokyo: University of Tokyo Press.

1986 The Expansion of the Inka State: Armies, War, and Rebellions. In *Anthropological History of Andean Polities,* ed. John V. Murra, Nathan Wachtel, and Jacques Revel, pp. 49–58. Cambridge: Cambridge University Press.

1988 El aymara libre de ayer. In *Raices de América: El mundo aymara,* ed. Xavier Albó, pp. 51–73. Madrid: Alianza Editorial.

Murúa, Martín de

[1590] 1922 *Orígen de los reyes del Gran Reino del Perú.* Ed. H. H. Urteaga. Colección de Libros y Documentos Referentes a la Historia del Perú, vol. 4 (2d ser.). Lima.

[1590] 1946 *Historia del origen y genealogía real de los reyes incas del Perú.* Ed. Constantino Bayle, S. J. Madrid: C. Bermejo, Impresor. J. García Morato.

Nachtigall, Horst

1966 Indianische Fischer, Feldbauern und Viehzüchter. Berlin: Beiträge zur Peruanischen Völkerkunde.

1975 Ofrendas de llamas en la vida ceremonial de los pastores. *Allpanchis* 8:133–140.

Nash, June

1979 *We Eat the Mines and the Mines Eat Us.* New York: Columbia University Press.

Núñez del Prado, Juan Victor

1985 The Supernatural World of the Quechua of Southern Peru as Seen from the Community of Qotobamba. In *Native South Americans: Ethnology of the Least Known Continent,* ed. Patricia J. Lyon, pp. 238–251. Prospect Heights, Ill.: Waveland Press.

Núñez del Prado, Oscar

1984a Una cultura como respuesta de adaptación al medio andino. In *Q'ero, el último ayllu inka,* ed. Jorge A. Flores Ochoa and Juan V. Núñez del Prado, pp. 14–29. Cuzco: Centro de Estudios Andinos.

1984b El hombre y la familia: Su matrimonio y organización político-social en Q'ero. In *Q'ero, el último ayllu inka,* ed. Jorge A. Flores Ochoa and Juan V. Núñez del Prado, pp. 106–130. Cuzco: Centro de Estudios Andinos.

1984c La vivienda inca actual. In *Q'ero, el último ayllu inka,* ed. Jorge A. Flores Ochoa and Juan V. Núñez del Prado, pp. 82–86. Cuzco: Centro de Estudios Andinos.

Núñez del Prado Bejar, Daisy Irene

1975 El poder de decisión de la mujer quechua andina. *América Indígena* 35(3):623–630.

Oberem, Udo

1968 Amerikanistische Angaben aus Dokumenten des 16. Jahrhunderts. *Tribus* (Stuttgart) 17:81–92.

Orlove, Benjamin

1977 *Alpacas, Sheep and Men: The Wool Export Economy and Regional Society in Southern Peru.* New York: Academic Press.

Ossio, Juan M.

1986 Los mitos de origen en la comunidad de Andamarca (Ayacucho, Peru). *Allpanchis* 10(2d ed.):105–113.

Ossio, Juan M., ed.

1973 *Ideología mesiánica del mundo andino.* Lima: Edición de Ignacio Prado Pastor.

Pachacuti Yamqui, Juan de Santa Cruz

[1613] 1927 *Historia de los Incas y relación de su gobierno.* Lima: Imprenta y Librería Sanmartí y Ca.

[1613] 1968 *Relación de antigüedades deste el reyno del Perú.* Madrid: Biblioteca de Autores Españoles.

Paerregaard, Karsten

1994 Why Fight over Water? Power, Conflict and Irrigation in an Andean Village. In *Irrigation at High Altitudes: The Social Organization of Water Control Systems in the Andes,* ed. William P. Mitchell and David Guillet, pp. 189–202. Society for Latin American Anthropology Publication Series, vol. 12. Jeffrey David Ehrenreich, General Editor.

Palacios Ríos, Felix

1988a Tecnología del pastoreo. In *Llamichos y paqocheros: Pastores de llamas y alpacas,* ed. Jorge A. Flores Ochoa, pp. 87–100. Cuzco: Centro de Estudios Andinos.

1988b Pastores de llamas y alpacas. In *Raices de América: El mundo andino,* comp. Xavier Albó, pp. 133–151. Madrid: Alianza Editorial.

Palomino Flores, Salvador

1968 La cruz en los Andes. *Revista de Artes y Ciencias* 8:63–66.

1984 *El sistema de oposiciones en la comunidad de Sarhua: La complementaridad de los opuestos en la cultura andina.* Lima: Pueblo Indio.

Pantigozo de Esquivel, Dina, comp.

1995 *Yachasun: Experiencias en medicina tradicional andina.* Publicado por YACHAQ, Qosqo. Cuzco: Editorial Mercantil.

Pease, Franklin

1972 *Los últimos incas del Cusco.* Lima: Ediciones PLV.

Phipps, Elena

1992 Response to Sophie Desrosiers' article "Las técnicas de tejido   tienen un sentido?" *Revista Andina* 10(1):39–40.

Platt, Tristan

1986 Mirrors and Maize: The Concept of Yanantin among the Macha of Bolivia. In *Anthropological History of Andean Polities,* ed. John V. Murra, Nathan Wachtel, and Jacques Revel, pp. 228–259. Cambridge: Cambridge University Press.

Polo de Ondegardo, Juan

[1561] 1916 *Los errores y supersticiones de los indios.* Ed. Horacio Urteaga and Carlos Romero. Colección de Libros y Documentos Referentes a la Historia del Perú, ser. 1, vol. 3, pp. 3–43. Lima: Sanmartí.

Poole, Deborah

1991 Rituals of Movement, Rites of Transformation: Pilgrimage and Dance in the Highlands of Cuzco, Peru. In *Pilgrimage in Latin America,* ed. N. Ross Crumrine and Alan Morinis, pp. 307–338. New York: Greenwood Press.

Quijada Jara, Sergio

1957 *Canciones del ganado y pastores: Recogidas y traducidas por Sergio Quijada Jara.* Huancayo, Peru.

Ramírez, Juan Andrés

1969 La novena al señor de Qoyllur Rit'i. *Allpanchis* 1:61–88.

Randall, Robert

1982 Qoyllur Rit'i, an Inca Fiesta of the Pleiades: Reflections on Time and Space in the Andean World. *Bulletin de l'Institut Français d'Etudes Andines* (Lima) 11(1–2):37–81.

1987 Del tiempo y del río: El ciclo de la historia y la energía en la cosmología incaica. *Boletín de Lima* 54:69–95.

1990 The Mythstory of Kuri Qoyllur: Sex, Seqes and Sacrifice in Inka Agricultural Festivals. *Journal of Latin American Lore* 16/1: 3–45.

Reichel-Dolmatoff, Gerardo

1978 The Loom of Life: A Kogi Principle of Integration. *Journal of Latin American Lore* 4(1):5–27.

Reinhard, Johan

1992 Sacred Peaks of the Andes. *National Geographic* 181(3):84–111.

Remy, María Isabel

1991 Los discursos sobre la violencia en los Andes: Algunos reflexiones a propósito del Chiaraje. In *Poder y violencia en los Andes,* comp. Henrique Urbano, ed. Mirko Lauer, pp. 261–275. Cuzco: Centro de Estudios Regionales Andinos Bartolomé de las Casas.

Rick, John

1988 Identificando el sedentarismo pre-histórico en los cazadores recolectores: Un ejemplo de la Sierra Sur del Perú. In *Llamichos y paqocheros: Pastores de llamas y alpacas,* ed. Jorge A. Flores Ochoa, pp. 37–43. Cuzco: Centro de Estudios Andinos.

Rivero Luque, Sara Teresa

1995 Coca. In *Yachasun: Experiencias en medicina tradicional andina,* comp. Dina Pantigozo de Esquivel, pp. 240–241. Publicado por YACHAQ, Qosqo. Cuzco: Editorial Mercantil.

Rivero Luque, Victor

1990 *La Chakitaqlla en el mundo andino.* Lima: Herrandina Proyecto de Herramientos e Implementos Agrícolas Andinos.

Rösing, Ina

1990 *Der Blitz—Drohung und Berufung—Glaube und Ritual in den Anden Boliviens.* Munich: Trickster Verlag.

Rostworowski de Diez Canseco, María

1983 *Estructuras andinas del poder: Ideología religiosa y política.* Lima: Instituto de Estudios Peruanos.

Rowe, Ann Pollard

1987 *The Junius B. Bird Andean Textile Conference.* Washington, D.C.: Textile Museum.

1992 Response to Sophie Desrosiers' article "Las técnicas de tejido tienen un sentido? *Revista Andina* 10(1):40–42.

Rowe, John

1963 Inca Culture at the Time of the Spanish Conquest. In *Handbook of South American Indians,* ed. Julian H. Steward, 2(143):183–330. New York: Cooper Square Publishers.

Rozas Alvarez, Washington

1984 Los Paqo de Q'ero. In *Q'ero, el último ayllu inka,* ed. Jorge A. Flores Ochoa and Juan Núñez del Prado, pp. 143–157. Cuzco: Centro de Estudios Andinos.

Ruiz de Castilla Marin, Mario

1994 Camelicultura: Alpacas y llamas del sur del Perú. Qosqo: Municipalidad y Editorial Mercantil EIRL.

Ryden, Stig

1934 Note préliminaire sur l'archéologie de la région de la Candelaria. *Congrès International des Américanistes Sess. 25, La Plata 1932* 2:149–163.

Sallnow, Michael J.

1987 *Pilgrims of the Andes: Regional Cults in Cusco.* Washington, D.C.: Smithsonian Institution Press.

1991 Dual Cosmology and Ethnic Division in an Andean Pilgrimage Cult. In *Pilgrimage in Latin America,* ed. N. Ross Crumrine and Alan Morinis, pp. 281–306. New York: Greenwood Press.

Sarmiento de Gamboa, Pedro

[1572] 1907 *History of the Incas.* Trans. and ed. Sir Clements Markham, K.C.B. Cambridge: Presented for the Hakluyt Society.

[1572] 1942 *Historia índica.* Buenos Aires: Espasa-Calpe Argentina.

[1572] 1947 *Historia de los Incas,* 3d ed. Buenos Aires: Emece Editores.

[1572] 1960 *Historia índica.* Madrid.

Schaedel, Richard

1985 Discussion: An Interdisciplinary Perspective on Andean Ecological Complementarity. In *Andean Ecology and Civilization,* ed. Shozo Masuda, Izumi Shimada, and Craig Morris, pp. 505–509. Tokyo: University of Tokyo Press.

Seibold, Katharine E.

1992 Textiles and Cosmology in Choquecancha, Cuzco. In *Andean Cosmol-*

ogies through Time, ed. Robert V. H. Dover, Katharine E. Seibold, and John H. McDowell, pp. 166–201. Bloomington: Indiana University Press.

Seligmann, Linda J., and Stephen G. Bunker

1994 An Andean Irrigation System: Ecological Visions and Social Organization. In *Irrigation at High Altitudes: The Social Organization of Water Control Systems in the Andes,* ed. William P. Mitchell and David Guillet, pp. 203–232. Society for Latin American Anthropology Publication Series, vol. 12. Jeffrey David Ehrenreich, General Editor.

Sharon, Douglas

1978 *Wizard of the Four Winds: A Shaman's Story.* New York: Free Press.

Sherbondy, Jeanette

1982 El regadío, los lagos y los mitos de origen. *Allpanchis* 20:3–32.

Shimada, Izumi

1985 Introduction to *Andean Ecology and Civilization,* ed. Shozo Masuda, Izumi Shimada, and Craig Morris, pp. xi–xxxii. Tokyo: University of Tokyo Press.

Silverblatt, Irene

1987 *Moon, Sun, and Witches: Gender Ideologies and Class in Inca and Colonial Peru.* Princeton: Princeton University Press.

Silverman-Proust, Gail

1991 Iskay Manta/Kinsa Manta: La técnica de tejer y el libro de la sabiduría elaborado en el Depto. del Cuzco. *Boletín de Lima* 74:49–66.

Sotomayor Berrio, Marco

1990 *Tecnología campesina en el pastoreo altoandino.* Puno, Peru: Proyecto Alpacas INIAA-CORPUNO-COTESU/IC.

Spalding, Karen

1984 *Huarochirí: An Andean Society under Inca and Spanish Rule.* Stanford: Stanford University Press.

Stastny, Francisco

1993 El arte de la nobleza inca y la identidad andina. In *Mito y simbolismo en los Andes: La figura y la palabra,* comp. Henrique Urbano, pp. 137–156. Cuzco: Centro de Estudios Regionales Andinos "Bartolomé de las Casas."

Stein, William W.

1961 *Hualcan: Life in the Highlands of Peru.* Ithaca, N.Y.: Cornell University Press.

Sumar Kalinowski, Luis

1993 *La kiwicha y su cultivo.* Cuzco: Centro Bartolomé de las Casas.

Taussig, Helen B.

1968 "Death" from Lightning and the Possibility of Living Again. *Annals of Internal Medicine* 68:1345–1353.

Tomoeda, Hiroyasu, and Tatsuhiko Fujii

1985 Marriage Relations Between Punaruna and Llaqtaruna: The Case of Pampamarca Parish, Apurímac, Peru. In *Andean Ecology and Civilization,* ed. Shozo Masuda, Izumi Shimada, and Craig Morris, pp. 301–309. Tokyo: University of Tokyo Press.

Tupayachi Herrera, Alfredo

1993 *Forestales nativos andinos en frutos.* Cuzco: Universidad Nacional de San Antonio Abad del Cusco.

Turner, Victor

1969 *The Ritual Process: Structure and Anti-Structure.* Chicago: Aldine.

Ulloa Torres, Liliana, and Vivian Gavilan

1992 Proposiciones metodológicas para el estudio de los tejidos andinos. *Revista Andina* 10(1):107–134.

Urbano, Henrique

1974 La representación andina del tiempo y del espacio en la fiesta. *Allpanchis* 7:9–48.

Urton, Gary

1984 Chuta: El espacio de la práctica social en Paqariqtambo. *Revista Andina* 2(1):7–44.

1993 Moieties and Ceremonialism in the Andes: The Ritual Battles of the Carnival Season in Southern Peru. In *El mundo ceremonial andino,* ed. Luis Millones and Yoshio Onuki, pp. 117–142. SENRI Ethnological Studies no. 37. Osaka: Museo Nacional de Etnología.

Valcárcel, Luis E.

1959 *Etnohistória del Perú antiguo.* Lima: Universidad Nacional Mayor de San Marcos.

Valderrama Fernández, Ricardo, and Carmen Escalante Gutiérrez

1975 El Apu Ausangate en la narrativa popular. *Allpanchis* 8:175–184.

Van Kessel, Jan

1982 *Danzas y estructuras sociales de los Andes.* Cuzco: Centro de Estudios Rurales Andinos Bartolomé de las Casas.

Vargas Ugarte, Rubén, S.J.

1951–1954 *Concilios limenses.* Lima. 3 vols.

Villagomes, Pedro de

[1649] 1919 *Exortaciones e instrucción acerca de las idolatrías de los indios del arzobispado de Lima (1649).* Ed. H. Urteaga and C. Romero. Colección de Libros y Documentos Referentes a la Historia del Perú, ser. 1, vol. 12. Lima.

Walker, Charles

1991 La violencia y el sistema legal: Los indios y el estado en el Cusco después de la rebelión de Tupac Amaru. In *Poder y violencia en los Andes,* comp. Henrique Urbano, ed. Mirko Lauer, pp. 125–147. Cuzco: Centro de Estudios Regionales Andinos Bartolomé de las Casas.

Weberbauer, A.

1945 *El mundo vegetal de los Andes peruanos.* Lima: Ministerio de Agricultura.

Webster, Steven S.

1977 Kinship and Affinity in a Native Quechua Community. In *Andean Kinship and Marriage,* ed. Ralph Bolton and Enrique Mayer, pp. 28–42. American Anthropological Association Special Publication no. 7. Washington, D.C.

West, Terry L.

1988 Rebaños familiares y propietarios individuales: Ritual ganadero y herencia entre los aymara de Bolivia. In *Llamichos y paqocheros: Pastores de llamas y alpacas,* ed. Jorge A. Flores Ochoa, pp. 191–201. Cuzco: Centro de Estudios Andinos.

Wing, Elizabeth S.

1975 La domesticación de animales en los Andes. *Allpanchis* 8:25–44.

Winterhalder, Bruce

1994 The Ecological Basis of Water Management in the Central Andes: Rainfall and Temperature in Southern Peru. In *Irrigation at High Altitudes: The Social Organization of Water Control Systems in the Andes,* ed. William P. Mitchell and David Guillet, pp. 21–67. Society for Latin American Anthropology Publication Series, vol. 12. Jeffrey David Ehrenreich, General Editor.

Wolf, Eric R.

1982 *Europe and the People without History.* Berkeley: University of California Press.

Wright, Ronald

1984 *Cut Stones and Crossroads: A Journey in the Two Worlds of Peru.* New York: Viking Press.

1992 *Stolen Continents: The New World through Indian Eyes since 1492.* Toronto: Viking Press.

Yaranga Valderrama, Abdon

1979 La divinidad Illapa en la región andina. *América Indígena* 39(4): 697–720.

Zapata Rodríguez, Julinho

1995 Una estructura funeraria del Horizonte Medio en Batan Orq'o (Cusco). *Revista de Ciencias Sociales* 2:205–220.

Zorn, Elayne

1987 Un análisis de los tejidos en los atados rituales de los pastores. *Revista Andina* 5(2):489–526.

Zuidema, R. Tom

1964 *The Ceque System of Cuzco.* Leiden: E. J. Brill.

1967 El juego de los ayllus y el amaru. *Journal de la Société des Américanistes, Paris* 56(1):41–51.

1973 Kinship and Ancestorcult in Three Peruvian Communities: Hernández Príncipe's Account of 1622. *Bulletin de l'Institut Français d'Etudes Andines* 2(1):16–33.

1977 The Inca Kinship System, a New Theoretical View. In *Andean Kinship and Marriage,* ed. Ralph Bolton and Enrique Mayer, pp. 240–281. Special Publication of the American Anthropological Association, no. 7. Washington, D.C.

1982 Bureaucracy and Systematic Knowledge in Andean Civilization. In *The Inca and Aztec States 1400–1800,* ed. George A. Collier, Renato I. Rosaldo, and John Wirth, pp. 419–458. New York: Academic Press.

1990a *Inca Civilization in Cuzco.* Trans. Jean-Jacques Decoster. Austin: University of Texas Press.

1990b The Royal Whip in Cuzco: Art, Social Structure and Cosmology. In *The Language of Things: Studies in Ethnocommunication,* ed. Pieter ter Keurs and Dirk Schmidt, pp. 159–172. Leiden: Rijksmuseum voor Volkenkunde.

1991 Batallas rituales en el Cuzco colonial. In *Cultures et sociétés andes et meso-amérique: Melanges en hommage à Pierre Duviols,* 2:811–834. Aix-en-Provence: L'Université de Provence.

1992 The Moieties of Cuzco. In *The Attraction of Opposites: Thought and Society in a Dualistic Mode,* ed. David Maybury-Lewis and Uri Almagor, pp. 255–275. Ann Arbor: University of Michigan Press.

Zuidema, R. Tom, and Gary Urton

1976a Constelación de la llama en los Andes peruanos. *Allpanchis* 9:59–119.

INDEX